Sunflower Under

A Kyiv Memoir

RICHARD W. COAD

MAPLE
PUBLISHERS

SUNFLOWER UNDERGROUND - A KYIV MEMOIR

Author: Richard W. Coad

ISBN 978-1-83538-532-6 (Paperback)

Published by:
Maple Publishers
Fairbourne Drive, Atterbury,
Milton Keynes,
MK10 9RG, UK
www.maplepublishers.com

A CIP catalogue record for this title is available from the British Library.

1

ABOUT THE AUTHOR

Richard Coad grew up in the Oxfordshire Cotswolds and went to Burford School. Today, he lives in Surrey with his family.

For Oliver, Thomas and James

"After he got the promise, there was a span of twenty-five years between the promise and the fulfilment of that promise" – *Genesis 21*

Contents

Prologue

9th February 1998

As the lights dimmed, the invited audience hushed in anticipation. The concert was about to begin, and with it, the future of Ukraine's relationship with the European Union.

I took a deep breath and walked onto the stage, black folder in hand, the sound of my dress shoes echoing through the hall. As Olga took her place beside me, I could feel nervous energy radiating off her. We exchanged a quick smile before I turned to address the audience.

I wondered if I was ready for this momentous occasion. The weight of expectation was heavy, the eyes of the world were upon us. Despite my heart pounding in my chest, I knew that I had to keep my composure and deliver the introduction flawlessly. Together, we introduced the first set of European music arias performed by Misha, the young Ukrainian tenor, mentored by the legendary Lady Miroshnichenko.

As the first notes of the orchestra filled the air, a sense of excitement and anticipation washed over me. This was a new beginning for Ukraine, a chance to showcase its rich cultural heritage to the world and to forge new relationships with its European neighbours. And I was honoured to be a part of it all. Little did I know, however, that this concert would be the start of a journey that would take me down a path I never could have imagined; a path that would test my courage, my loyalty, and ultimately, my very sense of self.

But for now, as the music swelled around me, I knew only one thing: this was a moment I would never forget. After all, this was not just a concert, but an opportunity to show the world that Ukraine was ready to embrace its European future.

Chapter 1. 9:15 to Lvov

3rd December 1995

I awoke in the early afternoon from what was to be my last comfortable sleep for two days, in East Dulwich, south London. I had a quick shower and went down for breakfast.

"Do you want brown or red sauce?" asked *Slackbladder* as he cooked me a bacon sandwich. I could hear on the radio that England were crashing to defeat in the second test match in South Africa. At least there was some hope of a draw if captain Micheal Atherton was still at the wicket.

"Brown, thanks, and if you're making coffee, white with one sugar," I joked. I had met Slack in Plymouth university as a Fresher in our halls of residence on Milehouse Road at the beginning of our degree courses five years earlier. Our halls of residence, *Brightside*, was a huge, converted Edwardian house accommodating nearly twenty of us students, six per floor. I was on the top floor with an accountant called Sophie; a business student called Rachel; a psychologist; a marine studies student and a second-year big boy scout, who thought he could manage us. There was a sixth room on the top floor which seemed to be occupied with a different student every term. Slack's room was on the ground floor next to the kitchen which he shared with three psychologists, an architect, and a civil engineer. He was given the name of *Blackadder* by us because of his rather close-cut haircut reminiscent of the haircut adorned by the infamous *Blackadder* in the early 1980s (series one, to be sure). The name soon morphed to *Slackbladder* and then just *Slack* for short. He had done a degree in Transport which we all found hilariously boring, but he loved his music, and he carried great boxes of records with him everywhere. There was a whole other floor of psychologists, and we often argued, but we all had the best time in our *Fresher* year which none of us have ever forgotten.

I recall an early anecdote in the second term at Brightside, I thoughtlessly poached what I thought were chicken nuggets from Sophie's plate one evening; breaking out in a hot rash as I chewed them, I soon realised they were fish nuggets. Being very allergic to fish, I was swiftly ferried to the local Derriford hospital in Rachel's car where I spent the night recovering. It was the night that the first Gulf War's *Operation Desert Shield* started and was brought to us live in the hospital ward via an old roll-around television wheeled in by the staff nurse. I apologised to Sophie the next day and we ended up going out with each other. *That was 1991.* Two years later we travelled around Indonesia together, riding horseback up volcanoes, riding motorbikes into the jungle and riding waves in Bali. The trip ended with me getting food poisoning on the train from Bandung to Jakarta, consequently transported by ambulance to the general hospital where livestock was being sold at the entrance. Inside I got a few extremely expensive and unnecessary brain scans, the doctors concluding that an operation through my eye to clear a non-existent blood clot was required. Sophie called the British Embassy to rescue me as I was going under the knife. This they promptly did. *Forever grateful to her.*

I remember 1991 for two other events: the first was a stage performance in which I participated in the amateur dramatics' society at Plymouth university, in Willie Russell's *Stags & Hens,* playing a hapless scouser called *Billy* who campaigned for *CAMRA,* the Campaign for Real Ale; the second was the fall of the Soviet Union and the independence of a new country, called Ukraine, somewhere in Eastern Europe. I had watched the fall of the Berlin Wall in 1989 on television with huge interest as a teenager and became enthralled in the subsequent events. *That was then.*

After lunch, we went for a beer at Slack's local pub *The Forest Hill Arms* and caught a bit of the Newcastle v Wimbledon game.

"Cheers!" we cracked our pint glasses together.

"So, are you worried about going to Ukraine?" Slack asked, wiping a frothy moustache from his top lip.

"No, I've been to Indonesia remember, it can't be as exciting as that." *I felt little apprehension; did I realize what I was about to embark upon?* "Let's have a drink when I get back and I can tell you if I was right not to be apprehensive," I joked.

"You'll never get back; you'll spend twenty years in a labour camp for some minor crime," Slack laughed.

Having no fear, I was relieved to be finally going. We finished our beers and returned to Slack's house for some dinner. At 7pm Slack and I headed to Victoria Coach Station to check-in. It was a damp and dreary evening. The air was thick with the scent of diesel fumes, the ground was slick with rainwater. Passengers hurried about, dodging puddles, and clutching their luggage tightly.

"Thanks for all your hospitality, mate, "I said shaking his hand.

"I may come out to Poland in January for some snowboarding," he said, "I'll call you."

"Sure, I'll be just a short hop over the border," I joked." Farewell, mate." The goodbye was beginning to linger. I picked up my rucksack and rushed over to my gate in good time for my 9:15pm departure.

Amidst the flurry of activity, a lone figure stood out. He was a young man with a backpack slung over his shoulder, as I was; his eyes fixed on the departure board. The destination was Lvov, a city nestled near the Polish border in the western Ukraine. At the gate, I was met by a Russian woman who helped me with my baggage.

"That will be an extra charge of fifteen pounds," she said in a strong accent, "but you can give me five pounds and I won't tell the driver." *What sort of an operation was this?* As I passed through the gate, the bus loomed before me like a giant beast, its engine growling impatiently. The driver, a gruff-looking bear of a man, barked out instructions in a thick Russian accent to the passengers. "*Bistro! Bistro!*", he exclaimed.

I was relieved to hear the Russian woman talking to the lone figure in English. He looked like a student, and I started chatting to him as we boarded.

"I'm Warren, are you going out to Kyiv to teach English?" He gave the impression that this was not the first time he had done this journey.

"I'm Richard, and yes, how did you guess?" I asked.

"Why else would anyone go to Ukraine? I did the English Teaching Program in Kyiv last year but I'm returning to teach privately. You can make more money that way and manage your own clients, time and lessons." He clearly knew what he was talking about and I was glad to be sitting with him on the coach all the way to Ukraine.

The coach departed on time 9:15pm exactly and we were on the way to Ramsgate. It was full of Ukrainian students apart from one elderly English man – we joked he was a spy – and Warren and me of course. We sat at the back of the coach next to the drinks machine and the toilet, thinking that we would then have easy access to both for the duration of the long journey, later finding the drinks machine didn't have any drinks in it and the toilet didn't flush properly.

"Did you do an English teaching degree?" I asked him.

"No not at all, I did Economics at Edinburgh. None of the English teachers I met in Kyiv had done an English degree."

"Ah, good, neither have I. For me, Maths at Plymouth promptly followed by postgraduate punishment at Reading," I joked.

Warren and I settled in for the long journey ahead. We watched as the landscape outside the window gradually changed from the bustling dark wet city streets of London to the rolling green hills of the Kent countryside. *There was no snow yet, but I was headed to a place which guaranteed snow.*

4th December 1995

10

We arrived at the Ramsgate ferry terminal after midnight. Warren and I went for a coffee in the terminal building and talked about what was expected of me on the teaching program in Ukraine. Apparently, he only did fifteen hours per week last year. I quite liked the thought of that: a mere three hours a day, with the rest of my time to explore. After boarding the ferry at 1am, we immediately went to the restaurant for some highly expensive Belgian food. We proceeded to the bar for a Belgian beer where we met three English girls travelling to Brussels, and the European Parliament, as part of their A-level Politics course. That's where we stayed until the ferry arrived in Ostend at 5:30am. We boarded the coach and began the drive across Belgium.

As the coach driver prepared to continue his journey, he glanced out the window at the winter wonderland outside. For a moment, he looked less gruff. But then, with a shake of his head, he turned the key in the ignition and set off once again, his bus trundling down the lightly snow-covered ramp into Belgium.

The coach rattled along out of the ferry port, its headlights piercing through the morning mist. The windows were foggy, and the heater was on full blast, but the chill in the air still managed to seep through. As the bus made its way through the Belgian countryside, the scenery outside was a blur of white and grey. The passengers were a motley crew, bundled up in coats, scarves, and hats. Some were chatting quietly, while others dozed off, their heads resting against the window. Four hours later, we crossed into Germany.

Travelling across Germany in a coach during winter was a novel experience for me. The air was crisp and chilly, but inside the bus, it was warm and cosy. Sitting by the window, the scenery passed by like a silent movie. The villages and towns looked like postcards, their colourful houses and wooden chalets adorned with Christmas lights. People were walking on the streets, bundled up in jackets, scarves, and hats, their breath visible puffs and whirls. Sometimes, the bus would stop in a small town, and we would have a break to stretch our legs and grab a coffee or a pastry. The shops were full of seasonal treats, gingerbread cookies, marzipan, and mulled wine. Some fellow travellers were chatting and laughing, sharing stories and snacks. Others sleeping, their heads resting on the seats, faces peaceful. I felt a sense of adventure and freedom, being on the road, exploring a new country. As the bus made its way across Germany, I found myself lost in thought. *I thought about the adventures that awaited me in Ukraine, the people I would meet, and the experiences I would have.*

5th December 1995

Hours passed, and the sun began to set on the horizon. At midnight, we eventually arrived at the Polish border, we got off and had more coffee and hot food. Immediately, I noticed how much colder it was. The thermometer on the coach showed minus ten degrees centigrade and it felt like it. We quickly got back on the coach and set off through the darkness across Poland. The temperature dropped significantly, and the snowfall became heavier. The gruff bus driver had been replaced by another; the new, happier driver navigated the slick roads with an air of calm reassurance. I felt a little anxious as we made our way through the treacherous terrain. Poland had had a troubled history and I had always been fascinated by this and its stoic people. Despite the cold, the coach was warm and cosy, if not a bit smelly, and I found myself lost in thought as we travelled through Krakow, the cultural capital of Poland.

At 9:30am we reached the Ukrainian border; it was minus fourteen degrees centigrade. I felt a knot form in my stomach. I had never been to the former Soviet Union, and the thought of crossing into one of the former Soviet states in the dead of winter was both nerve-wracking and exhilarating. The bus slowed down as it approached the border checkpoint. Tall fences and barbed wire separated the two countries. We watched as the Ukrainian border guards approached the bus, their breath visible in the cold winter air. The guards boarded the bus and began checking passports and visas. I held my breath as they approached my seat. I handed over my passport, heart pounding in my chest. After a few tense moments, the guard handed it back and motioned for the bus to continue. Relieved, I settled back into my seat.

Sooner than I had anticipated, we were entering the territory of Ukraine. My first impressions were that it was a desolate and bleak landscape and not a place where one would live comfortably. However, this was a short stretch of the journey, and we would arrive in Lvov by midday.

"You shouldn't call it Lvov," Warren affirmed. "This is the Russian name, and the Ukrainians don't like it."

"What should I call it then?"

"Lviv," he enunciated the short 'i' sound, "only Lviv." There seemed to be an intensity in Warren's eyes that I had not noticed before.

As the journey continued, the Ukrainian landscape outside the bus began to take on a surreal quality. The beautiful snow-covered fields and forests were a stark contrast to the bustling cities and towns we had passed through. As we approached this old Ukrainian city of *Lviv*, the bus driver honked his horn and the other passengers began to stir, gathering their belongings, preparing to disembark. I felt a sense of relief and excitement as we pulled into the *Lviv* coach station, knowing that I had made it through the coach journey.

Looking back on that journey - exactly thirty-eight hours after leaving London - I realized that it was a microcosm of the entire trip. There were moments of discomfort and uncertainty, but also moments of beauty and connection with others.

A thrill of excitement rushed through me as I gathered my rucksack, eager to see all that Ukraine had to offer. The coach door opened, the winter air was biting and crisp, but now I didn't mind. It was midday when Warren and I emerged from the coach, picking up our bags from the pile on the pavement. Immediately, a young lady appeared and threw her arms around Warren.

"This is Liena," Warren said, "Liena this is Richard." She looked at me and smiled.

"*Ochen priyatna!*" she said shaking my hand.

"Nice to meet you too," I replied, not brave enough to test my Russian out just yet.

"We are going straight to our hotel nearby; can we give you a lift?" asked Warren.

"I have a pre-arranged driver to take me to my hotel, so I had better wait," I said. "The Hotel George."

"OK that's in the next street to ours so I'll come over to *The George* at 3pm," he insisted, *"to check that you arrived safely and haven't been kidnapped."*

Chapter 2. George and the Underground

The quaint streets and colourful buildings under snow looked like something out of a fairy tale. The sound of church bells were ringing in the distance.

The car slid to a halt; we had arrived at The Hotel George. Nestled in the heart of Lviv, the hotel stood as a magnificent testament to the city's rich history and architectural splendour. With its grand façade and a legacy spanning centuries, this iconic establishment offered a relatively unique blend of luxury, comfort, and cultural immersion. The cold winter wind whipped at my face as I approached the imposing hotel entrance. I shivered, not just from the cold, but from the sense of foreboding that seemed to emanate from the very structure itself.

Pushing open the heavy metal door, I was met with a blast of warm air and the sound of muffled voices. I was glad to get inside the lobby away from the biting cold. Upon entering, I was greeted by a reception with high ceilings, crystal chandeliers, and refined furnishings, transporting me to an era long gone. This was more than just a place to rest. A reception desk stood before me, an austere-looking woman in a grey suit and horn-rimmed glasses stared back at me. I stepped forward and was met by a rather sallow chap who appeared from nowhere.

"Hello Richard, I am Dmitry," his voice as awkward as his appearance. I smiled as he announced that he was to be my guide, and apparently my bodyguard, for the rest of the journey to Kyiv.

""Welcome to *The Hotel George,*" the austere-looking woman said, her voice flat and emotionless. "May I help you?" Her English was good. I hesitated for a moment, wondering if I had made a mistake coming here. She then squared her shoulders and coughed as if to hurry me along.

15

"Yes, I have a reservation," I said, trying to keep my voice steady, "for a single room." Dmitry nodded at the woman as if to confirm what I had said was true. The woman typed something into her computer and handed me a key.

"Room 309," she said, "the elevator is down the hall to your left." I lifted my rucksack rather than put it back over my shoulders.

"Can we meet in the restaurant in one hour for some lunch and to discuss the onward journey to Kyiv tomorrow?" Dmitry requested in a business-like manner, which didn't really suit him.

As I made my way to the lift, I turned back to the Reception to see Dmitry still chatting with the woman. What on earth were they discussing? They seemed a most unlikely pair. On the way to my room, I couldn't help but feel a sense of unease. Unlike the opulence of the lobby area, the hallways on the bedroom floors took on a more Soviet-era hue, dimly lit, with flickering fluorescent lights that cast strange shadows on the walls. The carpets were worn and stained, and I could hear the distant hum of machinery somewhere in the building.

Finally reaching my room, I was relieved to find it clean and comfortable, if a bit spartan. Out of the window I could see the city's cobblestone streets and colourful buildings; I felt a glimmer of excitement at the thought of exploring Lviv after lunch. But as I settled onto the bed, I couldn't shake the feeling that I was being watched. The hotel seemed to have a life of its own, a sinister presence that loomed over it like a shadow. I closed my eyes, trying to push the feeling away, but it lingered, possibly a reminder of the dark history that had taken place within these walls.

After a short snooze I sat up, remembered where I was and made my way back down the lift to the Reception area. I crossed the desk and noticed that there was a different, more pleasant and smiley, lady there. I asked her where the restaurant was, and she subtly indicated to keep going straight ahead.

Dmitry was already sitting at one of the nearside tables on the left of the restaurant; awkwardly, he stood up when I entered, and I acknowledged the gesture. We sat down at the same time and enjoyed the buffet lunch that was on offer, mainly bread, meat and water. It was all my stomach could handle after the long coach journey across Europe.

After my third lump of meat, I heard Warren's voice in the lobby behind me and turned to see him walking towards the restaurant entrance. Liena was two steps behind him with another man.

"Priyatnovo appetita!" he said as he approached the table. "Warren, Liena and her husband, Roman," he introduced. I reciprocated by introducing myself and then Dmitry.

"I can see you're eating so we'll go and have some lunch and come back and pick you up at 5pm," Warren said having satisfied himself that I hadn't been kidnapped.

"I will be ready in the lobby when you come," I replied.

Dmitry didn't acknowledge any part of the conversation and even seemed somewhat annoyed that I was making plans without his permission. We sat in an awkward silence after they stepped out of the restaurant. As soon as I had reached a place where I could simply eat no more meat, bread and water, I thanked Dmitry and rose from the table.

"You must stay safe and return to the hotel before 9pm as Lviv can be dangerous for westerners. I'll see you at 8am for breakfast." Dmitry offered this warning as I turned to leave the table and return to my room.

After a second snooze, I grabbed my coat and got to the lobby just as Warren, Liena and Roman entered the hotel. It was dark now and we left together into the freezing early evening air.

Sunflower Underground: A Kyiv Memoir

Warren's knowledge of the old town and its secret places likely came from his previous visit; his passion for exploration and his love for the city seemed to surpass that as if he had a deeper connection. He might have spent countless hours wandering through its narrow streets, uncovering hidden corners and tucked-away spots that many others had overlooked. Perhaps Liena and Roman had a network of friends and locals who shared their knowledge, revealing the hidden doorways that are known only to a select few.

"This way!" Suddenly, we turned off the main road, walked through a narrow alley and knocked on a door that looked like it led into an abandoned building. The cold winter air stung my face as we waited. I guessed we were arriving at the secret underground bar Warren had mentioned he knew of on the coach.

The heavy metal door opened; we stepped inside a dimly lit room. The cozy fire burning in the corner was the only source of light. The room was filled with smoke and the sound of raucous laughter stopped as we entered. A group of men in leather jackets huddled around a table, playing cards, and drinking *horilka*, a type of Ukrainian vodka. Others sat at the bar, nursing their drinks, and talking in hushed tones, watching us. The walls were covered in vintage Soviet-era posters. In the intimate and edgy atmosphere, I felt like I had stumbled upon a secret world. At the end of the bar, a door creaked open, revealing a staircase that spiralled down into the darkness.

"Come on in," Roman beckoned. We all filed through the door. A portal to a hidden world had been opened, and we couldn't resist the urge to explore. With each step down the spiral staircase, the air grew colder and the darkness more intense. I couldn't see anything except for the occasional flicker of light from a lantern mounted on the wall.

Descending deeper, strange noises from below our feet - whispers, rustling, a distant cry - floated up. But I pressed on, driven by my curiosity and a sense of adventure. Finally, after what felt like an eternity, we reached the bottom of the staircase. I counted thirty-nine steps.

Standing in a vast underground chamber, lit by flickering lanterns scattered around the walls, my eyes could make out strange objects - ancient relics, mysterious artifacts, and strange contraptions that I couldn't begin to guess the purpose of. As my eyes explored the chamber, I couldn't shake the feeling of being watched. Every shadow seemed to hold some hidden threat, the whispers grew louder and more insistent. *My instincts were screaming at me to get out of there.*

Roman and Liena had brought us to an underground club. Moving across another chamber to a door with a 'Members Only' sign above it, Roman slipped the doorman, what appeared to be, a coupled of packets of cigarettes. Yet another door opened for us and this time we entered a world of light, music, dance, drinking and fun.

We made our way to the bar and Roman ordered coffee and shots of horilka. The bartender, a burly man with a thick moustache, eyed me suspiciously.

"You're not from around here, are you?" he asked, with a pirate's grin. I shook my head.

"No, I'm just passing through." He nodded slowly, then leaned in closer.

"You should be careful," he whispered, "this place is not for foreigners." I took my drink and wandered around the room, taking in the scene.

"This is a gathering place for nationalists - men and women who believe in the independence and sovereignty of Ukraine," Warren muttered in English.

"There is a big black market and many mafia gangs in Ukraine, especially in Lviv," Liena explained, then glanced at Roman.

"Only last week a car followed us with four men inside and, after half an hour, stopped us and told us that we owed them seventeen dollars and it must be paid or else we would be killed, and our car sold,"

Roman continued. The story was chilling and so we had another horilka. We drank several more horilkas. As the evening wore on, the crowd grew rowdier. A group of men began singing patriotic songs, their voices rising in unison. *I couldn't understand the words, but the passion in their voices was unmistakable.*

Suddenly, the door burst open, and several policemen stormed in. The room fell silent as they surveyed the scene. The nationalists stood their ground, refusing to back down. There was a tense standoff as the police officers checked some identification. The nationalists sitting closest to the door presented their papers which seemed to be instantly at hand as if this often happened. After what felt like an eternity, the police officers finally left, and the room erupted in cheers and applause. Who were these people? What were they so passionate about? *Was the struggle for Ukrainian independence a reality?*

As we left the underground bar and stepped back out into the cold night air, I felt a sense of awe at what I had witnessed. The bravery and determination of those nationalists was inspiring - and I knew that their fight would continue, no matter what obstacles they may face. The bitter cold of the winter night hit me like a slap in the face. I pulled my coat tighter around me, wishing I had worn another layer or two. The streets of Lviv were deserted, except for a few brave souls, smoking under the awnings of closed shops.

We started walking back, my boots crunching on the snow-covered cobblestones. The horilka had warmed me up, but I still felt a little lightheaded from the potent drink. Old buildings glowed in the dim light of the streetlamps, their facades decorated with intricate carvings and mouldings. A gargoyle peered down at me from above, adding to my mounting paranoia.

Turning a corner, we were back on the street of The George Hotel. The glow of a fire in the distance piqued our curiosity; we quickened our pace and soon found ourselves outside a cosy-looking café next to the hotel. The windows were steamed up and I could smell the aroma of freshly brewed coffee. This time we were greeted by the light warmth of the room and the sound of friendly chatter. The cafe was packed with people, all bundled up in scarves and hats. We found an empty table and sat down, drinking more coffee. At this point Warren and Roman stood up, both extending their open hands to mine. Suddenly, Warren was off to catch a train, the overnight sleeper to Kyiv.

"Whoever gets to the British Embassy in Kyiv first should leave their telephone number," Warren said decisively. Horilka still flushing though my veins, I bear-hugged Warren and Roman. "Good luck!" Warren said then they both left. Liena remained sitting. It was only 9pm but it seemed like midnight; *how could I be so drunk so early in the evening?* Sipping my coffee, I watched the people around me. I felt a sense of camaraderie, a shared struggle that transcended language and culture.

"We feel persecuted in Lviv," she said, "and we're in a great hurry to leave." Warren had said that Liena was going to have a baby next year. "Please don't think that Lviv wasn't a nice place, because it is," she continued.

"Why don't you leave Lviv and go to somewhere like Kyiv?" I asked. "Roman can't. He has many business interests in Lviv and couldn't leave them," she replied, "anyway, our problems would follow us to Kyiv."

Roman appeared at the doorway; it was time to go. I finished my coffee and stood up to leave, feeling a sense of sadness wash over me. The experience of the secret underground bar and the cosy cafe had given me a glimpse into the heart of Lviv: a city that was both beautiful and welcoming, but also dark and intimidating; a city whose vibrant culture was as much a part of its charm as its struggle. Stepping back out into the cold, I knew that this was a feeling that I would remember for a long time to come. A sense of nostalgia had been ignited for a place I had never known.

After further bear-hugs, Liena gave me her telephone number, telling me to contact her if I were ever in Lviv. *I hoped to see them both again - preferably alive. I felt myself becoming a part of the city's story, leaving behind my old life and embracing a new adventure in this brutally enchanting place.*

6th December 1995

Early the next morning, I awoke to a loud ringing telephone in my bedroom. It was Dmitry phoning to make sure that I hadn't been kidnapped, again, and that I was getting up for breakfast. I still had an hour which I used for a scalding hot shower, as there was no option of cold water. I entered the restaurant to see Dmitry sitting at a far table, waiting for my arrival. He pointed to a coffee pot and some fried eggs which looked as though they had been run over but tasted fantastic. *So began the interrogation.*

"Did you enjoy yesterday evening?" he asked, "where did you go?"

"I have no idea," I replied, "not from drinking. I literally do not know where I was yesterday evening." *I certainly couldn't remember the name of it and, anyway, I felt that I was not obliged to tell him.* I killed the conversation there. Accepting my answer, Dmitry changed subject to the lighter topic of the Cold War during the 1980s. On more solid ground, we discussed the topic for a full hour until the waiters began to lay the breakfast tables for lunch. We had discussed the international relations between the USA, UK and Russia. I had a strong sense that he was not a great fan of the end of the Soviet era; a good Russian if you like, even though he now had liberty and was able to travel abroad quite freely.

"It would be a good idea if we bought some water and wine for the journey to Kyiv," Dmitry suggested, "we will be on the train for ten hours."

We left the hotel, stepping back out into another blizzard and walked down the same street that we had taken the previous evening. However, we didn't turn down the secret alleyway where I had entered the underground club the night before. I made sure not to glance that way in case Dmitry picked up on it. A minute later, we arrived at a door in a rather plain-looking building. I followed a

22

flustered Dmitry through the door. Incredibly, I found myself in a sort of grocery shop. The shelves looked like filing cabinets and there were only a few different items being sold: bottles of water, wine, gherkins and bread. *The worst stocked grocery shop in the world had everything that we were looking for, so we bought two of everything!*

At midday, Dmitry and I stepped out of the cavernous ticket hall onto the platform at Lviv railway station. I was hit with a wave of cold air. It was the beginning of an exceptionally cold winter in Ukraine and the temperature outside was already well below freezing. I stepped carefully along the heavily salted platforms as I followed Dmitry towards our carriage.

The train appeared like a huge grey metal slug, partly as boarding occurred from ground level rather than a platform. It was a relief to climb aboard this cold metal beast which had a certain Soviet-era charm to it. I shuddered as I made my way to my seat, grateful for the warmth inside. People were bundled up in jackets and scarves, all trying to stay warm. The seats were worn, the windows were fogged up, but I could still see the salt-covered platforms below.

Dmitry and I settled into our cigarette-scented compartment and laid out our food and drink on the small table under the compartment window. As we prepared for the journey, the train awoke and lurched forward as it tugged the carriages into motion. Dmitry perched on the lower bunk of the compartment, and I sat opposite him. Without asking, he passed me a glass of wine, which was the last thing I wanted to drink, *apart from more horilka*.

As the train made its way through the snow-covered landscape, everything looked bleak in the winter. The trees were bare, the fields blanketed with snow. It was a beautiful sight, but it also made me realize how harsh the winters were in Ukraine. The train grew quieter before stopping at a couple of towns along the way. I bought a cup of thick black coffee and watched as the snow fell outside. People settled into their seats, wrapped up in blankets and sleeping bags. I pulled out a book and started to read, but I couldn't concentrate. *The sound of the train moving along the tracks was soporific and I drifted off to sleep.*

Chapter 3. Gangsters Paradise

The sound of the train gently braking woke me. It was late evening and we gathered our belongings and made our way to the door of the train, expecting the blast of the freezing cold winter air. The approaching station looked foreboding, almost like something out of the *Second World War*.

It was easy to imagine Kyiv station during that time as a place of chaos and fear. *It would have been a place where people were constantly on the move, either fleeing the city or being deported to concentration camps. The sound of train whistles and the screeching of metal wheels on tracks echoed through the station, creating an eerie and unsettling atmosphere. As the war raged on, the station would have become overcrowded with desperate people trying to escape the violence and destruction. Families huddled together, clutching their belongings, waiting for their turn to board a train. The air would have been thick with smoke from burnt-out buildings and the smell of fear; soldiers patrolling the platforms, keeping a watchful eye on the crowds, their guns at the ready. Amidst the chaos, moments of hope and humanity. Strangers helping each other carry their bags and comforting those crying. Children playing games to distract themselves from the harsh reality of the war. And every now and then, a train would arrive that was filled with food, blankets, and medical supplies, bringing a glimmer of hope to the weary and exhausted crowds.*

As Dmitry and I stepped off the train, my heart raced with excitement, this was my first time visiting Kyiv. I scanned the bustling platform, searching for my contact.

"Richard! Over here," called Andrey. "Dima, let's go". I turned to see a tall, well-built man waving at me. With a weary smile, I hurried over to meet him.

"Welcome to Kyiv!" Andrey grinned, clinging onto a baggage trolley. "I hope you had a good journey."

"Thank you, yes, all good," I replied and followed him out of the station to a sleek black car parked nearby. Climbing into the passenger seat, Dmitri got in behind. As we drove through the busy streets of the Ukrainian capital, Andrey told me about his city; he pointed out some of the most famous landmarks in the city. The golden domes of St. Sophia's Cathedral sparkled in the snow, and the neon lights of Independence Square illuminated the night sky.

The snowflakes danced in the headlights and the city was transformed into a winter wonderland. The occasional building had a Christmas decoration, and the streets were empty apart from a few cars. Despite the cold, some people were out and about, but the holiday season had not reached Kyiv yet. As the car turned a corner, we caught a glimpse of the Dnipro River frozen over, with snow-covered boats and a lone ice fisherman braving the cold night.

"I used to play ice-hockey there as a boy," Andrey remarked. "The river freezes like this every winter."

The sights and sounds of the city under snow and lights were unforgettable but this soon became a never-ending series of blocks of flats in the *Svitoshin* region. The car turned through several narrow streets between the blocks and stopped in a courtyard. As I got out of the car, Andrey handed me my rucksack from the boot of the car then walked towards an entrance. The bitter cold seeped into my bones and the icy wind whipped through my hair. The grey buildings loomed above me, windows frosted, and walls covered in a layer of snow and ice.

Andrey and I made our way up the steps, my breath visible in the frigid air; I was struck by the desolate feeling of the place. The only sound was the crunching of my boots in the snow and the occasional shout of a child playing in the courtyard. A stray cat slid up against the grey, bleak wall in the snow-covered courtyard.

Andrey knocked on the door of the third-floor apartment which was to be my home for the next three months. After a moment, it was

26

opened by a kind-looking woman, bundled up in several layers of clothing.

"Good evening, Maria. This is Richard, your English teacher," Andrey introduced me to her in Russian. She welcomed me inside, and I was immediately hit by the warmth of the apartment.

"Maria," the woman said, pointing to herself. The heat was blasting, the cosy interior was a welcome respite from the bitter cold outside. Maria returned to the kitchen which appeared to be the heart of her home. A bearded man replaced her in the hallway.

"Volodymyr," said the man, who I assumed to be Maria's husband. The aroma of garlic and onions wafted through the air as Maria sautéed them in a cast iron skillet. She quickly added chunks of juicy tomatoes from somewhere and let them simmer. Volodomyr took my rucksack into a bedroom across the hallway.

"Good evening, my name is Taras," a tall, slim boy appeared. "How was your journey?" To my relief, he seemed to have reasonably good English. A mop of unruly blonde hair fell over his eyes, which he habitually brushed away with his hand. His blue eyes were curious, always scanning his surroundings.

"Hello Taras, I'm pleased to meet you," I said. "Ihe journey was very long and a tiring."

"I think you are OK now, so I'll say goodbye," Andrey said as he turned to leave. "Let me know if you need anything. I'll see you in the English school in a few days."

"Thanks Andrey," I replied as he closed the apartment door behind him. That was it. I was on my own.

"Can I show you to your room," Taras gestured with a hand. He was just fifteen years old but, despite his young age, he was very engaging and polite. *I had found a Ukrainian "Jeeves".*

"I am fifteen years old," he said, "and my brother is eighteen years old." Taras was already quite tall, my height, and with long limbs that seemed to have a life of their own. He sometimes tripped over his own feet as he walked. The older brother was sitting at a desk studying and looked up as Taras and I entered.

"Sergei," he smiled genuinely, holding his hand out to shake mine. "Sorry, I must work."

"He has an exam tomorrow," Taras explained as we left Sergei, "and he needs to pass. My brother's English is not as good as mine," he asserted. I understood that Taras' English was fluent, but Sergei's English was broken and heavily accented. Both were eager to practise and improve.

The apartment of this traditional Ukrainian family was cosy and warm. The walls were adorned with colourful tapestries and embroidered tablecloths. The living room had a comfortable sofa and armchairs with a long dining table.

"Richard, please sit down for dinner," Taras requested. The family had waited for me before having dinner. I took my seat at one end of the table with Volodomyr sitting at the other end, the head of the table.

"My father is an engineer," Taras began as Maria brought in plates of food from the kitchen." Volodomyr exchanged a few words with him in Ukrainian.

Taras translated. "He told me that Ukrainian nuclear missiles were better designed and built than Russian nuclear missiles."

"So I hear," was the only response I could think of. *Who was I to argue with that?* Taras translated my comment back to Volodymyr who responded.

"He is angry that Ukraine is getting rid of their nuclear weapons," Taras paused, "because someone can invade us."

"I agree with your father," I replied. "Nuclear weapons have prevented world wars since they were invented." Volodomyr looked up in respectful acknowledgement as Taras told him my reply.

"My father often brings home fish from a river fisherman," Taras announced, changing the subject, "do you like fish?"

"I'm allergic, so he needn't bring any on my behalf," I responded. Taras translated and Maria responded in Ukrainian.

"My mother says that fish allergies do not exist in Ukraine," Taras explained. I didn't feel like chancing it. I had a bowl of borscht, a hearty soup made with beetroot, cabbage, potatoes, and meat, then a big plate of potatoes with a side of pickled vegetables.

Before we sat down for dinner I had felt cut off from the world, as if I had been transported to another planet. *That sense of isolation was soon replaced by an appreciation of the warmth and kindness of my Ukrainian family.*

8th December 1995

That second day, Maria was always making sure I had enough to eat and drink, insisting that I try every Ukrainian dish she prepared. Despite the language barrier, we managed to communicate through gestures and simple phrases. The family were proud of their country and its culture, eager to share it with me.

Maria took me to the local market where we shopped for fresh ingredients for a traditional Ukrainian meal. She pointed out different fruits and vegetables, explaining how they were used in Ukrainian cuisine. She taught me how to make *varenyky*, a type of dumpling filled with mashed potatoes and cheese. We spent hours in the kitchen, rolling out the dough, shaping the dumplings, and boiling them in a pot of water. As we sat down to eat the *varenyky*, Maria beamed with pride at my attempts to speak Ukrainian and my enthusiasm for her country's cuisine. For dessert, she would prepare a sweet *varenyky*, filled with fruit or cheese, or a honey cake made with layers of sponge cake and creamy frosting.

The traditional food served in the *Korol* family's apartment was more than just sustenance. It was a reminder that sometimes the most meaningful moments happen around the dinner table. I learned that their family name 'Korol' meant 'King'. I joked with them that they must be related to our royal family.

Maria and Volodymyr were keen to tell me about their boys. At school, Taras was a bit of a clown, but he was a good-hearted boy with a strong sense of loyalty and family. He was a gifted linguist who excelled in his English classes and was often called upon to help his classmates. He loved spending time with his older brother and helping his parents around the house. He dreamed of one day traveling the world and experiencing all it had to offer. For now, he was content with his life in Ukraine and the adventures he could find right in his own backyard.

Sergei's exam had gone well that day, he was a natural when it came to Maths and Science. His skills were already recognized by his teachers and peers. He'd decided to follow his father and pursue a degree in Engineering at the local polytechnic institute. However, despite having studied English for years, Sergei found it difficult to speak fluently and write coherently. He knew, as most academic books were written in English, that his lack of proficiency could hinder his success.

In an attempt, to find a common ground that didn't involve translation, Sergei showed me his favourite computer game: Caterpillar. He watched in awe as I navigated the game I had played as a boy fifteen years earlier. I found myself immersed in the simplicity of guiding a string of pixels through a maze, the bleeps and bloops of Sergei's primitive computer added to the charm of the game. I briefly lost myself in a world of retro gaming, emerging victorious with a high score that surpassed Sergei's best efforts. *When I went to bed, still racing through the mazes of the game in my mind, I felt at home in this Ukrainian family.*

9th December 1995

After an extensive Saturday morning lie-in, the brothers and their dad encouraged me to come for a walk with them around the local area to familiarize myself. The snow was heavy and we headed out of our courtyard towards the local tram station, called *Hnata Yuri*. As we entered, I was amused that Coolio's *Gangster's Paradise* was playing on the underground speakers. The sound and lyrics of this song were perfectly suited to the surroundings. Tiled walls in shades of grey and white, with occasional pops of colour in the form of advertisements. The ground was slick with melted snow and slush. I had to be careful not to slip as I made my way to the platform.

I could see my breath in the frigid air as we waited for the tram. The only sounds were the distant rumble of trains and the occasional announcement over the loudspeaker, replacing the sound of Coolio. Despite the bleak street level atmosphere, there was a sense of community among the commuters underground. An elderly woman smiled kindly at me and a group of teenagers laughed and chatted animatedly.

"You must always stamp your ticket," Taras explained, "and stand up for an elderly babushka." His etiquette was flawless. While the two brothers took turns in providing me with new snippets of information, Volodymyr sat back quietly letting his sons be the tour guides, getting more English practice. We spent a couple of hours hopping on and off trams and trolley buses. Had they abandoned me, I would not have any chance of finding *Hnata Yuri* again. We found ourselves at a road crossing. A man dressed in a thick brown overcoat stopped and almost stood in front of me to block my route.
"Do you speak English?" he asked abruptly.

"Yes," I glanced at Volodymyr, hoping for a sign, as I replied, "do you?"

"Yes, I am a businessman," he announced. Still needing guidance, I saw Sergei staying silent, keen to see how I handled this situation.

"I am tomato businessman," the man continued, "would you like to buy my business for fifty thousand dollars?"

31

"Er...no, tempting but thank you, though." I made a move and family Korol followed me, clearly not engaging with this Ukrainian businessman.

"To promote tomatoes is to promote Ukraine!" he yelled after me. Those final words ringing in my ears.

At dinner that evening we talked about our walk and how, I as Ulysees, had been stuck on the island of the siren *Tomato Man*, with his temptation. It was Maria that voiced her concern.

"He was a gangster!" Maria exclaimed," you should have helped Richard." Volodymyr, Taras and Sergei all found the stunned look on my face amusing, and I understood their previous silence. I had passed a test, I'm not sure what, but from that day forward I was a *Korol* family member.

11th December 1995

My daily journey to the English school started. After lunch I passed through the little subway, Coolio's *Gangsters Paradise* looping as usual, and headed to the tram stop at *Hnata Yuri*. I could see the buildings growing older, the streets busier, the air thicker with the smell of exhaust fumes as I drew closer to the city. This routine would become very familiar to me. There was a stark contrast between the suburban moonscape of *Svitoshin* and the city centre.

Exiting the tram at *Politeknik Institute* became the preferred route as it got me out of the cold tram into the warm underground Metro system sooner. The green *M*, shining like a beacon, had a metaphorical significance as a portal to another world, an underground labyrinth that connected the city's disparate parts.

Entering the station, the warm air was a welcome reprieve from the biting cold. I descended the escalator, struck by the sheer scale of the station. The sound of trains rumbling through the tunnels echoed through the cavernous space. It was like a city within a city, with its own set of rules and customs. Commuters rushed past me; their faces set in determination as they headed towards their destinations. A train arrived with a screech of brakes, and I jostled my way on board, squeezing into a packed carriage. After four stops, I reached my destination, *Maidan Nezalezhnosti,* or Independence Square station. From there, it was a quick change to *Kreshchatik,* the main thoroughfare, then two quick stops south on the blue line to *Respublikanski Stadium,* latterly *Olympiiska,* station.

I emerged from the station into the afternoon sunlight, to see the grandeur of *Respublikanski Stadium* looming over the surrounding buildings, a behemoth of concrete and steel that seemed otherworldly. It was a short walk to the English school where I was teaching for the next three months.

"I was born in the same year that the Olympics were here," Taras had told me, "a hundred thousand people can sit in there." In 1980 the stadium was a marvel of modern architecture, used as a training ground for the Moscow Olympics. The stadium was more than just a place for sports - it was a symbol of community and unity. It seemed as though anything could fit within the walls of the *Respublikanski Stadium.*

The old Soviet school building, adjacent, had seen better days. Its faded yellow bricks and cracked windows spoke of a bygone era, one where the ideals of Communism had been etched into every facet of daily life. It was no longer a place of indoctrination, but one of education. The building had been transformed from a symbol of oppression to one of hope and possibility. It was a testament to the resilience of the human spirit, and a reminder that even the most unlikely places can be filled with the promise of a better tomorrow.

Arriving at the entrance, I saw *'School No.17'* on the sign outside. I opened the creaky metal and wooden door and stepped in, disappointed that the drab exterior carried through to the inside. At the end of the dimly lit corridor, Andrey sat at his desk in the main office.

"Welcome to School no.17," he said, standing up. "How is your Ukrainian family?

"Thank you, they are all very hospitable."

I noticed he was passing me something which turned out to be teaching worksheets. Surprised and a little confused, Andrey ushered me to follow him out of the office, halfway back down the corridor then up a staircase. We entered one of a pair of tall thin doors, into a classroom where there already sat eight students. The classroom was spacious with old desks and peeling paint.

"Good evening, everyone this is Richard, your new English teacher," Andrey said in a quick introduction in English and Russian. "I will leave you to it," then he promptly left. *Was that all the training and induction done? I'd done the Teaching English as a Foreign Language (TEFL) course but never taught a real class before!*

"Good evening, everyone," I began.

Eight pairs of eyes fixed on me, waiting expectantly. They were a diverse class, ranging from older school age students to more mature middle-aged students.

"Why do you all want to learn English?" I asked. The first thing I could think of to ask.
"I want to improve my job prospects," replied one.

"I want to broaden my horizons and travel the world," added another.

"All good reasons," I responded. As the lesson progressed, the students grew more confident with me and in their own language skills. They stumbled over words at first, but soon found themselves speaking basic sentences. After the first lesson I met a few of the other teachers and the camaraderie kicked off straightaway. We were a motley crew, hailing from all corners of the English-speaking world. We all arrived in Ukraine with a sense of adventure and a desire to share their language and culture.

34

For the next few weeks, I followed the same journey between *Hnata Yuri* and *Respublikanski Stadium* as the winter became harsher. I did manage to work out an alternative route from the school by either walking directly to *Ploscha Lva Tolstogo,* missing out the change at *Kreshchatik,* or heading up to the next street to catch the tram directly. The latter meant a sore backside on the hard plastic moulded tram seats by the time I reached *Hnata Yuri.*

As the temperatures dropped, the streets became quieter and the snow started to pile up. People walked with their heads down, trying to shield their faces from the biting wind. Despite the cold, the city still had a certain charm. The snow-covered buildings and Christmas lights, compensated for the lack of advertising, except for *Guinness* adverts, which were everywhere. Clearly a favourite with the locals when they were not drinking litres of homegrown horilka.

On the occasions I chose to walk up to *Ploshcha Lva Tolstogo,* I would pass through a narrow alleyway where a large *Guinness* sign lit the way. The *Guinness* sign was placed over the entrance to one of the many small street-level bars which had popped up in recent years. Opposite, across the alley way, was an *obmin valyut,* or currency exchange, where I could get my *kupons,* the currency in Ukraine at this time. I could change a fifty dollar note and get one hundred million *kupons.* With these beer tokens, I could buy ten pints of *Guinness* which for a young twentysomething was the only currency in Kyiv that held any value at that time. Today, the *kupon* is a relic of Ukraine's past. But for those who lived through that time, it remains a symbol of hope and determination in the face of economic adversity.

On an occasion I took the tram directly to *Hnata Yuri* I walked up to the street in between *Respublikanski Stadium* and *Ploshcha Lva Tolstogo* to the tram stop. The tram stops were located on opposite sides of the road depending on whether you were going east or west. *Hnata Yuri* was west so I would stand on the high side of the road under a streetlight.

Sunflower Underground: A Kyiv Memoir

The snow was falling softly, blanketing the street with a pristine white layer. People were hurrying along, bundled up in their warmest coats and scarves. I stood under the lamp light, watching the flakes dance and twirl as they drifted down. Waiting for the tram, my fingers started to feel numb, despite my thick gloves, and I stamped my feet to keep the blood flowing.

As I waited, a black limousine pulled up on the lower side of the street opposite. Within a minute, a second limousine pulled up on the high side, my side of the street. Both cars across the road from each other. Then simultaneously the roadside back doors of both cars opened, and a lady exited one car and walked briskly across the road, entering the open car door of the other. Both cars drove away in opposite directions.

Shrugging this odd event, I snapped back to reality as the tram pulled up. The sliding doors hissed open. I stepped inside, grateful for the warmth and the chance to escape the snow. As the tram rumbled away down the street, I looked back at the lone streetlamp in the snow and the enigmatic arranged meeting of the two cars reminded me of a scene in *Narnia*. *More secret portals in this fascinating city.*

Another day, while waiting for the tram, I noticed an old man sitting on a bench. He was wrapped up in a thick coat, scarf and hat. He was a tall man with a shock of white hair, and he spoke perfect English with a faint accent.

"I've lived in Kyiv all my life," he said. "It is more dangerous now than ever before." I told him about what I had seen previously with the black limousines. The tram arrived. We got on together and sat together. The old man eyed me closely.

"Listen, this tram stop especially was dangerous," he warned quietly. "If you ever see an exchange between two limousines again, just look at your feet. The occupants, often gangsters, inside the car might think you can see them through the blackened windows." Then, most chillingly, he said, "The consequences of being invited into such a vehicle wouldn't bear thinking about."

"Where did you learn to speak such good English?" I asked.

"I was a foreign diplomat for many years. I've seen the world," he smiled. "I've been to places most people here can only dream of."

He then proceeded to tell me stories of his travels, of diplomatic missions to Africa, Asia and Europe, and of negotiating with foreign governments. I respected his wealth of knowledge and experience, including the many leaders he had met. The old man spoke with quiet dignity of the challenges representing his country abroad.

"Leonid Kravchuk. I liked him, he was born in a small village in western Ukraine in 1934 and became a prominent Soviet politician in the 1980s," he explained, as I noted Kravchuk was the same age as my mum. "When Ukraine gained independence from the Soviet Union in 1991, Kravchuk was elected as the country's first president." *I imagined Kravchuk in the Lviv underground bar.*

"Kravchuk was known for his efforts to establish Ukraine as an independent and democratic state. He played a key role in negotiating the dissolution of the Soviet Union and securing Ukraine's independence. However, Kravchuk's presidency was marked by political instability and economic hardship." I listened intently. "Kravchuk faced criticism, and he was ultimately defeated in last year's presidential election by Leonid Kuchma." The old man_paused, concerned that he had missed out an important fact.

"So here we are, President Kuchma is the second president of Ukraine. Similar age, but he was born in a town in eastern Ukraine and had a career in the Soviet military before entering politics." He smiled at me." He was elected on a platform of economic reform and anti-corruption measures. He is pushing the gangs out of Kyiv to Odessa, and they will soon be all gone."

When my tram arrived at *Hnata Yuri*, I stood up to leave, but the old man held out his hand and shook mine. "Thank you for listening," he said. "It's not often that I get to share my stories with someone."

"Thank you, for sharing your experiences," I replied, humbled. "Good luck, I wish you well."

Transfixed by the conversation, I hadn't even noticed that my backside was sore from the hard seat. From that day on, I made it a habit to chat with locals. *Ukraine had changed so much in the last five years, and I knew it held more secrets yet to be uncovered.*

Chapter 4. Students and the Secret Papers

22nd December 1995

As any English teacher will know, it is challenging to come up with lesson plans that are engaging, interesting, and catered to the individual learning needs of each student. I soon realized that many of my students had different learning styles and preferred different modes of instruction. To cater to these different learning styles, I started incorporating a variety of instructional strategies into my lesson plans. I used videos, visual aids, hands-on activities, and group work to engage my students. I also made a conscious effort to get to know each student. By learning about their interests, hobbies, and passions, I was able to tailor my lessons to their individual needs and make learning more enjoyable and meaningful for them, and me.

I used the educational facilities available at the British Council. The office was located just off the near end of *Kreshchatik*, behind *Bessarabski Market*. The office manager, Sveta, was always very helpful, supplying coffee and biscuits, and after a couple of visits had wanted English lessons from me. She had also directed me to the British Consular at *Arsenalna*, "go and see Inna in the Consular there" she had insisted. I kept that in mind. *Where was Arsenalna?*

As the days turned into weeks, I saw an improvement in my students. Teaching at *School No.17* had been challenging yet rewarding experience. I was genuinely grateful for the opportunity to make a positive impact on the lives of my students and help them understand English, and *the English*.

It was a two-way process as I started to learn more of the native language. I found myself slipping in Ukrainian words and I could- read signs and order food without hesitation. Every time I spoke, I felt a sense of pride and accomplishment. But it wasn't just about the language, it was about the connections I had been making with the people here. They opened their homes and hearts to me, and I had learned. I gained a new perspective on life and a newfound appreciation for Ukrainians. Two of my students, Vadim, of school age, and Kateryna, a professional lady, were more confident, motivated, and eager to learn than some of the others. Kateryna, better at English than some, would give mini lectures in my classes, while Vadim was just liked the sound of his own voice.

"The Ukrainian language has a rich history and culture dating back to the 9th century. During the Soviet era, our language was suppressed, and Russian was promoted as the dominant language in Ukraine," Kateryna would say. "However, after Ukraine gained independence in 1991, there was a renewed interest in Ukrainian language and culture."

"Many Ukrainian writers and poets began to write in Ukrainian, and their works gained popularity among the Ukrainian-speaking population," she exclaimed, "Novels, plays, and poetry in Ukrainian began to be published, and Ukrainian literature began to flourish."

"The breaking through of the Ukrainian language in independent Ukraine was a testament to the resilience of Ukrainian culture and its people," she continued, "despite centuries of oppression, the Ukrainian language managed to thrive." The rest of the class applauded her, in a way they never had me.

Occasionally, during my classes, I would throw in my newest Ukrainian or Russian word of the day to try and impress my students. Naturally I didn't know the nuances between the two languages, so I often strung together sentences which were a pidgin blend of the two. Bizarrely, I seemed to be understood. Invariably, they found my attempts amusing, getting points for trying.

"Are you trying to learn Ukrainian or Russian?" Vadim asked, "because I can't quite tell."

"Ukrainian," I replied sheepishly.

"Why?" he said. "Russian is more prevalent here." The class seemed to wait for my answer with bated breath.

"Because we are in Ukraine," I replied. Slowly, understanding a common aim to bring back the power of Ukraine's language, eight pairs of hands clapped unanimously, and my heart sang.

Kateryna saw this as an opportunity, "The similarity between Ukrainian and Russian is due to their close historical and cultural ties. Both languages belong to the Slavic language family and share many common roots in their vocabulary and grammar. However, there are significant differences. Ukrainian has more vowel sounds, which makes it sound more melodic and softer than Russian."

"In terms of vocabulary, there are also differences, with Ukrainian borrowing more words from Polish, German, and other Western European languages, while Russian has more borrowings from Turkic and Mongol languages. They share the same alphabet but have different sounds peculiar to each language." I deferred to her superior knowledge on the subject.

"So, Kateryna, while Ukrainian and Russian may sound similar, they are different languages with their own unique features?"

"Yes, you understand me, "she said. Therein lay a compliment.

I got to know the other English teachers who had travelled out before me and were already very familiar with Kyiv and regularly ventured out in the evenings for drinks. Alison was self-assured but very pleasant; she seemed to be in control of her life in Kyiv. She was an experienced teacher and knew how to get the best out of her students; she had long blonde hair and answered all my questions about life in Kyiv.

"Do you want to come out for a beer?" Alison popped her head in my classroom as I said goodnight to the last of my Friday students.

"Sure, I need a beer after a long week," I said. The girl standing next to Alison laughed.

"This is Veronica, she was a student of mine". They appeared to be very close girlfriends. I was happy to go out with some like-minded friends away from the usual routine of getting on the tram straight after the lessons.

We travelled on the metro to *Poshtova Ploshcha*, which was the next station beyond *Independence Square*. The Arizona bar was a themed establishment down by the river. For many Ukrainians, as for me, the bar was a welcome novelty, offering a glimpse into life in the United States. It was decorated with classic Americana, including neon signs, license plates, and posters of iconic American figures. The menu featured classic American dishes like burgers and hot dogs, as well as the usual selection of beers and cocktails. The staff spoke English, adding to the authentic American experience. Alison, Veronica and I enjoyed the vibe, the beer and the easy conversation. It was reassuring to know we could depend on each other in this city.

Returning home late was more than a little risky. For one, missing the last tram meant an expensive and dangerous taxi back to *Svitoshin district*. Secondly, it was always a little awkward with my Ukrainian family, as they would wait up for me to return, concerned that I got lost in a snowstorm or was abducted in the shadows by the local gangsters *or even eaten by street dogs.*

Maria welcomed me with open arms, inviting me to take a seat at the kitchen table for a meal, assuming all the time that I must be hungry. In the corner, a pot of borscht stood on the stove, filling the room with its rich, earthy scent. *In her kitchen domain, for the mother of the family, knowing food was more than just sustenance.*

"*Smachno?*" she asked. I knew that she was asking if I liked it.

"*Duzhe smachno!*" I replied, "*na ulitsa tak kholodno.*" I said saying it was very tasty and it was very cold outside.

"Your Ukrainian and Russian is improving," she clapped her hands in joy. I continued to mix the two languages. On the windowsill the radio was still switched on, in a low-level hum, constantly broadcasting discussions from the Ukrainian speaking parliament.

A few weeks into life with my Ukrainian family, Taras felt confident enough to invite me to his school.

"Richard, please may I invite you to my school," he asked cagily," to meet my class and my teacher."

"Of course, I will," I said, "I'm very happy you asked me."

The following day I walked into school with Taras and met his teacher. She was a very jolly lady who welcomed me into the school as if I were a visiting *Ofsted* inspector. She handed me the obligatory ultra strong coffee and we marched together to the class where I was greeted like something between an alien and a rock star. I spent a full hour with Taras' class, answering questions in English about life in England and how I was finding life in Kyiv.

"Richard, we thank you so much for coming today," the teacher said, "I had wondered why Taras' English had suddenly improved over the last few weeks. Please do visit us again." She beamed.

We were into the last week of English lessons at School No.17 before the winter break. As I entered the building, now feeling like a real teacher not an imposter, Alison approached me.

"Up for a beer after lessons?" she asked, already knowing the answer.

"Yes, meet you 8pm in the office" I confirmed, making my way up the staircase.

"Ok, I want to introduce you to someone," she replied. After another thought-provoking lesson, we left the school and walked up to *Palats Sportu*, or Palace of Sport, the twin station of *Respublikanski Stadium*.

Alison and I caught a train for one stop to *Teatralna*, located just off the central thoroughfare of *Kreshchatik*. *Teatralna* refers to the

43

nearby *National Opera and Ballet Theatre*, the Opera House, one of the most iconic landmarks in Kyiv. It is one of the busiest metro stations in the city, serving as a change point for the red and green lines. At one end of the *Teatralna* platform was a huge bronze plaque depicting Lenin's head in front of a flowing banner with words written into the metal sculpture. Standing underneath Lenin, a Russian looking lady wearing a very thick fur-skin coat and fur hat.

"Oksana, this is Richard," Alison said, "Richard, this is Oksana." Oksana smiled a very broad grin and introduced herself again.

"I am Oksana," she said, "I'm very glad to meet you." She spoke exceptionally good English but there was a slight nervousness to her disposition. I glanced at Alison who grinned back.

"I would like to know if you could do some translation work for me," Oksana asked.

"Sure," I replied over-enthusiastically," what text would I be translating?" Ignoring my question, Oksana pointed to the escalators travelling up to above ground and walked on. My curiosity piqued, I followed.

We exited *Teatralna* and walked a hundred metres up the hill to enter a cafe opposite the Opera House. A waitress approached the table.

"Three coffees please," Oksana politely asked in Ukrainian. The cafe was basic, but they clearly knew Oksana. She pulled a paper folder out of her bag, taking out the contents and passing them to me.

"I would like you to proofread these papers," she said. I saw immediately that the papers were ten pages of mathematical content. This was a research paper. Most of the paper was covered in mathematics equations, some of which I vaguely understood.

"Why are you asking me?" I asked, a little frustrated by the cloak and dagger routine.

"Alison mentioned that you studied Mathematics at university," Oksana said simply, still smiling, open for my response.

"I'm flattered but I'll need a week to review it as it is on top of my teaching work. I accept the challenge!"

"Devushka," Alison called the waitress, "three horilkas this time." We clinked our tiny glasses together, toasting this deal with the Ukrainian word for cheers: *"Budmo!"*

Chapter 5. Vodka and Sunflowers

25th December 1995

I feared Christmas Day would be a rather flat affair for non-orthodox Christians, such as myself, in orthodox Ukraine. Christmas in Ukraine is celebrated on 7th January, according to the Julian calendar, different from the Gregorian calendar used in most of the world. In Ukraine, the celebration of Christmas lasts for three days, and people may attend church services, visit family and friends, and participate in cultural events and performances.

Taras used his best English to explain, "One of the most common traditions in Ukraine is the preparation of a special meal on Christmas Eve. The traditional meal, called *Sviata Vecheria*, includes twelve meatless dishes, which represent the twelve apostles. After the meal, families may sing carols, exchange gifts, and attend Mass."

Taras enjoyed the role reversal where he got to teach me about Christmas in Ukraine, "Another important tradition in Ukraine is the decoration of the home with ornaments, including a special Christmas tree called *didukh*, made from stalks of wheat or other grains and symbolizes the ancestors of the family."

There were enough English teachers in Ukraine to have a half decent 25th December. So, we organised a couple of drinks in Arizona and then onto *O'Brien's,* a new Irish pub located off Independence Square. The pub had a lively atmosphere with a traditional Irish pub feel. The interior was decorated with Irish flags, posters, and sports jerseys with a warm and friendly staff. The pub featured live music, adding to the ambiance.

The pub was very popular with Brits who wanted to step out of Ukrainian life for an evening. So, it was here that I spent my Christmas Day, drinking Guinness, playing pool, singing, and dancing to live Irish music.

A week later, I was invited to a New Year's party in my Ukrainian host family's apartment block. Celebrating New Year is the main occasion in Ukraine. People gather with friends and family to celebrate. And there was me, an Englishman. The party was mostly Ukrainian students who were Sergei's school and university friends, in a flat three floors above ours. They had prepared a lot of traditional dishes, such as Olivier salad, herring under a fur coat, and *varenyky*, among others. There were sweets, a fruit platter, and champagne to toast the New Year. Ukrainian pop songs, as well as international hits, were played while we chatted and played games.

From my own alcohol-fuelled university days, I knew the key to surviving copious amounts of alcohol was to fill my stomach early with bread and meat. *This did not include fish.* A game which continued throughout the evening was to drink a glass of straight horilka every time the clock struck the hour, every hour, up to midnight. Each glass represented a different city on the next time zone across all time zones in Russia. Having started with Vladivostok some seven hours previously we were fast approaching the Moscow shot of horilka.

"I can't drink anymore," didn't even register and the shots kept coming. This seventh round of horilkas, to be honest, was my limit. I was now in unchartered territory of drunken mind over matter, but somehow trying to maintain a state of awareness so I would at least wake up in my own bed the following morning. The temperature outside was a chilly minus fifteen degrees centigrade and I had no intention of spending the night in a deep snowdrift either.

As the clock approached midnight for the eighth round of the *New Year's Horilka Time Zone game*, I unsuccessfully attempted the classic throw-the-vodka-over-the-shoulder trick to mitigate the percentage of alcohol already in my blood.

"Keep your eyes on the bottom of the glass next time, so you don't miss your mouth," Artem advised me as he re-filled my glass.

"There is no escape," he advised, "it is the Ukrainian way."

As the clock struck midnight, there was huge excitement, everyone filled their glasses, cheered, sang and danced. Before I could finish teaching everyone the words to *Auld Lang Syne*, everyone grabbed their coats and rushed out of the concrete apartment building into the fresh tumbling snow. Everyone was letting off fireworks that sounded and felt like hand grenades. *We welcomed in 1996 with a lot of snowy hugs and kisses.*

7th January 1996

In January, a few new English teachers arrived at the school. I was straight back into teaching my students for a short week then came Orthodox Christmas and Old New Year. Naturally, this was further excuse, had any been needed, to drink more horilka.

After this brief period of self-induced alcohol poisoning, normality returned. The snow showers were relentless. I struck up an instant connection with Ron, one of the new teachers. He had a small goatee beard and had arrived in Ukraine during the orthodox Christmas via the same route as I had travelled a month earlier. He was a Worcester man born and bred which meant that we were both from the Cotswolds and had much in common.

"Do you want to come for a beer in Arizona?" I asked as was tradition when a new teacher arrived.

"I would love a beer," Ron accepted, and we settled into an easy friendship. On the way we stopped in *Guinness Alley* where I often grabbed an emergency hot dog from an apparently closed kiosk there. I showed a puzzled Ron how it worked.

"Dva sausage sandwich pozhaulsta," I said as if I were casting a spell and a little hatch opened, where I put my money. The hatch closed. Ron watched, fascinated. Then half a minute later it would open again and there, as if by magic, was a Ukrainian hot dog. Ron had a go using the same magic words, with the same result.

In Arizona bar, with beers in hand, I gave him a brief insight into my life in Kyiv with the other English teachers. We compared notes between his and my adopted Ukrainian families.

"Do you want to go and visit Odessa?" he asked after a few pints. This immediately reminded me of the old man at the tram stop.

"Odessa is full of mafia gangs," I warned," are you sure you want to go there?"

"Yes," Ron said excitedly, "it sounds like fun." And so, we started planning a trip to the Black Sea. I also introduced him to the *River Palace* which was a nightclub on a boat on the Dnipro river.

"If you like the sound of Odessa," I joked, "you'll like the *River Palace*." I had always felt there was a slightly dark side to this establishment.

14th January 1996

I had completed the translation of the maths papers passed to me by Oksana before Christmas. How I had translated the papers into any meaningful form between all the celebrations and parties of the last few weeks I'll never know. But I had done. And now all papers with translation notes were neatly tucked inside the paper folder ready to be reviewed and edited or whatever. I still had no idea why Oksana had asked me.

Oksana had passed a note via the school to arrange a meeting time for me to deliver the translated papers back to her: midday at the Lenin sculpture in *Teatralna*.

I arrived at exactly midday to find that Oksana had not. While waiting, I observed the Ukrainian commuters as they moved through the station. The same as London commuters, but there was something different, they moved like pedestrians captured on old black and white films, something from the 1920s about them.

Oksana came rushing down the centre of the platform towards me. As she hurriedly approached Lenin in her thick coat and hat, I could imagine her carrying out his orders efficiently and quickly. I was still standing in the same place, and she immediately composed herself.

"I apologise for my lateness, and Happy New Year," she panted. "How are you?"

"No bother," I said politely. "Happy New Year to you!" She smiled.

"You are a proper English gentleman," she smiled again. I laughed, imagining the stereotype she was comparing me against. *James Bond or Hugh Grant in every film he's in?*

"Let's have lunch," she said, "I would like to review some of the translation work with you." We passed up the towering escalators and exited on the *Kreshchatik* side of the station and walked down the thoroughfare. Oksana led the way and knew where she was going. She was noticeably a foot shorter than me and so probably needed two steps to my one as we walked down the icy street. After five minutes, she turned in towards a door, set a step below the pavement.

There were plates of food displayed on glass shelves in the window, so I assumed this must be the restaurant. The display of dishes were samples from the menu, curiously actual food on plates in direct sunlight. Surely, these would not be consumed by the lunchtime customers. Oksana found a table in the corner near one of the windows displays and we sat down to browse the menu and order a drink. I handed Oksana the paper folder with the translated papers.

"What did you think about this type of work?" she asked as she skimmed through the pages.

"I quite enjoyed the subject matter," I said as the waitress placed a jug of water on the table. Oksana didn't look up. I acknowledged the waitress.

"Can I ask who the author of the paper is?" I enquired. "I'm assuming he is an academic in a university." She appeared to ignore my question then stopped on one page to question some of my translation work.

"I felt that some passages of the paper, and notable equations, should be better written in a slightly different way," I began saying, "because of the different way English language was written." She seemed to be reading and re-reading certain passages repeatedly as if to try and understand and reconcile my editing. She looked up at me and smiled.

"Excellent", she finally looked up. I felt like a student, waiting for my grade.

The waitress approached the table, "Please may I take your order." I let Oksana order first.

"I'll just have some borsht," Oksana replied.

"I would like the chicken fillets with the potato salad," I said as I pointing to the menu.

"Please can you order something else," the waitress asked.

"OK...er, I'll have the beef dish with French fries?" But again, the waitress hesitated.

"There is no beef left," she said. "But if you want, you can take the display dish from the window." Thinking she was joking I laughed, but she stood there stoney-faced which clearly meant she was being serious.

"Um, no thank you," I declined politely, mildly uncomfortable with the lack of food hygiene and unaware how long those display plates had sat in the window. I looked at Oksana. *This was not the high-class culinary reward I had been anticipating.*

"Please could I have the borscht soup, with some black bread" I asked. Without acknowledgement, the waitress took my menu and walked back to the kitchen.

"I will take the translated paper into the Mathematics Institute where the author will review it," Oksana said. She handed me a second paper.

"Here is another paper for you to work on," she said, "same author and subject matter."

"I will try and complete it by next week," I answered. "I'm travelling down to Odessa for a few days."

She nodded as the waitress brought two dripping bowls of borsht soup to the table. Most of it had stayed in the bowl. The feedback I was waiting for never came.

After lunch, we parted on *Kreshchatik*, Oksana turning up the hill towards *Teatralna*, while I continued walking up *Kreshchatik* towards Independence Square to post a letter.

There was a constant snow fall on *Kreshchatik* and the snow-clearers were busy shovelling, piling up the snow between the giant pavements and the street. The snow-clearers were all women. They were dressed in grey overalls and well built, with tree-trunk bodies and branch-like arms. Each team consisted of about eight women on one truck. A woman sat in the driver's seat of the truck while one woman stood on the back of the truck, directing operations above the team. The women on the road carried great snow shovels; some were shovelling from the pavement side into the great wall of snow and some shovelling from the road surface. As I watched in awe of the sheer muscular nature of the operation, the woman in the truck shouted some instruction. All the women on the ground leaned their shovels against the truck and took a glass from the back of it. The woman in the truck then proceeded to pour a clear liquid into each glass which the woman drank. Presumably this was their tea break, or rather, vodka break. Once the vodka was downed, the women picked up their snow shovels and resumed their work.

I reached Independence Square and immediately turned into the great door arch of the central post office. Snow was blowing in through the outer door but not the inner set of doors. Once inside the main hall, the noise of the snowstorm was replaced by the busy chatter of customers discussing their business at one of twenty different kiosks.

I approached the back of the queue which led to the nearest kiosk. The queue snaked past a large rack of postcards which all had a dated look of Kyiv during Soviet times, the postcards were more drawings rather than photos. I wanted to send a few postcards home, but most were just too dull to consider. Some postcards highlighted the struggles and challenges of the post-Soviet period, *joy indeed*, featuring illustrations of Soviet leaders, such as Lenin and Stalin. There were images of Soviet symbols, like the hammer and sickle or the red star, *enough to brighten up anybody's morning*. Many of the postcards also featured slogans or messages in support of the Soviet government or Communist Party. *No thank you.*

Some postcards celebrated the country's independence and featured the national flag, emblem, and other symbols of the newly formed state. Many postcards featured sunflower fields or just individual sunflowers. An eye-catching postcard with a vibrant and sunny backdrop was filled with a breathtaking field of sunflowers stretching as far as the eye could see. The sunflowers stood tall and proud, their golden petals shining brightly under the warm Ukrainian sun. The contrast between the bright yellow petals and the deep green stems created a vibrancy. These postcards captured the essence of summer with cheerful and uplifting vibes and were warming images in the depths of winter. These sunflowers were the perfect image to send to my mum and dad, letting them know about the beauty and positivity that the Ukrainian sunflower symbolizes.

Taras had mentioned to me that "Sunflowers hold a special significance in Ukraine. They have become a symbol of Ukraine. Firstly, Ukraine is one of the largest producers of sunflowers in the world. These bright, resilient flowers are a common sight throughout the landscape." As was usual during my cultural training, he would pause to see if I had understood what he had said. "Secondly, the abundance of sunflowers in Ukraine represents the country's rich agricultural heritage and fertile lands."

Maria added, translated by Taras, "Additionally, the sunflower's ability to turn towards the sun, following its path across the sky, is seen as metaphor for the Ukrainian people's resilience. Their ability to find hope and strength even in challenging times." Taras would pause to allow his mother to continue, then translated "During Ukraine's struggle for independence, the image of a sunflower was often used as a peaceful symbol of unity and freedom. It represents the desire of the Ukrainian people to grow and flourish, just like the sunflower itself." Maria was proud to have given me this information which had come from her heart. I understood the sunflower's connection to Ukraine's agriculture, it's symbolic meaning, and its representation of hope and unity made it an iconic beloved national symbol.

I picked out a handful of the sunflower postcards and, as I waited, started to write them in the queue. Every minute, the main door blew open with a burst of snow and cold air behind me. Every minute, I stepped forward one space as the person at the front of the queue was beckoned forward by the lady in the next available kiosk.

I noticed that there were only women in the kiosks, seemingly post-office work was not considered a male career in Ukraine. As I wrote the first postcard, I found that I had to write on a second then third postcard. After labelling them 'one of three', 'two of three' and 'three of three' I had reached the front of the queue. Another blast of cold air blew in.

"Next," beckoned the lady in kiosk number nine. She was a rather fierce looking middle-aged lady. "What do you want?" Customer service was not a strong feature in this country. I placed the three postcards on the counter, and she took them and turned them over one by one. She then placed them back on the counter and barked something at me which I didn't quite understand.

"Pochemu ty uzhe napisal na otkrytkakh?" she asked. The lady next to me in kiosk number eight had heard and seen the look on my face.

"She asked 'why have you already written on the postcards before paying for them?'"

"Sorry," I said to Number Eight, "I didn't know we couldn't."

"Well, you can't," she said. "You're in Ukraine now." I thought she might stick her tongue out at me. The whole queue was now watching. If I wasn't on the other end of it, I would have admired her bluntness.

I apologised to Number Nine in my best Ukrainian Russian mix, and she appeared to accept my apology and payment without any further grief. The door blew in another blast of cold air, slamming shut as if to end our exchange.

I quickly retreated from the kiosk and took refuge up a stairwell. I was curious to check out what was up there. Creeping up, I discovered a basic but very functional internet cafe. This was the first internet cafe I had seen in Kyiv, and I was slightly annoyed that I had not discovered it sooner. *I didn't have a mobile phone in those days, not many people did.* Anyway, I turned back down the stairs, feeling I had discovered the Lost Ark, and left the post office back into the snowstorm.

Postcards posted and job done! I decided to go for a pint at O'Brien's, across Independence Square, happy in the knowledge that my parents may receive some sunflower-festooned postcards from me in a few weeks' time, *in whatever order.*

Chapter 6. Ice

1st February 1996

The winter of 1996 in Ukraine was desperately cold. Temperatures dropped to minus thirty degrees centigrade in some areas, causing numerous deaths. It was, in just such temperatures, that Ron and I decided to take a trip down south to Odessa on the Black Sea coast.

We were joined by Anna, a teacher from Germany. She had grown up in Leipzig and had lived through the fall of the Berlin Wall. After completing her studies in English and German at the University of Leipzig, Anna moved to Ukraine to teach German. Anna enjoyed teaching both languages and felt that her experience of growing up in East Germany had given her a unique perspective. She was able to explain the nuances of the language to her students in Russian and share her experiences of living in Germany with them. Teaching both English and German was a way for her to bridge the gap between cultures and promote better understanding.

The stories of criminal gangs in Odessa had not put us off the trip. The man at the snowy tram stop had told me "During the 1990s they were able to operate with impunity due to corruption within the local government and law enforcement agencies. Many police officers and government officials were on the payroll of the gangs. This allowed the gangs to continue their criminal activities without fear of being caught. Despite the challenges posed by these criminal organizations, there were also efforts to combat them. In 1994, the Ukrainian government had established a special police force to combat organized crime. This *Berkut* force was able to make some progress in reducing the power of the criminal gangs in Odessa."

It was against the backdrop of this gangsters' paradise, during an unusually cold winter, that Ron, Anna and I boarded a train at Kyiv station, *Voxalna*, heading south. We took vodka, some bread and meat to immerse ourselves in the Ukrainian experience. Vodka, bread, and meat are indeed traditional snacks. But I had discovered *salo*, basically cured slabs of subcutaneous pig fat, to be eaten with cloves of garlic, which was now a particular favourite of mine. *In the confines of our sleeper carriage this proved to be particularly unsociable.*

Ron and I had the two lower bunk beds while Anna took one of the top bunks. The remaining bunk was used for storing bags, food and drink. We settled down with our hearty *Cossack* feast as the great train pulled out of Kyiv central station.

After a long day of teaching and getting to our train, we were ready to wind down with a few drinks. We decided to try some of Ron's *Hetman's* vodka, and let's just say, it packed quite the punch.

"The name *Hetman* comes from the same word, which means 'leader' or 'military commander' in Ukrainian," Anna explained. "It's a traditional Ukrainian drink, centuries old."

Ron had done his research too. "The recipe for Hetman's vodka is a closely guarded secret, but it is known to be made from high-quality Ukrainian wheat, rye, or barley. The ingredients are fermented and distilled multiple times to create a smooth and potent spirit."

As we sipped our drinks, we started to feel the effects of the *Hetman*. Our eyes were getting a little blurry, our words starting to slur. Before we knew it, we were completely hammered. We stumbled around our accommodation, giggling and laughing at everything. We decided to get into our beds but realized that we had forgotten to prepare them for our drunken state. As we attempted to climb into our beds, we kept falling off and rolling around. We couldn't stop laughing at ourselves and the ridiculous situation we had found ourselves in. Finally, we managed to get into our beds, but it was like sleeping on a waterbed, except we were the waves crashing into each other.

Early the next morning, we woke up feeling a little worse for wear, but we laughed at the memory of our drunken bed-making attempts. We learned a valuable lesson that night: *always prepare your beds before drinking Ukrainian vodka.* As we snuggled into our seats, with a surprisingly forgiving hangover and a revolting coffee, the sound of the train wheels clacking on the tracks, I thought about the stories I had heard about Odessa.

We arrived in Odessa at 7am, still feeling less than fresh, courtesy of *Mr Hetman*, glad that we were all wearing arctic thermals with additional warm clothing, including a hat, two layers of gloves, and a heavy jacket. That day, Odessa train station was minus twenty degrees centigrade with thick snow on the ground and solid ice all around. That winter, the snow and ice were especially thick. We took a moment to appreciate the icicles hanging from the early 20th century grand architecture, before taking a short taxi ride to our accommodation, the *Hotel Krasnaya*.

During the nineties, *Hotel Krasnaya* was a popular Soviet-style hotel in Odessa; built in the sixties, it had over two hundred rooms. While these hotels were often criticized for their lack of modern amenities and drab interiors, they were still popular with visitors to Odessa due to their central location and affordable prices.

Ron and I had a twin room while Anna stayed in another twin down the hallway on the same floor. The rooms were functional and basic in design. Ours had twin beds with plain white bedding and a simple wooden headboard. The walls had been painted in a neutral colour and there was a small desk with a chair. The small television had limited channels, a basic bathroom with a shower and bathtub. There were half used toiletries such as soap and shampoo left over from the previous occupants. There was little decoration in the room, other than perhaps a simple painting on the wall. The rooms had a single ceiling light and a bedside lamp. *This was communism.*

After dropping our bags, the three of us headed out into town. We only had two days in Odessa. So we headed straight for the *Potemkin Steps*, a giant staircase in the city of Odessa and one of the only landmarks I had heard about in the city. The steps connected the city centre to the port of Odessa consisting of 192 steps, arranged in a series of landings, creating the illusion that the staircase is longer than it is. The steps are famous for their appearance in the classic 1925 silent film, *'Battleship Potemkin'*, which I had watched before coming to Ukraine. About the Russian Revolution of 1905, the film features a memorable scene in which a group of soldiers march down the steps, firing on a crowd of civilians. Although the staircase offered stunning views of the city and the frozen sea, we found ourselves clinging to the ice-cold railings as we slid down step by step.

Reaching the shoreline, we noticed just how thick the ice was on the frozen sea.

"Walking on frozen Black Sea ice in winter can be a unique and exciting experience," I suggested to Ron.

"However, it is important to note that it can also be dangerous, and precautions should be taken before venturing out onto the ice," Ron countered.

"Firstly, it is important to check the weather and ice conditions before heading onto the ice. The ice should be at least ten centimetres thick to support a person's weight. Stay away from areas where the ice may be thin, such as near the edges of the ice or near areas where there is moving water," I joked.

"Secondly, it is important to dress appropriately for the cold weather. This means wearing warm, waterproof clothing, including a hat and gloves. One should wear sturdy, non-slip footwear to prevent slipping on the ice," Ron laughed, pointing to our worn-out trainers.

"Thirdly, it is important to bring along necessary safety equipment, such as ice picks or a rope, in case of an emergency. Let someone know where you are going and when you plan to return," I added.

"Fourthly, female Germans will stay on shore while British males play their stupid games," Anna joked.

Moderately hungover, Ron then I wandered onto the thick honeycomb-shaped ice sheets. Anna sensibly stayed in the snow-covered beach. "You're both mad," she shouted. Ron edged out ahead of me and the ice continued to feel sturdy and solid.

"How's the ice your end?" I shouted.

"Feeling sturdy," Ron replied. "How's the ice at your end?"

"Solid," I replied, tentatively edging along just in case it wasn't.

As we got to twenty metres offshore, we both marvelled at the horizon of cargo ships and oil tankers. During winter months, ports in the Black Sea region experience ice formation, which hindered the movement of ships. To avoid this, some oil tankers chose to anchor in open waters outside the port and wait for the ice to melt or be cleared. It also helps to avoid delays and potential damage to the ship caused by the impact of ice. However, anchoring in open waters also presents its own set of challenges, such as exposure to strong winds and waves. *Battleship Potemkin* may have experienced the same problems.

"Let me take a photo," Anna called from the shore waving a camera above her head. Ron and I turned towards her and shook hands as if we had just reached the South Pole.

"Did you just feel the ice move?" Ron asked. It *was* moving. Ron was sliding away from me.

"Run!" I shouted. We raced back to the shore, hopping and skipping over frozen ledges and joints between the ice. Back on *terra firma,* we realised how different the outcome could have been but were exhilarated to have done it. Never again. The *female German* was right.

Back in the warmth of the *Hotel Krasnaya,* we ate some dry chicken dish and headed to our rooms. Popping open a bottle of peach flavoured horilka Ron and I laughed about our near-death experience on the ice. It had been exhilarating. Anna ignored us and opened a deck of cards. "Poker, anyone?" she said. The losers drank a shot after each round. Somehow, that was Ron and me.

It wasn't long before we got stuck into British politics and the prospect of a Labour government for the first time in 18 years. "Tony Blair will win the election next year," Ron and I both concluded under the influence of a fruity Ukrainian vodka.

"John Major is just too boring," Ron said. We both pictured the grey, dull *Spitting Image* caricature we'd seen on UK television.

"Tony Blair seems to be the person I would most prefer to have a drink with," Anna said. There we were drinking horilka, playing cards, choosing the next UK prime minister in an old Soviet hotel in a gangsters' paradise, the adrenaline of dancing on the Black Sea ice in our veins.

Two days later, we had visited the market, ice skated safely at the city's outdoor rink, explored snow-covered parks and gardens, and visited museums and art galleries. Exhausted, we returned to Kyiv; we had been to somewhere special, and Kyiv felt like home. *It suddenly dawned on me that I would be going home to the UK in less than a month.*

Chapter 7. The Professor

28th February 1996

I had almost survived a Ukrainian winter - it was nearly March in the icy city of Kyiv; the anticipation was that March would arrive with a burst of energy and anticipation fuelled by the start of Spring. Usually, the snow would begin to melt away at this time of year but not this year. The snow and the ice remained. It looked like my last week in Kyiv would remain winter until my departure. *What would the next week bring?*

My Ukrainian family were happy that I had returned from Odessa, having seemingly expected me to be kidnapped by gangs then released only upon payment of ransom. But something was different now; something had either changed in me or my Ukrainian hosts. Maria and Volodymyr had adopted me as another son in the family, albeit an errant one, while Taras and Sergei had accepted me as a sort of half-brother, or at least a distant cousin. We were all aware that I would be gone by this time next week.

I had one last evening of English lesson to give at School No.17 and then I would need to say goodbye to my students. During the day I prepared my lessons as usual and walked through our tram station with Coolio's *Gangsters Paradise* blaring out of the speakers. I took the tram into *Politeknik Institute* as usual and changed to the metro so I could get into *Kreshchatik* just around lunchtime, early enough to meet with Oksana.

Our meeting place on this occasion was not under the Lenin sculpture in the *Teatralna,* but in the grand central hall of the *Kreshchatik* metro station. The walls of the station were adorned with intricate mosaics and murals, depicting some important moment in Soviet, or more specifically, Ukrainian history. The platform itself was wide and long, with tracks running in different directions. The station bustled with activity, people rushing to catch their trains or simply passing through on their way to work.

Despite its grandeur, *Kreshchatik* station was also incredibly efficient. The trains arrived and departed on time. The station was well-equipped with modern amenities such as escalators and electronic displays above each tunnel entrance showing the time since the last train departed. This was the opposite of the London underground where passengers see the time until the next train arrives. The Ukrainian underground overall seemed to work much better than London's system and was much cleaner and significantly more spacious.

Oksana was dressed for the Arctic as ever and welcomed me with her beaming smile. She was aware that this was my last week in the city, and this was likely to be our last meeting. We chatted all the way up the towering escalators about when spring might arrive.

"I've never known a winter quite like this one," Oksana insisted. "The number of people dying from flu and even diphtheria is terrifying me." I suddenly had the feeling it was time to go back to England. Oksana led me to the *Passazh.*

"I know a very nice new French restaurant that does great business lunches," she said. The *Passazh,* or Passage, on *Kreshchatik* is a shopping mall. Its great archway was constructed after the war. *Passazh* housed around twenty stores, boutiques, cafes, and restaurants. The buildings' architecture was impressive but somehow grey and devoid of the sparkle you would expect of a trendy shopping mall. However, *Passazh* was a convenient place to meet for lunch. That day, that's where Oksana was taking me, for the promised improvement on the previous restaurant.

We entered *La Passazh,* a French restaurant which had a refined and elegant atmosphere, with a focus on high-quality ingredients and traditional French cooking techniques. This was different from the last restaurant I had visited with Oksana; no dried-up window displays.

The decor included crisp white tablecloths, polished silverware, and beautiful floral arrangements, creating a sense of sophistication.

"Tres Bon!" I voiced as we meandered to our table. The waiter passed us a menu each as we sat down. The menu featured classic French dishes such as escargot, foie gras, bouillabaisse, and coq au vin, as well as a variety of meat, fish, and vegetarian options. There was an extensive wine list featuring a range of French vintages, carefully curated to complement the flavours of the food.

The service was attentive and professional with knowledgeable staff, able to recommend dishes and pairings to enhance the dining experience. My first experience of a French restaurant in Kyiv was that it offered an almost authentic dining experience and was perfect for a special occasion, including the bombshell to come.

"Are you ready to order?" said the Ukrainian waiter.

"I'll have the soup and then Beef Bourguingnon," I said knowing that they probably had it in stock unlike the previous place.

"I'll have the same," Oksana ordered politely. The waiter wrote down our order with a flourish of his pen, pretending a little too much to be a French waiter. As he turned to walk back to the kitchen, Oksana burst into life and pulled out the usual tatty paper folder from her bag.

"I have some great news for you," she declared, as if she was just about to tell me that she had won the lottery. Not that Ukraine had a lottery.

"The professor who authored the papers that you've been translating was very pleased with the work," she said almost out of breath. Now, had that been the end of the conversation, I would have expressed my pleasure and tucked into my soup which had arrived. But Oksana had something to say.

"He would be delighted if you could go and meet him to discuss the translation work," she continued to say, holding her gaze on me. I made a second failed attempt to taste my soup.

"He found it most interesting to see how you had expressed some of the equations that you had written," she explained.

"When would he be thinking of having such a meeting given that I have less than a week remaining in Kyiv," I quickly asked, preparing for my third attempt at the soup.

"This afternoon if you're not too busy?" she said. I nearly dropped the soup spoon. *I could have said I was too busy.*

"Can you tell me about this professor," I enquired. "What is his name? I haven't seen it written anywhere."

Oksana paused while she took a mouthful of soup. "His name is Korolyuk," she said. "And he is an amazing man. You really are very lucky that he has asked to meet with you."

I was really intrigued. "I would be delighted to meet with the professor," I confirmed. "If I will ever finish my soup."

The Beef Bourguignon was less than exceptionally good. I was not sure that the French would be happy to put their name to it. However, the service remained excellent throughout the lunch, and I hadn't been offered a window display meal. "Au Revoir!", the pretend French waiter called as we left.

We exited the restaurant and *Passazh* towards the subway to the left. Through the subway we exited on the opposite side of *Kreshchatik* directly onto the hill that led up towards the Opera House. We continued to negotiate the snow and ice as we climbed the hill past the entrance to *Teatralna* metro station. As we did so, Oksana took a left down a side street that I had never noticed before. Fifty metres down this side street, we approached the gates of a solid fortress-like building. I tried to decipher the sign on the left of the gatepost to understand where Oksana was bringing me.

"Welcome to the Mathematics Institute," she said. A more foreboding building I had not seen since watching the *Adam's Family* film in black and white. This was clearly a place that you entered but should not expect to come out alive.

"Please do not to speak with anyone inside as you are a foreigner," she advised. "Some foreigners are not to be trusted," she forced a smile. *This was getting better and better.*

We entered the outer gates and walked across the empty courtyard towards another set of double doors. I noticed another sign saying the same thing. Oksana led the way as I followed behind her with my mouth well and truly zipped. The lady at Reception sat at a long desk. She was clearly placed there to meet and greet.

"Hello Oksana, what do you want?" she asked politely, but her eyes fixed on me.

"Korolyuk, *pozhaluysta*," Oksana and she had a short conversation about which I understood nothing. Oksana beckoned me to follow her to the right of the reception towards a grand granite staircase. The stairs were beautifully lit by the winter sun pouring through the windows. We climbed four flights of stairs to the second floor. There were a further two floors above. Oksana continued to beckon me as I got distracted by the sheer solid structure of the building. She turned down a corridor which was dark compared to the sun-washed light on the stairs.

"Please wait here," she asked. I waited in the dark corridor as she opened one of the single doors leading off it. The enormous doors were thick and evenly studded, running the full perimeter to seal the padding. Oksana went through and the door closed behind her. After ten minutes, I started to wonder what my escape plan would be, if I could get out of the building on my own. Suddenly, I heard the door opening and out came Oksana.

"Professor Korolyuk is inside this room and is now expecting you," she announced as if she were his royal butler. I wasn't sure whether I should enter the room alone or with Oksana. She indicated with a smile and a nod to proceed through the thick padded door. As I entered, I noticed there was another padded door beyond that. As the outer door closed, I entered through the diminutive inner padded door.

Once in the room, it was not immediately obvious to me that there was anyone else in there. The room was akin to an old lecture theatre, incredibly musty; a long black board on one side to the right and a full wall of windows to the left. This was the same side of the building as the stairwell as the sun brightly poured through the glass. The sunlight shone onto a large painting on the wall with the name "Professor Korolyuk" embedded in the frame underneath. It was then that I noticed another figure seated in the room.

I rather Britishly said, "Good afternoon, Professor. Thank you for inviting me here. You must be busy." I felt that I was doing all the talking and I probed further, "what is it that you would want to see me about?"

Still silence reigned; it dawned on me that he may not even speak English. Maybe he hadn't understood a word I said since entering the room. He slowly turned around on the swivel chair he was reclining in and looked at me.

"You have been interfering with my papers, have you not?" he asked accusingly. The tone of the question led me to deny it.

"I have not been interfering with the papers but merely re-writing them," I replied, trying to keep my tone calm. "In a way to make them easier to read for an English speaker."

The professor smiled and stood up with his hand outstretched. Apparently, I'd passed another test I didn't sign up for.

"Welcome to Kyiv!" he said. "It is a great pleasure that you have been brave enough to come and visit me here in the Mathematics Institute."

The fortress, I thought. Professor Korolyuk had a friendly face with a natural smile; I was immediately relaxed in his company.

"How is life treating you in Kyiv?" he asked. "Do you enjoy living with your Ukrainian family?" He had so many questions, including what I thought about the food and the weather. I told him about our visit to Odessa and how much fun it was to go to the Irish pub in Kyiv. "I have never had a pint of Guinness in my entire life," he insisted," but dream of doing so."

"I invite you for a drink at O'Brien's," I said.

"I accept if you ever to return to Kyiv," he said. I thought this was a curious thing for him to say.

Professor Korolyuk pulled out a paper from his bag and showed it to me. It was one of the research papers that I had 'interfered' with. He turned to one of the pages.

"Please can you explain why you have reordered some of the sequencing of the equations," he asked.

"If I had left it, the reader would need to understand the mind of the author, but by doing it this way, it shows that the author is trying to understand the mind of the reader," I replied. "So, the reader feels empathy for what was almost an impossible sentence to understand."

"It is a way of expanding your readership to include simple people like me," I rather boldly said. He looked at me, smiled then laughed.

He stood up and wandered over to a cabinet and side-swiped the cabinet door with his fist. The door opened down and he reached inside for a half full bottle of vodka. He placed the two glasses on the desk.

"Have you developed a taste for Ukrainian vodka during your stay?" he asked.

"I have, for both vodka and horilka," I replied, and I had certainly drunk enough. He carefully poured the vodka to the top of the glasses and replaced the bottle back into the cabinet. He handed one of the full glasses to me.

"*Nashe zdarovye,*" he toasted. "To our health." And I knew what to do after that - straight down the hatch. He was clearly impressed and swiftly poured another one to which I responded in the same way.

"Easier to drink than Guinness," he joked.

"How would you know?" I responded and he laughed out loud. Professor Korolyuk sat down.

"Would you like to help write more papers on the same subject as you have been translating?" he asked. The subject was Probability Theory of which I had a passing interest.

"I would be interested but I'm leaving Kyiv to return to England in a few days," I said.

"Oksana told me the same, "he acknowledged. "I am aware of this. If you like, you could work with me in Kyiv?" he tentatively asked. "In the Mathematics Institute as a research student. I invite you."

I realised he was offering me to become a student under his guidance. It was a lot to think about. "I need to think about this on my return home. Thank you for the offer."

He smiled, reassuring me he wasn't going to retract the offer. Incredibly an hour had passed; Professor Korolyuk stood up, his hand outstretched.

"The correct decision. Always give yourself an option and time." Bidding me farewell, I shook his hand.

"Thank you for the chat and the vodka," I said.

Sunflower Underground: A Kyiv Memoir

"Just let Oksana know about your decision. I would be very happy to welcome you into the Institute."

I exited the big, padded door to find, to my slight surprise, that Oksana was standing waiting for me in the dark hallway.

"Were you waiting the whole time?" I asked her.

"Yes of course," she replied," how was the meeting?"

"He invited me to work with him." She probably already knew this.

"You are lucky to have met him," she said in surprise, "let alone be invited to work with him."

"If I work with him, will I drink vodka with him every time I meet him?" I joked. "He wants me to take him out for a pint of Guinness!"

"Professor Korolyuk is a very secretive person," she laughed. "He must have seen something in you that he liked."

We walked back down the dark, previously sunlit, stairwell back to Reception. The receptionist had already gone home. Oksana and I parted at the gate.

"I will let you know about my decision to work with Korolyuk," I said by way of goodbye.

Chapter 8. Intermission

1st March 1996

I awoke, it was the start of March, the start of Spring. However, when I drew the curtains back there was a fresh layer of deep snow again. My very own *Groundhog Day*.

If yesterday had been strange enough meeting Professor Korolyuk, then today was even stranger. I ate a big breakfast in the kitchen after Taras and Sergei had gone to school. At around 11am, there was a buzz at the door; Maria wiped her hands on her apron and hurriedly stepped into the hallway. She took off her apron as she opened the front door. A young lady entered the apartment and hugged and kissed Maria. She placed her handbag on the floor before removing her winter fur coat and hat. They entered the kitchen.

"Richard, Marina," she said. "Marina, Richard." Marina did do a better job at introducing herself, as her English was very good. Marina was Maria's niece. She had long, brown hair and clear skin; an attractive face, if a little plain.

Marina was from somewhere outside Kyiv, an unpronounceable city beginning with a "Z". Already six years my senior, I was clearly at a disadvantage; I had better be careful. She was vibrant and intelligent, looking for companionship. I quickly sensed there had been a discussion within the family that I could be that person. According to the mother, I needed a tour guide in Kyiv, rather oddly three days before I would be leaving the country.

I went with the flow and finished my breakfast of kasha, like a roasted buckwheat porridge, with an extra coffee before getting ready to go out. Marina and I left the apartment block, taking the old lift down and crunched into the deep untouched snow at the apartment block entrance. The sun was shining. The sky was a clear blue making the snow sparkle like icing.

We chatted as we made our way into the tram stop at *Hnata Yuri* and headed towards *Kreshchatik*. Marina was a pleasant enough person with a lively conversation but seemed to think that I had spent the last three months sitting in the apartment.

"You must be going crazy sitting in that apartment all day every day," she said. "I bet you're glad that I arrived." She explained things to me that I had already found out for myself, but I didn't have the heart to tell her about my nights out, the people I'd met.

Upon arrival at *Kreshchatik* station, I started to revisit the events of the day before with Korolyuk. None of this was out loud to Marina but my mind was beginning to consider the possibility of a return to Kyiv later in the year. I would tell Ron this evening, just to get an initial sense check from him about how mad I would need to be to return to the *frozen wasteland*.

As we crossed stations to *Maidan Nezalezhnosti,* then advanced up the long escalator to exit on to Independence Square, my attention switched back over to Marina.

"I've always envisaged myself as a loving wife and a caring mother," the sales pitch continued. She obviously felt a strong yearning to fulfil these roles.

"Most women in England are glad of the freedom," I joked. I did my best to empathise and joke with her but was careful not to tread on her sensitivities.

We emerged from the warm underground to the freezing air above ground, and Marina chose the direction of travel. We headed towards *Europa Square* at the end of *Kreshchatik*.

"*Europa Square* is a prominent public space, often hosting various cultural events, concerts, and festivals," Marina declared. "The square is characterized by its spaciousness with the grand iron gates of

Dynamo Stadium visible on the south side," she said pointing like a tourist guide.

"It's a shame that the Ukraine leagues can't play at the moment, with the pitches frozen," I proclaimed. Marina didn't care about football.

"The *National Philharmonic Concert Hall* is visible on the far east side of the square," she carried on. "Behind it is the *Arch of Unification* built in 1982, on the 1500th anniversary of the city." She glanced at me as if to check that I was listening. I was, she knew her stuff. "The arch was built to commemorate the 60th anniversary of the USSR and the 'reunification of Ukraine with Russia' in 1654."

She continued, "The arch is a symbol of unity and friendship among different nations, standing as a reminder of Ukraine's multicultural heritage." We entered the subway under the vast roundabout and crossed over towards the *Arch of Unification*. It was a popular spot to view the river and east side of the city.

"My circle of friends and family have already found their partners," she said, "which intensifies my longing for a husband." If she wasn't describing the sites in forensic detail, she was, what we would call now, oversharing. Despite her attractive qualities and apparently successful career, Marina hadn't found a suitable husband. An internal pendulum swung away from the desperation I sensed on her.

After a brief view across the river and east side of the city, we wandered into the park, taking us around the *Dynamo Stadium* into *Mariinsky Park*.

We appeared behind a building that had the outline of an English stately home, *Mariinsky Palace*. The irony was not lost on me at this point – my guide having the same name as the place she was showing me. I could see for myself; the palace was an architectural masterpiece exuding elegance and grandeur. The exterior of the palace was adorned with beautiful columns, ornate sculptures, intricate carvings, giving it a regal appearance. It showcased a majestic presence and significant cultural importance.

"The palace serves as an important historical venue," she explained. "It holds historical and political importance, serving as the official ceremonial residence of Ukrainian presidents and for hosting important diplomatic meetings." She finished by saying, "the palace is a symbol of the country's national identity." The pendulum swung the other way.

"In Ukraine, not being married by a certain age is a stigma for women," she told me. "I hope that an independent and free Ukraine would likely shake-off these cultural stereotypes." She was right to hope for this. *I began to hope that her wish would come true.*

We continued our walk through the *Mariinsky Park* until we arrived in *Arsenalna Square,* Marina put her tour guide head back on. So, this is *Arsenalna.* I recalled that I had gone into the British Council before Christmas to make myself known, the office manager, Sveta, had wanted English lessons from me and then had directed me to the British Consular at *Arsenalna,* "go and see Inna in the Consular there" she had insisted.

"A prominent feature of *Arsenalna Square* are the bullet holes still visible in the walls," she pointed to one of the old armaments buildings facing the square. "The bullet holes are a reminder of the city's turbulent past, and the sacrifices made during World War II when Kyiv was heavily bombed and occupied by German forces." She glanced again to make sure I was listening. Again, I was. She continued. "The area around *Arsenalna* witnessed intense fighting and was a strategic location during the Battle of Kyiv."

Marina and I then headed toward the entrance to *Arsenalna* metro station. The pendulum swung again.

"Traditionally, in Ukraine, marriage was seen as a significant milestone and an essential part of adult life," she insisted.

"I suspected that it might have been," I responded. *I was relieved that the tour was coming to an end.*

74

We entered the barriers and approached the top of the escalators. "*Arsenalna* metro station actually holds the distinction of being the deepest metro station in the world," Marina continued. There was no stopping her. "The station platform lies one hundred and five metres underground and needs two full escalators to get down. The station pays homage to the armaments factory in *Arsenalna*. Indeed, it used to be one of the largest arms and ammunition manufacturers in the old Russian Empire." It was a relief to be back in the warm underground, escaping the continuing freeze above. The pendulum swung back.

"I worry that as time passes, my chances of finding a suitable husband may diminish," she persisted, "and I may miss out on the opportunity to have a family." I suddenly felt sorry for her. *And guilty.* She described the fear driving her to pursue potential partners, often compromising.

We arrived back at *Hnata Yuri* tram stop under falling snow. We wandered back to the flat in a new layer of deep snow. It was already getting dark. Unbelievably, it was already dinner time, and Maria opened the door, this time in her kitchen apron, and beamed at us on our return.

"*Ah, dity povernulysya!*" Maria said. We had been out all day wandering around. It really had felt like a break from the previous three months.

"Thank you for the guided tour. You were an excellent guide," I said to Marina. "I would've liked to do the same walk in the springtime but alas I will not be here."

"Thank you, Richard," she said," I hope we will meet again if you ever decide to return."

"I will do," I replied. "I wish you luck with your dream." The door closed behind her and that was it; I never saw her again. My feeling was that the Maria had expected us to return almost engaged and so I

75

must have disappointed her. We weren't going to be relatives after all.

As I preparing to sit down for some home cooked Ukrainian cuisine, Ron phoned.

"Where have you been all day?" he asked," we wanted to meet up in *Kreshchatik* later."

"On a grand tour of Kyiv," I joked. "I'll tell you about it later."

"Great, let's say *Kreshchatik* station at 8pm," he replied. "We can get a bite to eat, after my English classes at *School No. 17.*"

"I'm just about to eat here," I said but he had put the phone down. Anyway, I sat down to eat some fresh borscht and an enormous plate of *varenyky.*

"I must meet my friend," I said to Maria and Volodymyr. "Thank you for the excellent food."

"Don't be late," Maria warned. "It is cold tonight, and I don't want you to catch a cold and die in Ukraine." *This was a stark warning which I couldn't disagree with.*

I had reached the top of the escalator at *Kreshchatik* station a couple of minutes after 8pm and immediately saw Ron chatting with someone. Ron, wearing his usual flappy Russian hat, turned round.

"Hey Richard! This is Tom," Ron said. Tom was the latest teacher to arrive and seemed very keen. We were always excited to meet a new teacher.

"Hi Tom. Welcome to Ukraine," I extended my hand. Shaking hands had become customary in Ukraine, for every meeting between males.

"Where can we grab something to eat?" he asked.

"Indian curry?" I asked.

There was a unanimous "yes".

"Let's go to *Himalaya*," I suggested, with all the authority of knowing where the only Indian restaurant in Kyiv was located. It was also the most convenient restaurant to where we were standing. We were suddenly three English lads in Kyiv. *It was revitalising.*

Himalaya was the standout restaurant on *Kreshchatik,* situated adjacent to the *Passazh* entrance. Not much more than a portacabin perched above one of the grand *Kreshchatik* fountains. The three of us climbed the heavy granite steps to the entrance and walked through the set of glass doors into another world.

Himalaya was a bold commercial venture given that I didn't know a single Ukrainian, or Russian, who enjoyed even the mildest of spice. Most Ukrainian dishes were boiled or fried, not spicey, only the usual garden herbs. *Himalaya* was completely authentic, the ambience of the restaurant was inviting, especially with temperatures reaching minus ten degrees centigrade outside. The beautifully adorned interiors reflected the colourful culture of the *Himalayan* region. We entered and felt a sense of tranquillity, partly because there was no-one else in there. A man in Indian outfit appeared.

"Good evening my name is Mr Kumar. I am the manager of *Himalaya* Indian restaurant." He greeted us with wide open arms and a wider smile as we entered the restaurant. Having eaten in *Himalaya* once before, I knew that the manager's name was Mr Kumar. He greeted everyone like this who walked through the door.

"How are you this evening?" he asked, then rather comically. "Which table would best suit you?" All the tables were vacant. It was a testament to the entrepreneurial enthusiasm of Mr Kumar that all the tables had lit candles and jugs of water sitting on them, as if he were expecting a British stag-do for a late-night curry. We sat down at a table in the middle of the empty restaurant.

"Three Indian beers, please," Ron requested as Mr Kumar gave us all a menu.

"I'm looking forward to this," I said. "Indian curry goes well after Ukrainian *varenyky*." I ordered a small curry dish while Ron and Tom ordered a proper curry.

Mr Kumar brought the beers and we all cheered *"Budmo,"* and swigged the imported lager.

"You went on a grand tour?" Ron asked. "What was that all about?"

"I was taken on a guided tour of the *Mariinsky Park* by my hostess' niece," I admitted.

"So, it was a blind date then?" Ron asked.

"Yes," I answered taking another swig of my Indian beer as a response.

"What have you been doing all day?" I asked, swiftly changing the topic. Since our trip to Odessa, Ron had been employed by the British Council in Kyiv to provide English lessons for several hours a week.

"British Council offered me an intern position," Ron said. "By the way, Sveta is waiting for your response."

"OK, I will pop in tomorrow. But clearly, they were impressed with your performance, mate congratulations," I said. "Another beer over here, Mr Kumar."

"This new role comes with higher levels of security and appears to involve me attending various drinks dos and full-blown dinner parties," he joked. "I spent today recovering from a dinner party."

"What sort of occasion?" Tom asked.

"A black-tie dinner party hosted by the British Embassy with a few British naval officers," he began, "as well as several Ukrainian naval officers."

"Sounds serious," I interjected.

"I had already felt completely out of my depth by the time the Ukrainian naval officers pulled out a few bottles of vodka and began toasting each other's navy," he said. "My last memory, before passing out, is holding a full glass of vodka saying, *'Splice the main brace!'* to a British naval officer - notable for helping to defend the Falkland Islands fifteen years ago – and *'Here's to the Falklands!'*" Ron cringed.

"Splice the main brace?" Tom repeated. "Was it an 18th century dinner?"

"Next thing I know, I'm waking up this morning, in my bed," he groaned. "I don't know how I got home."

"Could've been somebody else's bed," Tom joked.

"I only got out of bed a couple of hours ago to give an English lesson and then stagger into *Kreshchatik* to meet you boys," Ron admitted. Tom, who was quite young and fresh faced, was under the impression that this was normal life in Kyiv. He had only recently finished school and was in a gap year ahead of going to study Russian at Sheffield university. "I might join the Foreign Office here, then," Tom joked.

"You'll be a good man to have around Kyiv," I said.

"I don't know any Russian yet, not really," Tom replied. "Depends on what you mean by 'good man'."

Mr Kumar came out of the kitchen pushing a golden trolley. He placed the dishes, and more beer, on the table with an even bigger smile than before. We tucked in. *This was welcome relief from Ukrainian food.* We thanked Mr Kumar for his hospitality and left *Himalaya* for the freezing Ukrainian evening.

Keen to carry on, we decided to wander along *Kreshchatik*, up *Passazh*, and left around the corner to the *Rock Café*. Situated in a pretty tree-covered square with an impressive fountain, I thought how wonderful it would look in the Spring *I would never see.*

The *Rock Café* was where all our Friday evenings collided. As Ron, Tom and I stepped inside, we were greeted by a welcome symphony of British nineties music. It was popular with expats; we walked into a sea of friends from *School No.17*, their associates, host families and other foreigners we would know by the end of the evening. We met Alison, Veronica, Anna and her boyfriend Tobias near the bar and had a few pints more.

"Everyone's coming over to mine for a party tomorrow night," Anna shouted. "You have to come." This was turning out to be a long week. We agreed to go, it would be my last night before leaving Kyiv.

The next day, I got up late in the morning; my host family had already departed for the day. The radio was on as usual with the members of the Ukrainian parliament arguing as usual. *I wish I understood, about what?* I helped myself to the dishes laid out for me in the kitchen. After the curry, it tasted fantastic. My appetite had grown significantly over the winter. I must have been burning off the energy at the same rate, as my weight was the same. The curry and beers last night almost felt like a dream as I was happily tucking into an enormous plate of *Vermicelli Pavlovski*. The phone rang; it was Anna.

"Hi Richard. Everyone is meeting at *Lisova* metro station at 6pm. I'll walk us over to my host family's flat, not far from there," she said. "Bring a bottle and some food – those are the entry requirements." *She was very organized and to the point.*

Ron, Tom and I had met up at *Teatralna* before taking the metro to *Lisova*, which was the last station on the red line. Ron and I had brought a few cans of beer and some sausages, while Tom had brought a bottle of Coca-Cola and some bread. The train to *Lisova* seemed to take ages. When we arrived, we immediately saw our group of friends with Anna standing in the middle of the giant platform all clutching their bags of food and drink. When we'd all arrived, Anna led us out of the station like the Pied Piper of Hamelin leading away the children from the town. As we emerged from the station steps into the freezing winter air, I was awestruck by the desolate surroundings.

The tower blocks stood side-by-side, forming clusters or neighbourhoods. From a distance, the rows of towering buildings were a vast and uniform expanse, resembling a stark moonscape. *But appearances were deceiving.* These tower blocks were home to thousands of people, each with their own stories, lives, and experiences. Exploring the surrounding neighbourhoods there were hidden pockets of charm, community spirit, and resilience. Beauty is found in unexpected places.

Anna led us through the snow towards one of the giant tower blocks. We entered the vast twenty-storey building. The one working lift was only big enough for four people at a time, so we took turns in taking the solitary lift to the tenth floor. Those of us who waited at the bottom of the lift for the longest, opened their drinks. After half an hour, Ron, Tom and I were the last to enter the lift. There were two parallel rows of ten buttons but when we tried to press anything that said '10' on it; none of the buttons were numbered.

"Just count ten buttons from the bottom on the left row," Tom was happy with his idea. The lift doors closed, and we started moving upwards, still drinking our open beer bottles. When the lift stopped, we got out into a dark corridor, not knowing if we had arrived on the right floor. As our eyes got used to the darkness, we couldn't see any sign indicating which floor we had arrived on. The only light was around the rims of various front doors. I decided the only way we would find out where Anna's party was would be to knock the nearest door. I knocked while the others hid behind the corner.

"*Kto tam?*" a lady's voice called a whole minute later.

"Richard," I replied much to the amusement of Ron and Tom.

81

"*Kto?*" came the response.

Together we tried to work out how to say, "What floor is this?" We attempted just "*Etazh?*" which meant "Floor?". The response suggested an expletive in Russian which none of us knew, then she said "*militsia*" which we all understood, and decided to abandon this strategy before the lady did call the police. Ron and Tom were increasingly in hysterics.

"Let's go back into the lift and try again," I suggested.

This time Ron counted ten buttons from the lower left-hand row and counted across two each time until he had reached the right hand-button on the fifth row. Tom and I agreed this was entirely logical and the lift started to move downwards. As the doors opened, we walked out of the lift into a brightly lit floor but again we could see no number indicating which floor. This time Ron chose a door and rang the doorbell, and a large man opened the door. However, with the man, came an horrendous smell of a flat that had not been properly aired in months.

"Which *etazh* are we on?" Ron asked the man feebly.

"Come inside for some vodka," the man beckoned us in. We politely declined and ran back into the lift. Tom pushed the button for the next floor up. Again, we entered a brightly lit floor with no indication. Tom rang the bell on the next door. This time a good-looking young woman opened the door.

"How may I help you?" she asked. Jackpot!

"We are lost," Tom said politely, clearly affected by her beauty. "We are looking for the tenth floor."

"Well, this is the ninth floor," she chuckled," so you're pretty close." Anna must be on the floor above.

"Where are you all from?" she asked.

Like moronic triplets, we all answered "England" at the same time. She smiled.

"OK, goodnight and have fun!" she said before closing the door behind her. We all got back into the lift and pressed the next button of the random lift sequence we had worked out.

At the fourth attempt, the lift door opened to another well-lit hallway; one which contained Anna standing with a stern look on her face.

"What took you so long?" she asked, "have you deliberately tried to avoid the tenth floor?" We didn't mention that her lift was missing some key information, that we had already met some of her neighbours. Instead, we apologised and entered the party.

By midnight, the party petered out, most had gone on, leaving Ron, Tom and I sleeping in the living room. We all woke up at around 6am, hungover, and decided to get up for the first metro of the day. The beautiful girl from the flat below came in with a tray of coffees. We looked at her then at each other, as if we were sharing the same dream, then we all looked at Anna.

"Boys, let me introduce you to my landlady, Zhenya," Anna said. "She stayed with a friend of hers on the floor below, while she kindly allowed us to have the flat for a party".

"Good morning, boys," Zhenya looked at us and smiled knowingly. "Glad you found it." Anna looked quizzical, sensing we had all met before.

It suddenly hit me that this was the dawn of my last day in Kyiv; I had promised to get back to my flat to have breakfast with my host family before they all went out to work. Coffees downed, I grabbed a can of *Tango* and put it in my pocket on the way out of the flat. Ron, Tom and I thanked Anna and Zhenya for their hospitality and we made our way back to the *Lisova* metro station. There had been another heavy snowfall in the night and our footprints from the previous evening had been covered up. In the daylight, the moonscape seemed different, friendlier. We found our way back to the metro station and noticed a chain across the top of the entrance stairwell suggesting the station was 'closed for engineering work'. A workman emerged.

"*Metro, net?*" Tom asked.

"*Metro, net!*" replied the workman. "*Vsya ochered do tsentra goroda zakryta do poludnya!*" Between us, we understood the whole green line up to the city centre would be closed until lunchtime.

"Which direction to the centre of Kyiv?" I indicated one way or the other.

"*Idi tuda,*" he replied pointing down the main road. We began walking.

"In the spirit of Scott of the Antarctic," Tom cried. Ron and I glanced at each other knowing that didn't go well either.

Two hours later, we were still walking, the snow was still falling. It felt like we would suffer the same fate as Scott and his men. It didn't seem such a good idea now and we didn't have any money for a taxi, only the metro cards that we would scan at the metro barriers. We had crossed the *Dnipro River* and had reached the underpass. I was thirsty and remembered the can of *Tango* in my coat pocket. I opened it and had a sip. The dehydration eased after the walk and the party the night before. As soon as I'd had a sip, I felt like having a pee so I asked Tom to hold the can of *Tango* while I had a quick pee by the side of the road. No sooner had I finished, a police car pulled up behind us. A *militsia* got out of the car and approached us.

Now in Ukraine having a pee at the side of the road is not acceptable; the police will fine you for it. We all knew this but at 8am with hardly anyone on the roads, it seemed safe.

"*Shto ty delaesh?*" asked the *militsia* pointing at the yellow snow where I'd had a pee.

"We don't understand," I said, and we all shrugged. Clearly, he was going to fine us. Then Tom, still holding the can of *Tango* poured it into the snow. Strangely it was the same colour as my pee had been.

"*Tango!*" Tom said.

"*Shto Tango?*" the *militsia* asked. This had taken an unexpected twist, but Ron and I backed him up.

"Tango in the snow," I said.

"*Net!*" he said and waggled his radio at us. On very thin ice, we waited for the policeman to drag us into the back of his car and take us all down to the local jail. The sound of a car crashing into another car above us on the flyover distracted him. "*Blyad!*" he swore as he jumped back into his car and drove off.

"That was close," Ron said. A lucky escape! We ran the rest of the way over the bridge to the *Dnipro* metro station and, to our relief, it was open. We ran down the steps and scanned our metro cards at the barriers before the *militsia* could come back. We laughed in the warm carriage as it headed towards *Kreshchatik;* it was only 8am. As we passed through *Arsenalna,* I thought how I had been there with Marina only thirty-six hours before, but it had seemed like weeks ago.

At *Kreshchatik* station, still laughing, we all got out and grabbed a coffee from the kiosk. Heading down *Kreshchatik,* we bowled balls of snow as we went, much to the bewilderment of the women shovelling the snow, already out in force. Ron, Tom and I split up at *Teatralna* to head in our different directions.

"Meet at *Voxalna* station this evening to see you off," Ron said. It was a fun end to a long three months. I even got back to *Svitoshin* to catch breakfast with my host family.

That evening, I thanked them and said an emotional goodbye. It was goodbye to *Gangsters Paradise* for the last time too as Sergei and Taras escorted me to the railway station at *Voxalna.* We met Ron and Tom, as well as Veronica and Alison, who had all come to wave me off. I would miss Kyiv and wondered if I'd ever return. To me, Kyiv had been this frozen snowy moonscape, full of beautiful warm people who loved to have fun at every opportunity. I had felt the mystery of Kyiv and had only scratched the surface of something that lay beneath. As I boarded the train back to Lviv, I remembered I had never seen nor heard of Warren again; he'd completely disappeared. *I remembered starting these last three months with Warren; it was now time to head home.*

Chapter 9. The Oxford Dilemma

12th April 1996

It had been six weeks since my return to England from Ukraine. My mind was consumed with thoughts of the future and the potential opportunities that lay ahead. I had reflected on my time in Kyiv and realized how much it shaped me. The experience and exposure to different perspectives fuelled my desire to return, despite the freezing cold winter weather. It allowed me to forget about my dilemma: should I take up the opportunity that Professor Korolyuk had offered me, given that it would mean at least two to three years of hard slog in a difficult country with a language barrier. The detail of this dilemma is what I had penned in my letter to *'Whom It May Concern'* in the Mathematics Department at Oxford University, the day after my return. They would know Korolyuk, and they might advise me what to do next. *I was still waiting for a response.*

My parents were delighted to see me return after a long winter away in a far-off foreign country. They were there to meet me at Victoria coach station in March; it was comforting to be back in the Cotswolds ahead of Easter. Dinner in the local *Merrymouth Inn* on the way home from London cemented the feeling that I was back home. As the English winter frost gave way to warmer, wet days, the Cotswolds awoke with a renewed sense of life and beauty. The countryside came alive as Nature awoke from its great slumber.

In Springtime, the Cotswolds transform into a picturesque wonderland, bursting with vibrant colours and enchanting landscapes. Nestled in the heart of the Cotswolds, among the rolling hills, were honey-coloured stone villages, one of these villages was *Fifield* which I had called home since I was eight years old. The ancient village, just inside the county of Oxfordshire border, had been our family home since 1980. I appreciated its beauty since returning from the harsh bleak Ukrainian winter. The stone cottages in Fifield, with their charming, slated roofs and colourful gardens, exuded a sense of warmth and tranquillity against the backdrop of blooming nature. Our house, *Altarnun*, was named after a village in Cornwall, a link to my Dad's Cornish heritage. The house used to be the *Old Rectory* and stood opposite to what was now the much larger *New Rectory*, opposite the village church. Wisteria vines cascaded down the walls, filling the air with a sweet fragrance, while blossoming cherry and apple trees created a captivating floral display. Lush green fields stretched as far as the eye could see, dotted with grazing sheep and playful lambs. The meadows were a tapestry of wildflowers, their delicate blooms painting the landscape with hues of purple, yellow and pink. Bluebells carpeted the woodland floors, creating a breathtaking scene of vibrant blue beneath the budding canopy trees.

Mum and Dad both spent time abroad when they were younger. Dad did National Service in the *Royal Air Force* soon after the end of the second World War in 1947, spending most of his time posted in the Mediterranean at a radar station on the Maltese island of Gozo. After leaving the *RAF* in 1950, he joined Lloyd's bank as a junior clerk and was posted out to India to assist with the post-independence transition. Upon arrival in Bombay, he was posted out to what is now Pakistan and Bangladesh for five years, which he enjoyed from the stories and photos I'd seen as a boy. Meanwhile, Mum trained at *Seal-Hayne Agricultural College* in the 1950s and found herself working in Malta for a governmental department called the *Milk Marketing Undertaking*, running a new laboratory and modernising methods of sterilizing milk in remote communities. In the late sixties Dad proposed to Mum and convinced her to leave her work in Malta to get married to a bank manager and have a family in England. Of course, regularly throughout my childhood I would hear from Mum that she wished she had stayed in Malta and married someone else. My Dad would jokingly respond that he wishes she had too. Both had had their fair share of foreign experiences and were always keen to engage in discussions about international affairs. It was Mum, via a friend of hers, who had put me in touch with a *European Union* agency working with doctors in Romanian orphanages, in 1994. This led me to travel and work in the Transylvanian town of *Alba Iulia* that summer, for something to do after finishing my Maths degree at Plymouth. It was this experience that had given me the curiosity and confidence to go one step further East and teach English in Ukraine the following year.

My brother had just finished his Physics doctorate at Cambridge university and was now engaged in some pseudo-important post-doctoral work. So, I felt the inevitable isolation and restlessness returning home to a quiet Cotswold village after the thrill of a buzzing European capital city.

It was great to catch up with old school and university friends. My school friends were still around, some working but most were at university. We occasionally caught up in one of our favourite Burford or Oxford pubs. Burford was where I had spent my school life in the eighties, and I have fond memories of that time. The original school building at the bottom of the High Street by the church dated back to 1571. It was across the road from the Cotswold Arms. Many *ex-Burfordian* pupils would often descend from their respective universities at Christmas and Easter time and be found meeting up in the Cotswold Arms or one of the many other pubs on the High Street. In Oxford, I had worked in several cafés and restaurants on George Street, part of the city centre leading into St. Giles', where I was born. I'd enjoyed working with the Oxford students during the months immediately before my journey out to Ukraine; I was glad I had earned and saved enough money for the trip. On my return from Ukraine, I slipped straight back into Oxford life and the student parties, as if I had never been away – *Antiquity Hall, Rosie O'Grady's, The Turf* and *The Lamb & Flag* were all pubs that I frequented.

When I wasn't writing letters or out with friends, I liked to play a round of golf with Dad. This wonderful time together allowed us to discuss a multitude of affairs, often leaving me in tears of laughter from his stories about his time in India. The best advice came from Dad on the Burford golf course that Easter: "Follow your nose, son, and it will always lead to a good Indian curry!'

Ever since writing the *dilemma* letter, I expected a quick response. But waiting for a letter made the passing of time slow down. Each day felt longer than the last. My thoughts drifted towards the possibilities contained within that envelope.

Anxiously, I checked the mail each morning for a response. Days turned into weeks and still no response. Doubt started to creep into my mind, questioning whether I had dreamed it all. The uncertainty was challenging but I remained determined not to let it dampen my spirits. But on this day for some reason, I noticed the *sunflower* postcards I had sent my parents from the Kyiv central post office a couple of short months ago. They were held on by a magnet in pride of place on the side of the fridge.

Amid my wavering confidence, I received an unexpected phone call. It was a lady calling from the Mathematics Department at Oxford University asking, "Could I speak with a Mr Coad?"

I replied, "Speaking".

She continued, "My name is Helen. We received your letter. We would like to invite you to come to the department to speak with one of the academics."

Excitement coursed through my veins as I eagerly accepted the invitation. We set a date for the following week. *I hadn't thought for one second that they would respond to my letter with a phone call.*

Preparing for the meeting became my sole focus. I immersed myself in research into Professor Korolyuk's works, thinking that I would be tested on this during my meeting the following week in Oxford. Sleepless nights turned into early mornings spent rehearsing potential questions and refining my responses. The days leading up to the meeting were a whirlwind of nerves and anticipation.

The day of the meeting had finally arrived; I decided to put on a suit and tie. Dad drove me down the four-mile country lane to Kingham railway station. The train journey from Kingham to Oxford was a journey I had taken many times since I had become old enough at fourteen to travel on the train with friends, or by myself, into Oxford. Twenty-five minutes, later I was walking out of the station towards the river. Walking past Antiquity Hall five minutes later, then onto George Street, I started to relax on home turf. I felt a mix of awe and determination; *I was here on important business.*

At the top of George Street, I turned left past the Randolph Hotel and the Ashmolean Museum into St. Giles'. Born in the *Nuffield Maternity Home* at the far end of St. Giles' in 1972, *I was really on home turf now.* The Maternity Home closed at that time leaving me to be one of the very last babies to be born there. Mum always joked that as soon as they saw me come out, they decided to close the hospital. That was Mum's sense of humour. She was from *Hoylake* in Cheshire so inevitably had some of that famous Liverpudlian sense of humour.

I crossed over St. Giles' and walked past the *Lamb & Flag* pub, thinking about the fun times I had in there after finishing my A-levels, and how I could just do with a pint of the local *Morrells* beer. I came to the end of St. Giles'; I stood in front of the Mathematics Department and rang the doorbell. *Over the street from where I had been born.* A woman's voice asked my name and the door clicked open. I went through into the Reception area and I was asked to take a seat.

A minute later, a lady appeared introducing herself as Helen. She was warm in her welcome and asked me to follow her; we went up the stairs and entered a small room. The room had a window overlooking the street, St. Giles' church graveyard on the other side. It looked like a tutorial room where only a few people could have comfortably sat. Helen gestured me to sit down while she left the room and disappeared down the corridor in the opposite direction.

A couple of minutes later, there was a gentle tap on the door and a man entered. I stood up and he gently closed the door behind him, immediately extending his arm out.

"Good afternoon. I am Professor Harris. I am the one who invited you in today. Thank you very much for coming in." His genial manner put me at ease; I instantly relaxed. I thanked him for taking the time to meet with me as he must be a busy man. He indicated that it was still the Easter holidays and he had come back a few days early to prepare some lecture notes. "I have been busier," he chuckled.

A starling landed on the windowsill outside and it started to rain through the sunshine. We both sat down as Helen brought in two cups of tea. It amused me that I had not been offered a cup of tea but was brought one anyway. As I dropped a sugar cube into my tea and stirred, Professor Harris began talking.

"Thank you again for your letter and I apologise for taking so long to respond. Easter seems to have got in the way. It was passed to several of the lecturers in the department, including myself. I read it with great fascination. Please tell me how you met Professor Korolyuk," he enquired.

I told him about my life in Kyiv and the events leading up to that day when Oksana had taken me to the Mathematics Institute in the snow. He asked me how I was sure that it was him and I told him about the painting on the wall. I had no doubt he was the same man.

"If you don't mind my asking, why are you so curious as to Professor Korolyuk's identity?" I asked, trying to work out where this was going.

"Well, no-one in the West has been in contact with Korolyuk for nearly thirty years. He just vanished around 1970 around the time he took up a position in a nuclear weapons factory in the Dnipropetrovsk region. Korolyuk is one of the greatest mathematicians to come from the old Soviet Union. He has written hundreds of research papers and books over the last fifty years – and has been recognized by many universities for his groundbreaking theories."

I wasn't surprised by what Professor Harris had said. But he talked about Korolyuk as if he were a ghost from the past. *His tone described him as a mythical being.* He went on, "Many academics assumed Korolyuk had died some years ago which is why it is a surprise that you have met him."

"Korolyuk was alive and very real when I drank vodka with him in his study," I was amused to consider the different drinks I'd shared with two professors: same settings but a world apart – vodka versus Breakfast tea.

Professor Harris' tone turned to interrogation. "In your letter you mention that he had offered you a position to work with him?"

"Yes, and I'm still mulling over my options. That's why I wrote to your department, to ask for advice."

"OK. I'll tell you what I know about him. Professor Korolyuk was born in Kyiv in 1925 where he went to school and finished his secondary education before the start of the Soviet involvement in the Second World War. Or, as they refer to it, the Great Patriotic War." He paused, as if to collect his thoughts, offering me the chance to interject. I smiled to signal I knew this already and for him to continue.

"When he was seventeen, he entered the Red Army. In a year, he had graduated from the Kharkiv Military Aviation School and started to work as an instructor of practical training at the same school. In 1947, he joined Kyiv Taras Shevchenko University as a third-year student graduate in the Mathematics Faculty". *I noted this as the same year Dad joined the RAF.*

Professor Harris paused and took a sip of tea. The starling was still on the windowsill, as if listening into the story. He continued, "In 1954, Korolyuk defended his PhD thesis, from which time he was closely associated with the Institute of Mathematics at the National Academy of Science. This is where you say, in your letter, that you met him?"

"Yes, that's correct." I tried to sound assertive.

"This is where it gets interesting." We both took another sip of tea; the starling appeared to be taking it all in, like a spy in our midst. Professor Harris carried on. "Prior to this, Korolyuk travelled to Moscow with some of his peers including an academic called Skorokhod. They received much recognition and several prizes for their extraordinary work in Probability Theory. Here, they met Professor Kolmogorov, still widely held to be the greatest mathematician the Soviets ever produced. He is considered the father of subjects like Probability Theory, Statistics, Random Process, Mathematical Logic in Computing, Algorithmic Complexity Theory and the list goes on." He paused again and finished his tea; I knew what he would say next.

"Kolmogorov identified Korolyuk, and Skorokhod, and two others as his natural apprentices and, as such, they all fell under his direct supervision from 1953." I asked how he could be so specific on the dates. He smiled at me and continued, "Well, you see, as the most important mathematician of the Soviet Union, Kolmogorov often crossed paths with a certain Joseph Stalin who had placed Kolmogorov in key positions during the Great Patriotic War. He contributed to the Soviet war effort by applying Statistical Theory to artillery fire; he developed a scheme of random distribution of barrage balloons intended to help protect Moscow from German bombers during the Battle of Moscow. This was called the *Moscow defence theorem*. Stalin recognized the huge contribution that Kolmogorov had made during the war and rewarded him with many medals and honours. Interestingly, before the war, Kolmogorov had betrayed his own professor, Luzin, in the Great Purge after he became a high-profile target of Stalin's regime. Luzin was accused of being an enemy of the Soviet people and lost his academic position. But he was neither arrested nor expelled – this became known as the "Luzin Affair" and Kolmogorov was right at the centre of it. Of course, we know that Stalin died in 1953 and Kolmogorov went on to live a long and prosperous life until the late eighties."

I joked that we were moving away from the topic of Professor Korolyuk. "No, we are just coming to him, we know that the young Korolyuk and Skorokhod were also recognized by Stalin, under Kolmogorov's recommendation before his death in 1953. But we don't know why. Stalin died in early March 1953 so Korolyuk and Skorokhod might have been some of the last people to see him alive. Korolyuk and Skorokhod continued to bounce between Moscow and Kyiv universities until the late sixties when Korolyuk completely disappeared off the radar. Where did he go?"

We both sat in stunned silence holding empty cups of tea. The starling had gone; it had all the information it needed.

"So, you see, not many degrees of separation between Korolyuk and Stalin," he commented sarcastically.

Professor Harris resumed, "I would really encourage you to return to Kyiv and take up Korolyuk's offer to work with him. He is an extraordinary man who has lived an extraordinary life. He has been crucial to the developments in the USSR since Stalin's death. If you feel that you are able to, with my full support, please go and get to know this man. Write papers with him, understand his mind, then come back and tell us about him."

Needing time to reflect on what I'd learnt, I responded by saying, "I'll consider it. And, of course, let you know what I've found out on my return."

There was a sharp knock at the door. Helen popped her head round to say a visiting professor had arrived from America and was sitting in Professor Harris' study. He stood up, I stood up and we shook hands.

"Richard. Good luck and please contact me whenever you can. He left the room and Helen escorted me back down the stairs to the entrance hall.

I found myself outside on the St. Giles' pavement, my head still spinning from the encounter. Two hours had passed since I had entered the building and it had started to rain.

I ducked into the Lamb & Flag for a swift pint of beer. My mind was churning over the information and history that Professor Harris had given me. In one way, it made my dilemma sharper, and the way forward was becoming clear. As I placed my empty pint glass back onto the bar, my mind was made up.

27th May 1996

I had just returned home in the evening after a hot day on Burford golf course. Mum told me I'd had a phone call earlier from 'someone called Ron.' My brain kicked into gear, and I asked if he'd left a number. She had pinned Ron's number to the cork board hanging on the kitchen wall.

The next day, I was back down at Kingham station waiting on the platform catching a train to Oxford. I met Ron in *Antiquity Hall* and we had a great catch up with pints of Morrell's bitter and a vodka for old times' sake. He had returned from Kyiv only last week and looked thinner than I'd remembered him at the beginning of March. Ron had started his new role in the British Council with all the associated drinking and dining. He had accepted an offer from the British Council for a full-time teaching position in Kyiv but returned home to prepare for a new posting in *Tirana, Albania*. We drank to Albania. I was delighted for him, and he was thrilled to hear that I had now formally accepted the research position in Kyiv with Professor Korolyuk. We drank again to my return to Ukraine. Although there was no clear timeline yet, we started to work out where we could meet in between the two cities – Bucharest in Romania seemed to be the best mid-point. We continued drinking until we had nothing left to drink to before stumbling onto the return train; I got off at Kingham, and he carried on to his parents' home in Worcester at the end of the line.

I was heartened to see Ron again and hear how different Kyiv was during springtime without snow and ice. Tom had stayed on in Kyiv for the summer, right up to the start of his Russian degree. For the rest of the summer, I spent my days earning money doing restaurant work and other odd jobs. I knew I would shortly be entering the greatest challenge of my life. The occasional round of golf or pint of Morells with a friend kept me sane.

Towards the end of that summer, I managed to get over to *Worcester Cricket Ground* to visit Ron and have a drink, just before his posting to Albania. My return to Kyiv to work with Korolyuk seemed very real now. *Given that there was also such a thing as pleasant weather in Kyiv, I couldn't wait to return.*

Chapter 10. The Friendly People

26th January 1997

My flight arrived at 3pm at Kyiv's *Borispil* Airport. In the last of the daylight, I disembarked with a fellow passenger, Roger. We had been sitting next to each other, talking solidly since Gatwick. He was an engineer working with TACIS, Technical Assistance to the Commonwealth of Independent States, in Ukraine.

"There is a generation's worth of work required to bring the country's infrastructure in line with the rest of Europe," Roger spoke authority. He took pride in saying, "I'll be busy here until my retirement!"

As I stepped off the plane, seeing the frozen mid-winter landscape and the glum border guards, I felt like Rocky Balboa, in *Rocky IV,* before his fight with Ivan Drago in the USSR. *I was ready for the fight.* At Baggage Reclaim, Roger gave me his number and told me to give him a call so we could go out for a beer. I couldn't reciprocate with a telephone number because I didn't yet know my new address, and it was still before a time when mobiles were commonplace. Roger collected his bag from the conveyor belt and joyfully departed by shouting, "The British Embassy usually celebrate Australia Day around now, we can meet up there."

After passing through Passport Control and Arrivals, Oksana was waiting for me. She had a big smile and warm hug, with big coat and hat, waiting for me.

"Thank you for coming to meet me at the airport," were my first words.

She replied, "Welcome back to Ukraine!" Then we climbed into the taxi she had arranged parked outside the main airport entrance. The taxi skidded around the airport forecourt and headed out of *Borispil* to Kyiv.

We passed over the river and under the Motherland Statue before the taxi turned down a couple of side streets. We arrived at my new apartment in a district called *Druzhbi Narodiv*, meaning 'The Friendship of Peoples'. Oksana turned to the taxi driver and insisted, "I'll only be a few minutes; please can you wait for me."

The street was called *Professor Podvisotskovo*, yet another professor. It was a name I would be writing on many future correspondences. Oksana and I entered the building porchway and climbed the bare concrete steps to the apartment. She rang the doorbell of number twenty-five.

Without any wait, *"Kto tam?"* The voice asked.

"Oksana," she replied.

We could hear several bolts being unlocked, then the door swung open. A woman with shoulder length hair in her late thirties smiled back at us.

"Dobra pozhalavat!" she said. I already knew that meant 'welcome'. She urged us into the warm apartment, giving Oksana and me a big hug. Oksana did the introductions. Natasha spoke no English whatsoever – so apparently the onus to communicate in Russian was entirely on me. Natasha had already prepared a table of food and drink; Oksana apologised and declined.

"Apologies, my taxi is waiting outside," she demurred and departed, giving me a reassuring nod.

Natasha gestured to me towards the dinner table; we rather awkwardly sat down together. The table was laid out with six placemats. Soon after Oksana departed, there was another ring at the door. Natasha apologised, stood up and opened the door to a boy and a girl who could not have been older than seventeen. One was Ivan, Natasha's son, and one was Kira, Ivan's fiancé. The four of us sat down at the table, but there were still two empty place mats. There was another ring of the doorbell. Next through the door were an older lady and a young girl about eight years old – Natasha's sister, Teofila, and her niece, Snezana. All six of us sat down at the table and finally we began to eat and drink – the adults toasting my arrival with a vodka. The conversation around the table was largely information about where to find food, where the shops and the underground station were, what time I would like to get up in the morning. I worked this out with my pocket English Russian dictionary. None of my new family around the table spoke any English apart from Natash's niece, Snezana, who was already quite conversant. She looked rather sickly and malnourished, which explained why her mother, Teofila, seemed to have a nervous disposition.

The next day, I planned a visit to the British Embassy to register my residency in Kyiv and to review and approve my contract from the *National Academy of Ukraine* to work with Professor Korolyuk. Ivan and Kira accompanied me, I think out of curiosity more than anything, but it was good to start practising some Russian. *My new host family didn't speak Ukrainian.* The route from Natasha's apartment to the *Druzhbi Narodiv* metro station was no more than a five-minute walk and took me past a row of small shops, including grocery and bakery stores. The underground station was on the green line and only four stations from the centre with a one station change to *Kreshchatik*. To get to the British Embassy, we exited from *Maidan Nezalezhnosti* station, out of Independence Square and up the hill, past O'Brien's pub into *Mykhailivska Square* in which dominated *St. Micheal's Church* opposite *St. Sophia Cathedral*. The cathedral was adjacent to the *Ministry of Foreign Affairs* and one of the city's main police stations.

St. Micheal's Church was a magnificent sight to behold. The outside wall is adorned with beautiful frescoes of various religious scenes, including St. Micheal himself. The church building stood tall, exuding grandeur and elegance. The high arches and domed ceilings had been destroyed and rebuilt multiple times. Opposite, St. Sophia's Cathedral was, and still is, a symbol of Ukraine's rich history. St. Sophia's served as the centre of the Kyivan Rus, the medieval East Slavic state, and was the site of important ceremonies and religious events. Both landmarks were a visual feast and held historical and cultural significance for the people of Ukraine.

The whole area had a feeling of ceremony and government. The cobbled streets gave the area authenticity. The British Embassy was well hidden down a tree-lined street that ran alongside the Ministry of Foreign Affairs, called *Desiatynna Street*. The three of us arrived at the Embassy door.

"I'll be straight back out," I gestured to Ivan and Kira. They nodded their understanding. My *Maurice Mimer* impressions were not going to waste.

On the way out, after the British Embassy approved my contract, I noticed a group of students gathering outside the Embassy steps, British by their clothes and mannerisms. I acknowledged them as I exited down the Embassy steps. One of them responded in a broad Newcastle accent.

"Are we in the right place to register ourselves - we are from Great Britain?" he enquired.

I replied, "Yes, if you go inside the entrance, someone will help you."

"Thanks mate, do you work for the Embassy?"

I responded with a question of my own, "Are you teachers?"

A second chap with a strong Irish accent responded, "Yes we are all English teachers here – just arrived in Kyiv."

"I'm Greg, he's Rory," Greg interrupted.

Suddenly, feeling very experienced, "I'm Richard. I used to be a teacher in Kyiv a year ago." Ivan and Kira, still waiting for me on the pavement, were listening intently to this Anglo-Saxon exchange, naturally not understanding a single word of it. The group of English teachers, six in total, were all on the same programme I had been the previous winter. We ended the exchange by suggesting that we could all meet up at the Embassy on the Australia Day celebrations at the weekend.

"That would be amazing!" said Greg as he and the others disappeared into the Embassy door.

The following day, I went to visit the British Consular at *Arsenalna*, where the interests of British citizens in the country are looked after. *I was reminded of Marina's guided tour, I wonder if she'd found what she was looking for.* At the Consular I finally met Inna, who was a very smiley representative, in one of the consulting rooms.

"I'm fascinated to understand the reasons why you are in Kyiv," she said, the smile not breaking for a second. "And want to know more." We drank coffee and ate several biscuits.

"I can return each week and let you know my progress," I offered.

"That would be fantastic," she confirmed. "The Consular will be very happy to support you."

I stopped in at the British Council, behind *Bessarabski Market*, to visit Sveta for the first time since I'd left Kyiv the previous March and let her know I had connected with Inna. We grabbed another coffee then hit a bar to catch up. It had been a busy first couple of days settling into my new address, with my new hostess Natasha, re-establishing my links with the Embassy, Consular and Council. *I now felt confident enough to meet Professor Korolyuk again.*

31st January 1997

Friday had arrived and I'd almost completed the first week back in Kyiv. Snow was falling but it wasn't as cold as the previous winter. Natasha didn't work on Fridays so when I awoke, she was busy cooking in the kitchen. She asked me if I wanted any breakfast, demonstrating a range of freshly cooked Ukrainian dishes. I recognized the *Vermicelli Pavlovski* and so I opted for that with a strong cup of coffee – a strange breakfast but one I'd come to love.

After breakfast, Natasha asked if I wanted to learn some Russian. *Note: all our conversations were done with a combination of mime, English, Ukr-Russian and smiles.* I happily agreed. I had brought a book *Colloquial Russian* by Svetlana Le Fleming to purposely teach myself in the event there was no teaching assistance. So, Natasha became my formal Russian teacher, and she was very good. We started well completing Chapters One to Three of twenty chapters at the first attempt, the basic phrases including the Cyrillic alphabet I already knew. I wondered how long it would take me to get to the end of the book; six months was a reasonable expectation, especially if Natasha was going to be my live-in Russian teacher. In the afternoon, Natasha and I explored the vicinity around her apartment. She came with me because she was worried that I would either get lost on my own or I would get kidnapped (it was not the first time I had heard this – did I have *'kidnap me'* written on my forehead?). We went into a couple of the local kiosks to buy groceries, enroute to the metro station. Natasha introduced me by name to a couple of the shop assistants, who she knew. *Everyone knew everyone here.* They just called me *'The Englishman'* which they thought was funny; in a tight community I was concerned this would be the surest way of getting kidnapped.

By 5pm, we had returned to the flat with several bags of groceries. After a cup of tea, I rang Roger, of TACIS, to let him know that I would be at the Embassy by 7pm for the Australia Day celebrations. Living so close to *Druzhbi Narodiv*, which in turn was so close to the central stations, meant that I could get to and from anywhere in the city relatively easily at any time of the day or night.

It began to snow heavily. I arrived at the Embassy steps on time and entered the Reception. I saw Roger waiting inside. We were immediately directed downstairs towards the cellar bar under street level. The Embassy bar was called the *'Cave Inn'* and we began to drink the inexhaustible supply of free *Castlemaine 4X*. Australian flags adorned the *Cave Inn* walls and ceilings; stuffed kangaroos wearing hats with corks sat on the bar. There were several Australians in the bar too who had clearly begun drinking on Australian time (eight hours ahead) and were already singing their own version of *Waltzing Matilda*. The British Ambassador, *'Just call me Roy'*, had a pint in his hand at the bar, surrounded by several of his team – both British and Ukrainian. He was an experienced diplomat and Ukraine was lucky to have him.

Roger and I continued our conversation where we had left it, in Baggage Reclaim at *Borispil* Airport. Before long, we were on our second and third pints of *4X*. The Aussies were now playing another drinking game which involved a tongue twister *'How much wood would a woodchuck chuck if a woodchuck could chuck wood?'* This had to be said correctly within three seconds or a drinking forfeit was taken. The tongue twister defeated all-comers until it was the turn of a rather loud Scot called Fraser who was articulate, or less drunk, and so he won the bottle of whiskey. The English teachers I met a couple of days earlier appeared in the bar, looking slightly bewildered. We had a round of introductions before a fifth round of drinks. Australia Day celebrations went into the night and incredibly, we all got back home without any incident involving a can of *Tango* and the *militsia*.

1st February 1997

It was a beautiful freezing February day. The sun shone in a crystal blue Ukrainian sky, not a hint of snow. I felt mildly hungover from too much free Australian lager the night before, but I managed to get up for breakfast around 10am. I noticed that if I asked Natasha for food or drink in English, it was roundly ignored. The telephone rang and Natasha answered then called my name.

Taking the receiver, I said, "Good morning, Oksana."

She replied in an overtly happy voice, "How are you this morning? Are you settling in to your new flat and host family?"

"Very well thank you, but I notice that Natasha is not very responsive when I ask something in English. Do you know how I can get a better response from her?"

"You have to ask for anything only in Russian - this is an instruction from Professor Korolyuk to Natasha." Oksana chuckled. Now it all made sense. Oksana explained that "Korolyuk wants you to learn Russian quickly so you can understand some of the problems he will set for you – it will also make your life in Ukraine more rewarding." I agreed with her that immersion was the best way to learn a foreign language, even though my mealtimes were at risk. I was happy that plans were in place to prepare me for an extended stay in Kyiv – and Korolyuk was already ahead of me, training me, even though I'd yet to meet him since my return.

After lunch, Natasha took me on a journey into the pine forests in the southern outskirts of Kyiv, parallel to the Dnipro River called *Koncha-Zaspa*. Many of the new wealthier families were building their *dachas*, or summer houses, here. *Koncha-Zaspa* was also known for its scenic landscapes and tranquil atmosphere, making it a popular destination for fishing, nature lovers and those seeking a peaceful retreat, especially in summer. Even in winter, the snow made it beautiful. In the 1920s, the territory was the first state preserve in the Ukrainian SSR. The route to get from *Druzhbi Narodiv* to *Koncha-Zaspa* required one metro stop towards the river to *Vydubychi*, then a twenty-minute shuttle bus that ran past the very new *Dynamo Kyiv* training ground, to a bus stop that appeared to be in the middle of nowhere. From there, we walked.

A Ukrainian pine forest in snow is a truly magical sight to behold. The pine trees, adorned with a fresh coat, stand tall and proud, their branches delicately draped in glistening white. The forest air feels crisp and invigorating, carrying a hint of pine fragrance. The ground is blanketed in a soft, untouched layer of snow, creating a serene and peaceful atmosphere. The branches of the pine trees formed graceful arches, creating natural tunnels that beckon you to explore further. The sunlight filtered through, casting a golden glow upon the snowy landscape. It created a mesmerizing play of light and shadows, making the surroundings appear ethereal. The snow-covered boughs of the pines seemed to hold the weight of the winter world.

After a fifteen-minute walk, the pine forest suddenly opened up; towering over us was a newly built ten-storey apartment block. Because of its white facade, it looked like something out of the 'Lord of the Rings' against the forest backdrop.

"This is where my father lives," said Natasha. The outside metal door of the building opened. An elderly couple stepped out, carrying two heavy carrier bags each. Natasha introduced me to her father, Nikolai Ivanovich, and his wife, Natasha - *thereafter known as old-Natasha*.

"*Priviet, ochen priyatna,*" I said in my best Russian. Nikolai gave me a very warm shake of the hand and old-Natasha gave me a big smile in acknowledgement. No English speakers here either; I was becoming really immersed now. I asked if I could help them with the bags in Russian; they smiled and let me have all four of them.

I lugged the bags over to a small white *Zaporozhets* car which they had opened and were climbing into. I squeezed the four bags into the boot. Whatever was in the bags was heavy. The *Zaporozhets* was a rear-wheel-drive Supermini designed and built in 1958, and it was still popular in many former Soviet states. Like the *Volkswagen* Beetle or East Germany's *Trabant*, the *Zaporozhets* was destined to become a 'people's car' of the Soviet Union; it was the most affordable vehicle of its era. All four of us squeezed into the *Zaporozhets*, Nikolai in the driving seat. He started the ignition. I could hear the air-cooled engine in the rear spurting into life. We drove away from the white tower down a different track to the one we arrived on. The track was smooth and undulating beneath the light-covering of snow, and Nikolai moved at speed; I found this somewhat disconcerting given that the risk of smashing head-on into an errant pine tree was uncomfortably high. I thought about suggesting to Nikolai that he slow down, however neither Natasha, nor old-Natasha, were remotely bothered sitting in a high-speed rally *Zaporozhets* – I just tried to enjoy the ride.

Five minutes into *The Pine Forest Offroad Rally*, and it was about to get the better of my nerves, when as if by magic, the road reappeared. We reached our destination: a row of small dachas beside a lake. The exterior of the summer house was covered in a thick layer of snow, resembling a charming snow-covered cabin straight out of a fairy tale. We disembarked from the *Zaporozhets* and started unloading the bags from the boot and carried them into the kitchen. The four bags were all full of different foods – meat, vegetables, fruit and sweets – and bottles of a variety of drinks including homemade vodka, wine and juices. The kitchen was one of three rooms in the dacha. The shelves were lined with jars of pickled vegetables, homemade preserves, and jars of honey harvested from the nearby forest. On the windowsill, a row of herbs and spices basked in the sunlight, their fragrant leaves waiting to be added to the next dish.

The other two rooms were a dining room and a reasonable sized bedroom, with a double bed. Nikolai was immediately busy lighting the small stove in the kitchen which could likely radiate enough heat for the whole of the dacha, making it cosy and warm. When all the bags had been unpacked, Nikolai and old-Natasha urged Natasha and I outside while they prepared the dinner.

We left the dacha via the back door taking us out into the garden, ten times the size of the dacha itself.

"This half of the garden, on the right-hand side, is grass and flowers, while the other half is full of vegetables and fruits," explained Natasha. Naturally, the snow obscured the grass, but I noticed wooden frames from the allotments poking through the snow.

"You can't see it now, but when we come back in the spring it will be beautiful."

"I can imagine how beautiful it will be in spring and I look forward to seeing it then." I replied. She smiled back.

She led me through to the bottom of the garden to a rear gate. Passing through, we arrived at the edge of a lake, frozen solid.

"Is the ice thick enough to walk on?" I asked.

"This winter isn't cold enough for ice skating, unlike last winter which was very cold. The lake had remained frozen until April. Walking on it now would be too dangerous especially with your weight!" Natasha smiled at her own joke.

I thought about the day Ron and I walked on the sea ice in Odessa; it must have been twenty degrees colder than today. I glanced at her as if to say, "are you calling me fat?" To which she grinned, appreciating the repartee. We walked on the path around the lake which took us back to the garden gate. As we approached the dacha, I could see the light smoke rising from the chimney, hinting at the crackling fire that awaited us inside. We wandered back up the garden path, old-Natasha was there to greet us on the steps, inviting us to the dinner table.

Stepping inside, we were greeted by a welcoming atmosphere. The interior was adorned with rustic wooden furniture, exuding a sense of traditional charm. The dining area was now the heart of the dacha, with the adjacent kitchen stove turned into a roaring fireplace glowing with a mesmerizing dance of flames. The crackling fire cast a warm glow, bathing the whole living space in a comforting light. The dining table was immaculately set with crockery and brimming with traditional Ukrainian dishes. The aroma of hearty Ukrainian cuisine filled the air as a pot of *borscht* and *varenyky* simmered on the stove.

We all sat down at the table; Nikolai insisted that I sit to the right of him. I did as I was told, and he promptly opened a bottle of the homemade vodka. Nikolai poured four glasses to the brim with neat clear vodka.

"Richard, welcome to Ukraine!" We collectively cheered *"Budmo!"* and drank the vodka in one gulp. It was strong stuff, and Natasha pointed towards the plate of lemon slices in front of me. I took a slice, and this eased the punch of the vodka straightaway. I was passed a plate of black bread, salo and garlic cloves. All this helped to absorb the vodka; the first of at least half a dozen rounds through the course of the dinner. It was relentless eating, and we hadn't even started the main course yet. Miraculously, the hangover from the Australian beer the night before had been cleared by the purity of the liquid crystal glass vodka.

As we completed several helpings of the main course, which looked like battered beef fillets, mashed potato and a potato salad, Nikolai took out a box and placed it carefully on the table. We drank another vodka – took a lemon slice, ate black bread with salo and garlic. Inside the box were several medals. Nikolai took out one-by-one and started passing them around the table. I was fascinated by these medals.

"Are these your medals?" I asked. He smiled back at me without answer. Taking this expression as an affirmation, I continued, "Where did you win them?"

"Here, in Kyiv, during the Great Patriotic War," he responded. Natasha jumped in and spoke on behalf of her father.

"He fought in the pine forests of Kyiv when the Germans attacked in 1941." Natasha glanced at Nikolai, seeking permission to continue. "The memorial to the battle is in the forest, not far from here. The trenches are still visible, even today." My response was inadequate.

"That's incredible! Could I visit the memorial and see where he fought?" I responded inadequately. Natasha again glanced at Nikolai and asked him before she spoke.

"If we come back tomorrow, he will take us. Today, it is too late, too dark." Nikolai poured one final vodka, for this meal.

"What rank were you?" I asked, tapping my left arm trying to sign 'rank' with three straight fingers. Nikolai understood my question.

"Colonel, I was a Colonel after the war," he replied.

Vodka glass in hand, I toasted "To the Colonel!"

Natasha acknowledged the toast and downed her vodka. The Colonel then indicated to old-Natasha and said, "She was also decorated in the army as a nurse, but after the war."

"She still works in the Kyiv hospital even today as a Matron," Natasha confirmed. I understood that there was a strong military background to this family. Indeed, I learned Natasha herself was a trained sniper, although she had completed her service ten years ago, before the end of the USSR. I placed the medals back into the box and thanked the Colonel for showing them.

Natasha and her father then broached another family subject – from what I had understood Ivan and Kira were due to be married in only two weeks' time. They were discussing final preparations for the wedding.

"Aren't they a bit young to be getting married?" I asked, inappropriately.

Natasha smiled and swiftly responded, "That's what you do when you're seventeen years old and pregnant in Ukraine."

"Ah, Congratulations," I responded, knowing full well Kira's predicament presented awkwardness for the family. And there it was; I felt a real bond with my new Ukrainian family. *A bond that would last a lifetime.*

By evening, the dacha was illuminated by the soft glow of candles with warm, golden light. The summer house in the forest was a magical place where family and friends gathered, shared stories, laughed and cherished moments like this. That first visit to a Ukrainian dacha in winter was a haven of snugness and contentment. Board games, books, puzzles were at hand to entertain and foster a sense of togetherness – but nothing could beat the heart-felt stories combined with good vodka. The dacha in February was a place where the cold of the winter is kept at bay, replaced by the warmth of a crackling fire, delicious food and the company of friendly people.

Chapter 11. The Institute and Napoleon

6th February 1997

I had been back in Kyiv for nearly two weeks and had yet to see Professor Korolyuk. Oksana called after breakfast, and a morning Russian lesson.

"Professor Korolyuk can see you this afternoon," she told me as if he were the King and I one of his ministers. It began to feel very formal. I wanted to consider how I would tackle this and how research work was done in Ukraine. *Would Oksana act as personal assistant for my meetings with Korolyuk?* I didn't feel comfortable with this kind of micro-management and thought carefully about my strategy. Surely, Korolyuk would consider this, as my professor and mentor. I needed to sidestep Oksana to get a direct route to Korolyuk. I knew that, with a little creativity, preparation, and a positive mindset, I could be more my own agent. *I wanted to be more of a prince to Korolyuk's king.*

"Has he made some time for me then?" I replied sarcastically.

"Yes - he will be waiting for us in the Institute at 2pm," she said, choosing to ignore the sarcasm.

"Did you get the Embassy to review your contract?" she continued. "It needs to be signed before you can formally work with Korolyuk."

"Yes, it was all fully checked and signed on Friday. I'll make sure I bring it with me," I confirmed proudly; the week had flown by in a haze of vodka, beer, Natasha's family and some of the wedding arrangements.

"OK great – see you at 2pm under Lenin. Don't be late." I noted the irony as she was invariably late most of the time. As she rang off, I assumed she meant the bronze Lenin in *Teatralna*, where we first met.

There were still plenty of Lenin statues in Kyiv, including the big one opposite *Bessarabski Market*.

As expected, I arrived at Lenin before Oksana, who was a few minutes late. I suggested that we meet in the Mathematics Institute to save time.

"No that's not possible. You must be accompanied by someone known to the Institute, at all times," Oksana stressed the words 'at all times', a little like a school teacher.

"Why?" I pushed.

"There are some people in the Institute who disagreed with you being offered a place there," Oksana admitted, wishing she hadn't let this cat out of the bag.

"Why on earth not?" I replied quizzically.

"Sure!" she responded, not quite getting the hang of this expression. "The Institute is renowned for pushing the boundaries of mathematical research and attracting all sorts of brilliant minds from around the world. You are the first to occupy a research position from the UK – and not only the UK but a NATO country."

"I like the 'brilliant minds' bit but why the suspicion from some?" I was becoming more and more intrigued by the world of secret staircases and professors that went AWOL for thirty years.

"At first glance, the Institute appears like any other academic institution. Professors and researchers can be seen discussing complex mathematical theories, scribbling equations on blackboards, and collaborating on cutting-edge projects. Hidden within the Institute's corridors are highly classified research rooms, dedicated to military applications of Mathematics. Cryptography is a thriving field here; our mathematicians work tirelessly to develop unbreakable codes and encryption techniques. These codes are intended to be used to secure sensitive military communications, safeguard national secrets, or even protect critical infrastructure." She paused to capture her breath and glance at my expression.

"Am I scaring you?"

"No, but I'm already planning my next stiff drink," I joked, she smiled and continued.

"Projects can focus on optimization algorithms; mathematicians devise advanced models to solve intricate logistical problems. These models can aid military operations, determining the most efficient deployment of troops or optimizing supply chain management during critical missions."

"OK you're scaring me now," I tried to break her flow. She demonstrated a grasp of English not evident five minutes earlier. Not only was she more fluent in English than most English people, but she was also exceptionally smart.

"Moreover, the Institute's mathematicians are working on developing complex simulations and predictive models. These tools could be utilized to analyse battlefield scenarios, simulate the behaviour of enemy forces, or even predict the outcomes of various military strategies." Oksana paused to think; appropriately, it was snowing again, just as the conversation became frosty. *I thought back to Professor Harris' words in Oxford.* He'd spoken of Kolmogorov's work at the Battle of Moscow.

"The Institute's researchers are experts in their respective fields of Mathematics, Computer Science and Engineering. Their collective intellect and innovative thinking will shape the future of military drone technology." I was starting to think Oksana was an artificial intelligent human like 'Ash' in the 1979 *Alien* film, imagining that she'd bleed white blood.

"While the existence of these secret military projects may seem unconventional, the fusion of Mathematics and Defence serves as a testament to the power of interdisciplinary collaboration. By harnessing the brilliance of mathematicians, the military gains a strategic advantage in an ever-evolving world." She suddenly stopped as if her battery had switched off.

"OK Oksana, pump the brakes – I get it; I understand why I need to be accompanied by someone," I submitted, still in disbelief that she was able to explain all that in a language that was not her mother tongue.

"What is *pump the brakes*?", she asked. It didn't need an answer.

We entered the gates of the Institute and walked across the courtyard, under full glare of the offices above.

She continued, "Please don't go up to the third and fourth floors unaccompanied; that is where many of the military projects are active."

"Noted!" I confirmed. I needed Oksana with me whenever I wanted to enter the Institute to visit Professor Korolyuk. *This was going to be harder than first thought.*

We entered the Institute together and were nodded through Reception. This time, we went up one flight of stairs to the second floor (or first floor from where I came from). Our first stop was the Institute's Administration Office. This office had three desks; at each desk was a female administrator, again clearly not a male job in Ukraine in the nineties. The desk by the window was occupied by the head administrator, her name was Galina. As we entered, she glanced over her monitor.

"Oksana, my dear, for what are we so deserving of your visit?" Galina's personality filled the room. The other two administrators were not in Galina's league: silent and expressionless, possibly as a result of spending their working days with her.

"We are here to return the contract of our English student," Oksana replied. I pulled out the folder with the signed contract and handed it over to Galina.

"My name is Richard and I'm very pleased to meet you," I said intuitively with an outstretched hand. Galina reciprocated by reaching out her hand, but in a peculiarly limp-wristed response. I thought for a moment she might want me to kiss her hand. Maybe she had a preconception that Englishmen still behaved as they did in the Victorian times. She took the contract and reviewed my counter signature on the back page.

"Thank you very much. We will get this registered with Samoilenko. Richard can start work when he wants to," she directed to Oksana. "What other business do you have in the Institute today?" she asked Oksana, while looking at me.

"We are seeing Professor Korolyuk now, so Richard can commence his research work," she replied.

As we turned to leave the Administration Office, Galina said "Richard, if you need anything, please do not hesitate to visit us." I thanked her but didn't quite feel her tone and expression fitted with the words. Maybe she was allied to those in the Institute that did not want me there. We were back in the corridor.

"Who is Samoilenko?" I asked Oksana.

"Professor Samoilenko is the Director of the Institute," she said as if I should I already know this.

"Actually, he voted with Korolyuk to allow you into the research department," Oksana elaborated.

"Sorry, I'm not sure I quite understand, you will need to explain this to me," I urged, sensing that a lot had happened behind the scenes during my return to Oxford.

"When a new research student enters the Institute, the four heads of department vote with a simple majority – if there is a draw then, Samoilenko, as Director, casts the deciding vote. He voted with Korolyuk which is why you were approved by three votes to two."

116

"And if Samoilenko had not voted as he did?" I checked.

"Then you would not be here – simple really," Oksana smiled. "Now let's go in to see Korolyuk. We are due in his study now".

"Lead the way," I said, still contemplating the behind-the-scenes politics of the Institute, the entry test I had unwittingly taken. As I understood, there we some senior academics in the Institute that had actively voted against my entry. I would now be guessing who they were, looking over my shoulder for them, anxious just how difficult they could make my life during my time here. Galina would be aware of this as she would have needed to process the paperwork.

Oksana and I walked down to the end of the corridor on the same floor and approached Professor Korolyuk's study. Not all the rooms had the secure double doors I encountered when I first met Korolyuk nearly a year ago. Oksana knocked once and Korolyuk's voice could be heard saying, "Yes, please come in."

We entered Korolyuk's study to find him watering the plants on his windowsill. He put down the watering jug and greeted me with a warm handshake.

"It is wonderful to see you return to Kyiv, Richard. Welcome back!" His words felt as genuine as Galina's words were false.

"Thank you. I can't tell you how delighted I am to be back in Ukraine and Kyiv here with you." I managed to express from the heart, even with my head swirling from Oksana's recent revelations.

"Vodka?" Korolyuk smiled.

"Why not?" I rejoiced. Maybe every tutorial would start with a shot of alcohol into the veins. Maybe that's how the Soviets produced so many good scientists and mathematicians over the years; they were all drunk.

Oksana watched us drinking the vodka, smiling, making it clear that she would not partake in such male activities.

"Do we have any business to complete today, Oksana?" he asked her.

"Just one signature for the publication of your latest paper, if you please," she said, pulling a form out of her leather folder. Korolyuk signed it without checking anything, then gave it back to her.

"You can come back and collect Richard in two hours," Korolyuk ordered.

"That's fine. I have some printing to be done and people to see. Richard, I will see you at 4pm. OK?"

"Why wouldn't it be, OK?", Korolyuk joked with Oksana, ushering her out of the door.

"See you then," I managed to reply as she left the study.

"Another vodka?" Korolyuk said, sensing the freedom we now had. I thought it prudent to stick with the one vodka.

"Maybe after we have finished our work?" I replied, thinking that it could be a test.

"Very wise."

Korolyuk walked over to his desk and picked up a pile of several books. One-by-one, he handed them to me.

"This one is on General Probability. This one on Stochastic Laws. This one has several marked research papers that you need to read." He placed the pile of books in front of me.

"We will meet the same time every week for a tutorial and any questions you may have for me." I took out my notebook and began jotting down salient details.

"Have you ever heard of the *Wright-Fisher* Model?" he asked. Fortunately, I had been tipped off by Oksana about it during the translation of papers; he said at the time that this was one of Korolyuk's key interests.

"Yes, I have – they applied Probability Theory to Population Genetics," I said feeling smug with myself waiting for Korolyuk's reaction.

"Good, you are correct. I think everyone in the UK must know about the subject of Genetics; this is where it was first discovered by *'Watson & Crick'*. Am I right?" he enquired mischievously. It was also a stereotype that Ukrainians held of British people.

"You're right about *'Watson & Crick'* but not so much about everyone in the UK knowing the science," I retorted. Professor Korolyuk showed me the Wright-Fisher problem of Population Genetics; this would be the first mathematical problem I'd work on with him.

At exactly 4pm, Oksana tapped on the study door as Korolyuk and I put down our glasses from the second vodka. "It looks like you two have been having fun?" she smirked as Korolyuk hid away the vodka glasses in the top draw of his desk.

"We have been working hard, Oksana," replied Korolyuk. "It is your fault that you enter the moment we stop."

"Are you ready to go?" she asked me. I finished placing all the heavy books from Korolyuk's desk, with my tutorial notes, into my rucksack.

Shaking hands with Korolyuk as I departed his study, I was relieved that our tutorial session had been so positive. I was looking forward to writing my first paper with the *great Professor Korolyuk.*

As we walked through Reception, out into the frozen courtyard, Oksana invited me over to her flat.

"Would you come over for lunch tomorrow?" she asked, in a way I couldn't possibly refuse.

"Yes please that would be nice," I insisted, knowing that she lived near *Svitoshin*, where I used to live with my previous host family. I returned to *Druzhbi Narodiv* to a dinner of *Vermicelli Pavlovski* at the flat. I guzzled it down with some tomato juice. The tomato juice was sealed in a great bottle jar, having been prepared at the dacha in the summer

– it was delicious; all the natural goodness settled in my hungry stomach. *I thought of the Tomato Man's offer.*

That evening, I went out for a drink at the *Arizona Bar* with Veronica, her friend a beautiful blonde girl called Luda, Greg and Rory from the current crop of TEFL teachers. Greg was pure entertainment; we became good friends that evening. I was a little more circumspect about Rory, partly because he held his handled beer glass in an awkward back-handed way, slurping the beer over his wrist. I assumed it was an Irish thing. Some British Embassy people were there too, including Fraser, the drunken Scot, who I remembered from the *Cave Inn* during the Australia Day celebrations.

The *Arizona Bar* was popular with the Embassy staff as it was a quick trip down the funicular from *St Micheal's Cathedral*. I noticed a couple of new faces, I was particularly mesmerised by a young Ukrainian student called Eugene, well dressed, smoked a pipe, *like my own Dad*, and spoke excellent English in what sounded like a South African accent.

After several beers, in addition to the vodkas with Korolyuk earlier, I asked Eugene, "Have you spent much time in South Africa?"

"No, I have never been to South Africa." He looked confused.

"But you have this incredible accent," I insisted.

"Do I? Then it's because my vocal cords have been blessed by a mischievous African genie," surreal was an understatement. "I just need to learn how to tame zebras and surf on lions, and I'll be the true embodiment of South Africa," he retorted. *Beyond articulate.* He was Ukrainian and well-cultured which was usually the case with most Ukrainians.

Eugene introduced me to a girl who had escaped from the war in Bosnia a couple of years before. Her name was Ilda. I remembered her name as it was like my grandmother's name, Hilda, still alive and living in Plymouth. My grandmother used to tell us about the second

World War, she as a young woman with my grandfather, bringing up three girls, near Liverpool which was heavily bombed. Ilda's story was very sad, she had lost her father, but she had found refuge in Ukraine and was keen to make her life there.

It had been an extraordinary day: I'd felt a whole gamut of emotions including anxiety, satisfaction and ending with exhilaration, knowing I was with an extraordinary group of like-minded friends in Kyiv. The country was being reborn in front of our eyes; it was exciting, and we were part of it. Typical night at the *Arizona*.

The following morning, Natasha and I carried on our routine of breakfast then a Russian lesson. We had become good friends and were already on *Colloquial Russian* Chapter Four. At midday, I got my winter gear on.

"See you later, I'll be home around dinner time," I called.

"As usual," Natasha responded from the kitchen. We were like a married couple.

"Say 'hello' to Oksana from me!" she called.

As I left the flat, I noticed Natasha's sister's door was wide open. Thinking this unusual, I knocked on the open door.

"Hello, anyone there?" trying to be a good neighbour. She suddenly appeared from one of the rooms into the hallway. She was surprised and a bit flustered.

"I just wanted you to know, your door was open," I said.

"Oh, thank you, thank you," she said nervously and closed the door, applying at least four locks on the inside. The door was shut. *I hoped it wasn't me who made her nervous.*

The journey from *Druzhbi Narodiv* to *Nyvky* metro station, where Oksana lived, was forty-five minutes, including a change from the green to the red line at *Zoloty Vorota*, or Golden Gate. This was a journey of ten stations. I was late.

As I approached *Nyvky* station, I remembered travelling up and down this line to teach at *School No.17.* As I exited the train, I was tempted to stay on for one more stop to visit my old host family, especially Taras and Sergei at *Hnata Yuri.* I was in too much of a rush; going through the barriers, I noticed Oksana waiting at the top. She didn't seem that happy to see me.

"Why are you so late?" Straight in there.

"My apologies! I had some neighbourhood duties to carry out with Natasha's sister," I embellished.

"Is everything OK? I forgot that her sister now lives next door to her", Oksana enquired with a hint of *knowing* in her tone.

"Yes, all good I think, Natasha's sister always seems a bit nervous. I don't know whether that's me?"

"No, it's not you. There are good reasons why, but it is not for me to say," she said mysteriously. "Ask Natasha." *I stayed silent but curious; another Ukrainian riddle to solve.*

Oksana's flat was a short five-minute walk from *Nyvky* station. The station didn't derive its name from the nearby *Nyvky River,* rather from the name of an old farmstead with a dacha, or '*Nyvky*', at the heart of it. In the 1850s, this area was outside Kyiv but, by the 1920s, it had become part of the city's suburbs. The *National Pedagogical University* and *Dynamo* football school were located there, in addition to many parks, an airfield and a tank parts factory. Oksana was married but she lived with her mother. The seventh floor flat had the traditional décor of rugs on the walls and solid wooden sideboards.

"This is my mother," Oksana introduced us. *"Mama eta Richard."* Her mother smiled then promptly disappeared into another room. After a traditional Ukrainian lunch, including borscht, we moved into a study.

Oksana and I reviewed a couple of research papers she was translating into English.

"Would you like some tea?" Oksana asked after an hour while I was in mid-review.

"Yes please, I'd love a cup. Milk, one sugar please," I kept my eyes on the paper. When the doorbell rang, Oksana left the room.

I was engrossed in the research paper when Oksana returned to the study.

"Richard, would you like to come through to the Dining Room, "she enquired like an English butler. Tea, akin to the sort you would receive at the *Ritz,* was laid out on the table. It must have been Oksana's mother; did she do anything else?

As Oksana was pouring the tea, a young man entered the Dining Room.

"Richard, let me introduce you to Misha," Oksana exuded joy as she mentioned his name.

"And Misha, this is Richard, Professor Korolyuk's new student from England, "she said excitedly. The energy in the room had shifted since Misha had entered the building.

"Pleased to meet you, Misha," I said in my best Russian. He returned the pleasantries. Misha was a dashing young man, on whom I was certain Oksana had a crush. She finished pouring the tea and lifted a cover to an enormous white cake, layered with puff pastry and whipped cream.

"Would you like some Russian *Napoleon* cake?" Before I could answer, she had cut into the cake.

"Misha is an opera singer at the National Opera," Oksana said, carving the cake into huge pieces.

"What sort of operas do you sing?", I asked. Misha didn't speak any English whatsoever, so Oksana acted as interpreter.

"He's a tenor at the National Opera House and the Musical Conservatoire," she said. He came across as humble, maybe thirty years old, with great skin and teeth. So, he was a singer.

Oksana put the huge pieces of Napoleon cake on to plates and passed one to me. We tucked in with our shiny silver cake forks.

"Misha just won an award for the *Best Tenor of Ukraine,"* Oksana elaborated. Oksana's excited tone signalled this was something special.

"That's fantastic, Misha! Congratulations," I gushed, trying not to be patronising. We took awkward bites out of our giant slices. I could taste evaporated milk; it made the cake taste slightly off but I knew I had to eat the whole slice not to offend. I washed every chunk down with a mouthful of tea.

"Misha is trying to learn an English song," Oksana broke the silence, somehow finishing her slice before us.

"Oh, excellent, which one?", I asked, taking another giant bite. "Strangers in the Night." she said.

"Frank Sinatra?" I knew Frank Sinatra didn't write any songs but only sung them. *And sung them well.*

"Yes exactly, you know it? It was written by *Bert Kaempfert*, the famous German conductor," Oksana clearly knew her music as well. I placed the last piece of Napoleon into my mouth but realised too late that I had no more tea to wash it down with.

"Richard, would you like more?" Oksana asked.

"Yes please." I replied, mouth half full, thinking she meant more tea. To my horror, she cut another slice of Napoleon cake and put it on my plate. It was bigger than the first. And then poured me another cup of tea.

"Would you be able to help Misha sing *Strangers in the Night*?"

Now, I remembered being in the Junior Choir and had even sung in the shower, but I was not going to be able to advise Misha on how to sing.

"How may I help Misha, exactly?" I enquired, seeking some clarification.

"We think that you would be able to translate the lyrics into Cyrillic," she said. This was going to be tricky. She was asking for a translation of the lyrics for *Strangers in the Night* from the English alphabet to Cyrillic script. The letters would be Cyrillic, but the words would be sung in English, a language that Misha did not speak. Not wishing to be rude, again I accepted the challenge.

"Yes, I think that would be fun," I tried not to groan as I swallowed down the last mouthful of cake with more tea.

We finished the evening with a small glass of vodka. Seemingly, if I agreed to anything in Ukraine, it was cause for celebration and a glass, or two, of vodka.

It was 9pm by the time I returned to *Druzhbi Narodiv.* Natasha was waiting for me with some dinner ready on the table. She had prepared a Russian *Napoleon* cake for dessert.

Chapter 12. The Marriage and the Mouse

14th February 1997

The day before Ivan and Kira's wedding was Valentine's Day. I felt fortunate that I had no obligations to any lady on this day. I watched as Ukrainian men grabbed last minute flowers and chocolates from local kiosks, hoping to avoid domestic wrath. Ukrainian weddings take place over a weekend, starting on Friday night when the bride and groom, close friends, relatives, go to the church for the blessing. The whole wedding celebration takes three days. Those who respected the old traditions made it a week, but this is rare; most people have jobs and couldn't take a week off. Still, three days is a whole lot of partying and Ivan's and Kira's wedding began on the Friday morning.

After breakfast, Ivan invited me to go on a walk with him, Kira and Ivan's friends, Sasha, and Vlad, in the National Botanical Gardens. I presumed that one of them was going to be the Best Man at Ivan's wedding, always having to remind myself that they were still more boys than men. It was 10am and Sasha and Vlad had a bottle of *Obolon* beer in their hands. Sasha's ruck sack was full of beer. *Obolon* was a local beer named after the district of Kyiv where it was produced. The morning felt like it was turning into a stag-do. Also with us, but not holding a bottle of beer, was 'Funtik', Vlad's dog, a deranged mongrel terrier. The Botanical Gardens covered about three hundred acres, one stop from *Druzhbi Narodiv*. We disembarked at *Percherska* metro station towards the garden entrance. Once inside, Funtik was eager to get off his lead and have a runabout. Vlad popped open another *Obolon* and released Funtik who promptly stampeded off into the bushes. That was the last we saw of him that morning.

For the next three hours, we wandered around calling out his name, drinking Sasha's *Obolon*. If losing a deranged mutt had been the plan for Ivan's stag-do, it was turning out to be a success. Sometime after midday, we found Funtik lying on a park bench, shattered after being lost for three hours, but happy to let Vlad clip his lead back on. The snow came and we returned to the apartment cold, tired, hungry, and drunk.

"Did you have fun at the Botanical Gardens?" Natasha greeted us on the doorstep. Without waiting for an answer, she ushered us inside towards another big lunch table.

After lunch, we all went on an excursion to a market located on the airfield at *Nyvky*, near Oksana's apartment. We bought some last-minute wedding items. We arrived at the local church after dark, exhausted and a little deflated. At 7pm we congregated to see Ivan and Kira receive a blessing from the local priest followed by another vodka-fuelled dinner. By the end of Friday night, we were all ready for bed.

Wedding preparations were well underway by the time I emerged from my bedroom on Saturday morning. Natasha, her sister, and some neighbours were collecting food and packages to take to the wedding venue. Natasha's father, the Colonel, was helping Ivan get his shirt and bow tie on. There were bouquets of flowers being delivered and placed on the open balcony – the cool temperatures would keep them fresh. The temperatures were above zero, unheard of the previous winter. Luckily, some flowers were left after yesterday's Valentines Day flurry. After several coffees, I dressed in the only suitable clothes that I had brought with me: my dad's tweed jacket, a white collared shirt, and some dark blue chinos. I found a flowery tie to go with it.

The groom disappeared to meet with the bride and sign papers at the local Kyiv Authority (the official state issuers of marriage stamps, and not the most revered of Kyiv institutions) ahead of the start of the actual ceremony. We were all transported in taxis to a venue which appeared to be more like a production line of wedding couples. When one newly married couple left the building, Kira and Ivan were called in.

Usually, as was the case for Ivan and Kira, the couples were from the same school. We followed as their entourage. Vlad was the Best Man and he reminded me of 'Lurch', from *the Addams Family*. He was clearly suffering from yesterday's activities, and he'd brought Funtik with him. The wedding party were the bride and groom's families, their friends were all from the same class at school. If couples weren't from the same school, then they were at least from neighbouring apartment blocks. It was considered bad form to marry somebody from a different region in Ukraine.

The ceremony was quick; the priest blessed the newlyweds as they promised to be together forever. Photos of the wedding party followed, including one of me with the bride, which I felt slightly uncomfortable with. Then, the cutting of a giant *korovai* took place. *Korovai* is a wedding bread, intricately woven and decorated with unleavened dough, marshmallow, or whipped egg whites. Once the ceremony was complete, the wedding party left the church, and Kira threw sweets and small change to the assembled pack of children for good luck. Ivan and Kira then installed themselves in the doorway of an adjacent building to welcome everyone through to dinner.

The Ukrainian Wedding dinner has its own rules and traditions. A particular set of dishes eaten in a specific order, the positioning of guests, and, of course, the complex and specific toasting ritual must all be adhered to. If you get lucky, you may be permitted the honour of drinking champagne from the bride's shoe. I found myself seated among several attractive young ladies and felt somewhat the centre of attention. The different ladies were keen to practise their English and to enquire if I was already married.

For extra entertainment throughout the feast, guests yelled the words *"Girko! Girko!"*, translating literally as 'bitter', meaning that the drink is 'bitter' and the couple have to kiss to make the drink 'sweet'. This was the cue for the newlyweds to start kissing. It always happened without warning, and I only ever managed to raise my glass at the third

"*Girko!*" much to the amusement of the ladies next to me. Snezana occasionally popped over to say, "Hello."

"Where is your mother?" I asked. She just shrugged. I hadn't seen her since the apartment that morning. Maybe she had been at the church, but I couldn't recall.

The moment of the speeches arrived and the Best Man, *Lurch*, looked particularly nervous. I didn't understand a single word of his speech; it was a short one and everyone was thankful for the brevity. After the father of the bride's speech, there were several speeches from various friends and family including the Colonel. Each speech was followed by a glass of vodka. I sat and listened and drank and laughed at the appropriate pauses. After a longer pause, to my horror, I was invited to speak by the bride. *What would I say?* One hundred wedding guests were staring at me. I hadn't prepared any speech whatsoever, but declining wasn't an option. *It was probably the Ukrainian way or something.* I realised that, given most people in the room couldn't understand English, I could just about say anything. So, I did.

"Err...Ladies and gentlemen, bride and groom, thank you for inviting me to speak. As a fellow attendee at this wonderful wedding, I have the pleasure of addressing you all after several vodkas." I began, they all laughed as soon as I said 'vodka' – the only word they understood.

"I must admit, it's always a bit nerve-wracking to stand in front of a room full of strangers. Luckily, I'm standing in front of friends." I instantly regretted what I had said for being too cheesy, comforted by the knowledge that nobody understood a word of it.

"Weddings are a time of err... joy, celebration, and of course, love." I degenerated into a lousy Hugh Grant impression of *Four Weddings and a Funeral*. I glanced at Natasha, on the next table. She gave me an encouraging smile.

"And as we gather here to witness the union of two beautiful souls, I can't help but reflect on my own experience of love." *What was coming out of my mouth?* I needed somebody to save me before I corpsed. *I wondered if I could fake a heart attack.*

"It's a topic that has inspired countless songs, poems, and even some err... questionable fashion choices in the eighties. But hey, we've all been there, right?" *Maybe a choking fit or a mini faint.*

"Speaking of fashion choices, let's take a moment to appreciate the stunning bride and her impeccable taste. They say that a bride's wedding dress should be a reflection of her personality, and I must say, she looks absolutely stunning." *I could already see myself getting beaten up by the Best Man after the dinner.*

"It's almost a shame that we only get to wear these dresses once, isn't it? I mean, how amazing would it be if we could just casually stroll into the supermarket wearing a full-on wedding gown? Talk about a statement!" *I'd definitely get beaten up for being a cross-dresser. I needed an exit strategy.*

"But let's not forget about the groom. He cleans up pretty well too, doesn't he?" One hundred pairs of eyes stared at me. *A tumbleweed rolled by.*

"They say that behind every great man is a woman rolling her eyes, but in this case, I think ...ah...that behind this great man is a woman who's ...err...convinced him to wear a suit that fits!" I got a few polite smiles from the tone change. Funtik suddenly darted out from under the table, between my legs.

"Now...err...as we raise our glasses to toast the newlyweds, let's remember that love is a journey. It's not always easy, but it's worth it." *I had to stop. They could be divorced soon.*

"*Vodka!*", I said for the hell of it. There was laughter and applause. *This was the magic word!*

"And as we witness the start of this beautiful journey for our dear friends, let's also take a moment to appreciate the love and laughter they bring in our lives," Funtik was sniffing something assertively under the table. A girl screamed and a glass smashed onto the floor. Funtik had pulled a tablecloth off one of the tables, giving me the opportunity, I needed.

"*Girko!*" I tried to intone without squeaking.

"*Girko! Girko!*" came the response from my flock. The room erupted into applause. Natasha was beaming at me. *I Want To Dance With Somebody* by Whitney Houston signalled it was time for Ivan and Kira's first dance. Everyone stood up and started clapping. Ivan and Kira glided across the dancefloor. As the song came to an end, I took the opportunity to exit left to the toilet. But as I darted across the room, one of the young ladies from my table grabbed my hand and pulled me onto the dancefloor to do the *Macarena*. I was trapped on so many levels. The proceedings continued with a mix of dancing, more food and vodka late into the night.

Again, by 10am the next morning, preparations for another day of the wedding celebrations began. By midday, everybody was at the groom's apartment, where the elders, as is the tradition, came to wish the happy couple 'good luck', sing wedding songs and give them flowers and presents. Dinner was at Kira's parents'; I was fading fast through lack of sleep, alcohol consumption and massive over-eating. When everything finished, Ivan and Kira took a long rest to recuperate from their wedding celebration. Soon they would be celebrating their friends' weddings; seventeen was a popular age to get married in Ukraine. The whole ceremony, with a hundred guests, was a concession to tradition taking time and energy from the newlyweds. If it was up to them, they'd go to church by themselves, promise God to stay together forever, and use all that money to buy an apartment.

On Monday, Day Four of the wedding by my reckoning, I woke with a sore throat, we were invited to a post-wedding lunch at Natasha's brother's apartment in *Livorborezhna,* on the east side of Kyiv. *How many siblings did Natasha have?* Before that, I had a surprise appointment at the Opera House with Oksana and Misha. Oksana had called before breakfast.

"Richard, would you be able to get to the Opera House by 11am?" I had not been to the Opera House since last winter when I accompanied two thirtysomething ladies from my English class; both were looking for a husband, but I prided myself on being strictly professional. We had watched *Nabucco* by Giuseppe Verdi and drank a lot of Italian red wine in the Opera House bar.

"It's short notice but, yes should be fine. I'll need to let Natasha know as we have a post-wedding lunch at 2pm with her brother at *Livorborezhna,"* I insisted.

"Misha always arranges at short notice. No problem - you can take a metro directly from *Teatralna* to *Livorborezhna*. It's only five stops to get to lunch after." Oksana was good at organizing my life for me.

"What are we doing there?" I enquired.

"Misha wants to read through the lyrics of *Strangers in the Night* with you. Please can we meet outside the side stage door." It seemed that Oksana was acting as a formal assistant to Misha, as well as a one to Professor Korolyuk. Clearly, Oksana was someone who made things happen in these circles.

I told Natasha the altered plans and said she would meet me outside the station exit at 1:30pm, giving me two hours with Misha.

"Oh, one more thing," Oksana continued, "do you have a cold?"

"No. Why?"

"Your voice sounds hoarse. All opera singers ask about people's health before they can be in an enclosed space with them. Misha is paranoid about catching any virus which puts his throat out of action," Natasha explained.

"Understood. Yes - I'm 100% healthy," I confirmed before placing the receiver back on the phone. I gargled some salt water in the kitchen. I had heard this before; opera singers were high maintenance.

Natasha and I squeezed in a quick Russian lesson on *Colloquial Russian*, Chapter Five after breakfast. I took the opportunity to ask Natasha about her sister who always appeared nervous and timid. I told her about the 'open door' episode and asked why she had been invisible at the wedding.

"Teofila is always nervous," Natasha stated.

"Has she always been like this?" After three weeks of living in Natasha's apartment, we had become good friends.

"No, she hasn't. She paused then continued, "Teofila's husband was a very good nuclear physicist; in fact, he was one of Ukraine's finest. In 1978 he went to work at the new Chernobyl nuclear power plant, north of Kyiv."

"OK, he worked at Chernobyl?" I responded with shock. Everyone had heard of Chernobyl.

"Yes, and you know what happened in 1986?"

"Of course, the year of the disaster," I nodded slowly, part of me not wanting to hear the rest of the story.

"He was present during the nuclear testing of some of the reactors when an explosion happened," Natasha confirmed.

"Oh my god, now I understand why Teofila is like this."

"No, you don't understand. Teofila's husband *survived* the disaster but, of course, suffered from radioactivity after the initial clean-up. He became very ill; they had only just had a baby. It was an incredibly difficult time for everyone."

"The baby is Snezana?" I asked, knowing full well that it was her.

133

"Yes."

"Did her husband die from the exposure?" I asked.

"No. Five years after the disaster, he travelled to Moscow on business. The Soviet Union had collapsed, and Ukraine achieved independence in 1991," she paused. She looked at me as if to check that she could trust me.

"One evening, he was returning to his apartment in Moscow when somebody appeared around a corner and shot him dead." She stopped.

"Oh my god! That's terrible. How awful! He survived Chernobyl only then to be murdered in Moscow?" I was incredulous and understood why Teofila was so nervous.

"Yes, and she had a young baby to look after with no income after her husband was killed. Even after nearly seven years, she hasn't recovered from the trauma." Natasha paused, then changed the subject.

"You will be late meeting Oksana." It was already 10:30am; I had half an hour to get to the Opera House. I grabbed my coat and went out of the door.

"See you at 1:30!" she called after me.

I dashed out of the apartment building, past the row of kiosks, up the hill, past the pensioners selling milk and dacha vegetables and down the steps into the *Druzhbi Narodiv* metro. I was fluent with the process and got through the barriers and down the escalator in less than a minute. If I heard the moan of the underground train coming down the tunnel before I had reached the base of the escalator, I would accelerate the last few steps and sprint down the central platform, jumping on the train just before the doors closed.

"Uberezhna, dveri zachinaetsya. Nastupno stantsia Pecherska," was always the announcement from inside departing trains. It was

Ukrainian not Russian, as it would have been until independence: "Be careful, the doors are closing. Next station is *Pecherska*."

I arrived at *Teatralna*, exited the train and glanced across to the Lenin statue. *He was becoming a familiar friend.* It was nearly 11am and I had a few minutes to run up the hill to the Opera House. As I exited the station steps, I looked across to the Mathematics Institute gates. Maybe I expected to see Professor Korolyuk coming out. The Opera House was in sight. I never wanted to be late with Oksana. I arrived panting.

"Gosh you're unfit," she joked. I needed a couple of minutes to get my breath back.

"Twenty minutes from the flat is pretty quick," I responded, conceding that I had left later than I should have done.

"Thank you for getting here, no pressure at all. Misha thought it would be a good opportunity to read through *Strangers in the Night*. He has a concert at *Palats Sportu* on 11th March. He wants to sing it there."

"No pressure, then. We have three weeks to turn him into Frank Sinatra," I joked. This was no time at all given that he didn't even know the language he was going to be singing it in.

Recovered from my run, and concealing my hoarseness, Oksana led me through the stage door into the Opera House. We made our way through marble-floored passageways, down flights of steps, around sharp corners, and up flights of stairs. It was a well-organized space. We reached a door with Misha's name on it. Oksana knocked and the voice inside beckoned us in. It was Misha's dressing room, equipped with mirrors, costumes, and a makeup station to help Misha transform into his stage characters. "Welcome to my home!" Misha was already standing as we entered. *He had excellent teeth.* He gave Oksana the customary kiss on the check when greeting a lady in Kyiv.

"Would you like some tea or coffee?" I noticed two used cups already on the dresser: one with lipstick and one without. Maybe, Oksana had been here for some time already, which didn't tally with him just greeting her in the way that he did. I sensed that he was very popular with the ladies, especially in the operatic community.

"Coffee with milk for me, please Misha," I asked, knowing that you had to make it clear you wanted milk, otherwise it would be assumed that you wanted it black. He had a coffee maker in his dressing room and spent a couple of minutes making the drinks. Meanwhile, Oksana had taken out some printed scripts of *Strangers in the Night.* She passed one copy to me.

"I'll give you ten minutes to read through," she said, as Misha placed three coffees on the dresser in front of us. We sat in silence for ten minutes, interrupted only by delicate sips of hot strong coffee. It was cool in his dressing room, and we were below street level.

"Is everyone warm enough?" Misha asked coincidently. I told him I was fine.

"The Opera House always takes time to heat up in the mornings," he said.

"All the apartments here are so hot in the winter, the only way to cool them down is to open the balcony doors," I moaned. I finished reading the lyrics.

"All flats have communal heating in Ukraine," Oksana said. "It is the only way to regulate the temperature."

I read the first line of the first verse nice and clearly to try and maximise intonation for Misha:

"Strangers in the night exchanging glances," I said, contorting my face to express every sound clearly. The coffee had helped my throat. Oksana translated each line in Ukrainian.

"Wondering in the night," I continued. Misha listened and took notes.

"What were the chances we'd be sharing love," I almost broke out into song, but resisted.

"Before the night was through," I paused to let everyone catch up, sipping some coffee; it was brutally strong. Given that I was into Day Four of Ivan and Kira's wedding ceremony, it was needed.

By the end of the sixth, and last, verse of the song, it was already 1pm. I was on my second strong coffee.

"This is a good time to stop," Oksana said, remembering that I needed to leave. Misha was still writing notes.

"Yes, but this is excellent," said Misha. "Thank you both. Can we meet again in two days' time for a first rehearsal?" He wanted to spend some time familiarising himself with the meaning of the lyrics.

"Richard, can you convert the English words into Cyrillic script before then?" Oksana asked. I could and would be ready.

Misha showed us out of his dressing room. To my surprise, he continued to lead us in the opposite direction that we entered.

"I will show you to the door," He was clearly in a buoyant mood having now started 'Project Frank', as we began to refer to it. Everything had a codename here.

We walked into an area which housed props, costumes and set pieces. We were standing in the wings of the stage. The space was meticulously organized to ensure easy access and quick changes during performances. I imagined how chaotic backstage must be during a live show: technicians and stagehands working diligently to transport and set up the necessary elements of the production. To be a part of producing some of the world's greatest performances would be marvellous.

Misha walked us out onto the stage. We followed him with trepidation. The curtains were open and in front of us was the entire Opera House auditorium. *How it must feel to perform in a full house.*

137

Standing there for the first time was a moment of immense significance for me. The nerves I felt during *Stags & Hens* in Plymouth flooded back. I imagined the nerves and excitement of the young singers and dancers as they appeared here for the first time.

The idea of performing in front of an audience that size was impressive. I had given an impromptu speech to only a hundred people at Ivan's wedding yesterday and that had been terrifying enough. The Opera House could hold over two thousand people. I was in awe of the talent that performed on this stage. I had never seen Misha singing before, so I didn't know how good he really was. His recent national award said that he was good, really good.

We crossed the stage to another stage door entrance, opposite to the one we had entered.

"Goodbye," we both said as Misha hovered and closed the door behind us.

"That was amazing," I said as Oksana arranged her fluffy hat. It had started snowing again.

"Yes, Misha is very hospitable sometimes," she said.

"Only sometimes?"

"He is a complicated person, Richard. You wouldn't understand," her tone sunk, and I knew not to probe.

"I noticed you translating the lyrics in Ukrainian for Misha," I said, proudly demonstrating that I could tell the difference between the two languages.

"Yes, you're right. Misha prefers Ukrainian, in fact, he is a country boy really. He grew up in the regions in a village to the west of the country. He very much loves the Ukrainian language. It's much more melodic than Russian." *I related to Misha, he came from the countryside like me.*

138

"I need to catch a train from *Teatralna* to *Livorborezhna* in the next five minutes otherwise I'll be late meeting Natasha," I had to stop her explaining.

"Ok. Let's meet up again in two days. I'll call you to let you know where to meet. I'm headed toward the *Golden Gate* metro," Oksana replied, then she walked off in the opposite direction. I turned and headed down the slope back to *Teatralna*, the snow had started falling heavily.

Natasha was waiting on the other side of the barriers at *Livorborezhna*. The underground areas in winter were like warm subterranean village communities under the main city. I was a few minutes late getting from *Teatralna* but Natasha welcomed me warmly.

"How was Misha?" she asked. I had no idea whether she had met him or whether she was asking after an old friend.

"He seemed like a good guy, he even gave us a guided tour of the Opera House," I boasted, knowing that Natasha wasn't easily impressed.

"Do you know 'Misha' means 'mouse' in Russian? Come on, let's have lunch," she said, indicating with a smile and a nod to the station exit. Snow had settled on the steps going up to the street; from inside the station, it made the village community seem even warmer.

"*Mene zovut, Vasyl!*" Natasha's brother, Vasyl, welcomed us at the door of the apartment. He shook me warmly by the hand. He beckoned us to take off our snowy boots and coats and come into the living room; the table was laid out for another feast with Ivan and Kira at the top end.

Around the table were the wider family and friends of Natasha and her brother. Natasha gave everyone a brief introduction, 'This is Richard,' as we sat down, so that I wouldn't have to. *She was a rock like that.* The lunch began with speeches to the new bride and groom and the obligatory vodkas with wine. The dishes were delicious traditional

Ukrainian, and I was encouraged to 'eat, eat, eat'. As usual, I delighted everyone when I ate at least my own body weight. The dinner continued to early evening when Natasha and I departed, not before Vasyl presented me with his old army beret as a gift. I made a special note in my diary to *"avoid Ukrainian weddings where possible, they are bad for the health."* Indeed.

Chapter 13. Project Frank and the President

21st February 1997

It was a crisp Friday morning; the end of another week of reading and writing notes on Probability Theory. Natasha and I had completed *Colloquial Russian* Chapter Six. I wanted to accelerate my spoken language and be prepared for my first paper and my next meeting with Professor Korolyuk. As usual, I met Oksana at *Teatralna*, and she accompanied me through the gates of the Mathematics Institute, we checked into Reception and on to whichever room I needed to go to.

On this occasion, we bumped into Galina, the head administrator of the Institute.

"Good morning, Oksana," she eyed me suspiciously. "What is our student from England doing today?"

"Richard is meeting with Korolyuk at 11am," Oksana said on my behalf. "We are going to his study," she clarified. Oksana was nervous around Galina. Galina didn't take her eyes off me.

"Professor Korolyuk is not in his study. He is in Lecture Room Three with a visiting lecturer from Moscow," Galina said smugly. "He asked for you to join him when you arrived."

"OK thank you – I was not informed of this by Korolyuk," Oksana said, slightly puzzled. I got the feeling that there was a bit of a power game going on between Oksana and Galina.

"No, which is why I'm letting you know now," Galina insisted and, without waiting for a response, busily walked off down the first-floor corridor.

Oksana turned to me. "Please don't take any offence from her tone, that's just how she is."

We arrived at the outer door of Lecture Room Three. As Oksana opened the door carefully, we could hear faint voices coming from inside.

"Please go in quietly sit at the back of the room," she whispered. "I will come back in an hour." Oksana opened the door; inside several students and lecturers were seated, facing a white board covered in equations. Professor Korolyuk was seated in the front row. A man I had not seen before was standing in front of the white board presenting, what appeared to be, his research work. As I entered Korolyuk, acknowledged my presence. I moved quietly to the back of the room and sat down at one of the desks.

The visiting lecturer continued, speaking in Russian, without pausing as one or two other students entered the room after me. I was relieved not to be the only one entering during the presentation. He was coming to the end and appeared to be quite pleased with himself. He asked if there were any questions from the room. Korolyuk signalled that he had a query and asked him something which I couldn't quite understand. The visiting professor seemed a little annoyed but answered in a way in which he had to repeat in summary the last part of the presentation. Then Korolyuk asked him another short question. Visibly annoyed, the visiting lecturer repeated in summary the first part of the presentation.

Professor Korolyuk stood up and asked the visiting lecturer for his marker pen and then he commenced re-writing some of the central equations of the visitor's presentation. This further annoyed the visiting lecturer, and he began to raise his voice to Korolyuk. This was fascinating; there was clearly some disagreement with the theory that the visiting lecturer was presenting. It was like two intellectual bulls locking horns. Korolyuk then proceeded to change some of the initial conditions of the equations in the top left-hand corner of the white board; then he refined the solution at the bottom right-hand corner of the board. He gave the pen back to the open-mouthed visiting lecturer and said,

"Your theory was poorly thought through. I've corrected it for you, but it is now not a significant result." The room was silent. The visiting lecturer just stared at the reworked proof written by Korolyuk. He muttered something angrily at Korolyuk who snapped back at him. The lecturer picked up has bag, sweating heavily, and walked out of the room. Professor Korolyuk had demolished his theory in five minutes.

Professor Korolyuk calmly turned to his colleagues sitting in the audience, and asked if anyone had any questions. There were a couple of questions from another professor, but only to support Korolyuk's position. I certainly didn't have any questions from the back and wondered how easily he would tear apart any theories that I may try and present. The lecture room started to empty until only Korolyuk and I were left.

"We can stay in here," Korolyuk smiled. "How are you? How is life in Kyiv treating you?"

I told him about the extended wedding that I experienced and that I'd given a speech.

"I'm impressed," Korolyuk laughed. "It must have been daunting. What did you talk about?"

"Only about things I knew to be true," I said to him. "It is much safer ground in the face of doubters."

"Very true!" He patted me on the shoulder.

We spent the next hour running through several questions I had from the reading material and research papers Korolyuk had given to me a couple of weeks before. He provided counter notes to each of my queries then set me a few new tasks. There was a knock on the inside door. Oksana entered the lecture room.

"We are done for today", Korolyuk said, pre-empting what Oksana was going to ask.

"Was that Dr. Orlov presenting?" Oksana asked. She clearly knew the mathematics community, which was especially strong between Kyiv and Moscow state universities. *This is something that Professor Harris had touched on in Oxford.*

"Yes, but he was wrong, at best incomplete," Korolyuk smiled. I noticed; he did everything with a smile.

"Next time, we meet at my apartment," Korolyuk said to me. "Oksana, please give Richard my address and explain to him how to get there."

"Of course!" Oksana replied. I packed my rucksack; we all left the lecture room together. Korolyuk went back into his study. Oksana and I headed down the staircase to Reception.

"Lunch?" Oksana suggested.

"Yes, and you wouldn't believe what happened in the lecture earlier," I said.

"I would," Oksana replied knowingly. "Korolyuk is very critical of those who occupy high places but have low intelligence. Anyone who gets praise from Professor Korolyuk should be very proud. He can be devastating to those who haven't worked things through. He often finds academics from Moscow to be arrogant, especially when they are wrong," she smiled again.

"Thanks – I will take that advice onboard," I said. We headed out of the Institute gates, turning right towards *Kreshchatik* for lunch.

Friday night had turned into a *Rock Café* night with many regular friends attending in the early evening before heading off to another bar or a nightclub. Since last year, Ron and Tom had been replaced with a new crowd of *TEFL* teachers. I had received an email from Ron in Albania, to say he was enjoying life in the capital, Tirana; that I should come and visit Albania when I got an opportunity. I knew he was joking when his next email told me he'd been airlifted out of the British Embassy compound due to civil unrest. The previous year, Albania had been shaken by the dramatic rise and collapse of several financial pyramid schemes soon after its transition to a market economy. Ron had decided to leave the country. I had also heard from Tom that he was enjoying undergraduate life in Sheffield studying for his Russian degree. Alison was another of the teachers from last year no longer with us. *I was starting to feel like the Daddy of the group.*

But that night, at the *Rock Café*, Greg was celebrating his birthday weekend. His actual birthday was the next day and he'd invited everyone out to the *River Palace* night club. As a warmup, we had several *Obolons* and a few games of pool. I continued to feel the relief of the Friday *Rock Café* evening, it was a time where I could relax, be myself. No need to try and understand or speak any Russian. Alison no longer with us, it was nice to see Veronica, who now came either by herself or out with her girlfriends; she would always jokingly critique my Russian which she did admit was improving by the week. Our friendship pre-dated the current crop of teachers, and at times, we joked about some of the British naivety of the new ones. Kyiv felt more alive now than it had a year ago, less shadowy. More bars and clubs had opened. *There was more advertising, other than Guinness, and Kyiv was connecting to the internet.*

At 11pm we headed en masse towards the *Kreshchatik* metro and stayed on for two stops on the red line to *Dnipro*. From *Dnipro*, the *River Palace* night club was visible and less than a hundred metres to walk. Before boarding the gangplank to the boat, we had to be frisked by one of two giant bouncers. Once the bouncers were happy that none of us were carrying any drugs or lethal weapons, we were allowed on to the boat. We headed straight to the bar. Greg ordered a quantity of absinthe shots for those that wanted them and, in keeping with several twenty-something lads abroad, we downed them and had another. We joined the ladies on the dancefloor and embarrassed ourselves all night.

The late night made the next morning very tough. I had promised that I would help Natasha carry some parcels of food out to *Koncha Zaspa* for the Colonel. After at least three cups of strong coffee, and still feeling like death warmed up, we arrived at the dacha. Ivan thought it would be a good idea to go ice skating on the pond beyond the back garden. So, while still slightly hungover from the party the night before, I slipped on a pair of ancient ice skates, intending to do something that I swore I would never do and skate on a frozen pond. Ivan had his own skates, which looked a lot smarter than mine, and he was on the ice straight away. I had difficulty balancing on the blades and I still hadn't reached the ice. After five minutes of convincing myself that I could stand, I had seamlessly manoeuvred myself onto the smooth icy surface of the frozen pond. It immediately brought back memories of standing on the frozen Odessa Sea with Ron a year ago when we nearly floated away on the broken ice. *Today's danger was no less perilous.* Five metres from the bank, icy water lapped my feet, then my ankles, spreading up my lower legs until my groin was feeling the full effects of ice water. Sinking into the water, my reaction times must have dulled as the panic didn't set in as it should. Maybe the alcohol still flowing through my veins from the night before kept my body warm.

"Help!" I politely shouted in English, realizing that no-one would respond to that. Icey water was up to my waist now.

"Grab this," Natasha had appeared out of nowhere, holding a rope. She threw it at my face, and I grabbed the loose end with one hand, rubbing my nose with the other. Both Natasha and Ivan, who'd arrived, pulled me up out of the water, back onto the ice and to the bank. Suddenly warm again, I shivered as I walked back up the path to the warm dacha. "That was fun," I said, nose still throbbing.

Natasha's father had made a fire in the dacha stove, and I was relieved to be sitting in front of it. Natasha gave me a hot coffee. *I would not be ice-skating in Ukraine again.* The combination of late-night partying followed by a dip in an icy lake resulted in three days in bed with a cold. Strangely, spots appeared on my back a couple of days later. *I was in the wars.* Natasha insisted that I cover my back with a vodka-soaked cloth; she said the cloth would kill any virus I had contracted on my skin. Vodka was the medicine for most ailments in Ukraine, it seemed, so I gave it a try. It worked. The next day, my spots were gone. Apparently, Natasha said the 'vodka-cloth' also worked on a sore throat.

The next day I found out that Misha also stood by the 'vodka-cloth method' to cure his sore throats. He had been out of action for a few days with a sore throat as there was a lot of flu about now. *I hoped I hadn't been blamed for it.* He had spent two days with a vodka-cloth wrapped around his neck and apparently it had worked. Oksana called after breakfast.

"Richard, please can you meet us at *Ploshcha Lva Tolstogo* metro station at 11am. Misha has booked the recording studio and wants you there for Project Frank."

"Sure, I'll see you both then," I responded excitedly. This was reward indeed for delivering the adapted *Strangers in the Night* in Cyrillic for him last week. Luckily, he was still able to learn it while he had a sore throat. I was excited to take Project Frank to the next stage, but I was under no illusion that Misha would find it easy; English is a syllabic language and Russian is not. It was going to be trial and error.

I arrived at *Palats Sportu* to cross over to the sister station, *Ploscha Lva Tolstogo* on the blue line. As I passed through *Palats Sportu,* I saw the Davis Cup tennis advertised, I liked a bit of tennis – Ukraine versus UK in July – we had the mighty Tim Henman and, the not really English, Canadian Greg Rusedski. Making a mental note of this, I crossed over to meet Oksana and Misha. After Natasha told me that his nickname translated as *Mouse*, I smiled when I saw him again. The train wailed out of the underground tunnel, and we boarded for a couple of stations, south to *Lybidska.*

We arrived at a building two minutes' walk from the station exit. It wasn't obvious that this was a recording studio; I was already imagining Abbey Road Studios, famous for the Beatles zebra crossing photo. *This was not Abbey Road.* However, as we stepped inside, it began to look like a recording studio.

"This is the best recording studio in Kyiv," Oksana said. There was an acoustically treated control room. An audio engineer sat inside ready. In front of him was a mixing console, computer monitors, audio interfaces, and various other antiquated equipment necessary for recording and editing audio.

"Really?" I tried to conceal my surprise. Then I reminded myself it was not how it looked that mattered, but how it sounded. This was a preliminary recording session. No compact discs would be burned that day.

Misha was already setting himself up in the tracking room, where musicians or vocalists perform and record their parts. Also acoustically treated, it was big enough for probably four people with instruments, no more. There were wall racks with a variety of microphones, headphones, and musical instruments available for use.

"We can sit here," Oksana pointed into the control room. We sat in two black leather seats next to the audio engineer, who was playing around with the sound settings and testing the microphones, Misha with headphones on. We watched Misha through the soundproof glass separating the control room from the tracking room, waiting for his first attempt at *Strangers in the Night*.

Misha closed the door to the tracking room and the audio engineer, I wanted to call him Dave, started the familiar music. Misha could see the translated notes on a music stand in front of him to the side of the microphone. He began singing the first verse and I barely understood anything apart from *"Strangers in the Night"*. Everything else was a heavily accented mess. Misha was clearly not in his comfort zone of Italian opera.

The music stopped after the second verse. Misha beckoned me inside the tracking room.

"You need to conduct and mouth every sound for him," Oksana said. "I'll stay here."

In the tracking room, I walked Misha through the first verse, and, with a pencil, I accentuated where he needed make the correct sounds. This was a painstaking task and he prepared for a second run through. I put on a pair of headphones and the music started again. As Misha began to sing, I mouthed the words in front of him and conducted my pencil over the words as we moved through the verse. It got better; Misha clearly needed me in there supporting him.

"That was much better!" Oksana spoke through the control room microphone. It was now vaguely understandable but not exactly Frank Sinatra.

"Again," Misha said to me. The music began again, and we ran through only the first verse several times until he had got it right. We had been there an hour before we could say that the first verse was recognisably English. After four hours, we were all exhausted. Misha looked tired and he was even starting to sound a bit hoarse.

"That's enough,", Misha said. "I have a concert to sing in two days."

"Let's stop there, Richard," Oksana said. "We have another session in three days." I didn't know how Misha's voice would survive the next few days.

Incredibly, two days later, Misha did sing on stage in the Opera House for a televised concert. He had invited Oksana and me; we were sitting in the stalls watching as Misha sang his array of Italian and French arias. The concert was a success. It was the first time I had seen Misha in his comfort zone. On stage singing opera, he was an incredible singer, well deserving of the national award he'd received some weeks before.

1st March 1997

It was spring. Nature was starting to awaken from its winter slumber. A contrast to last year. The weather gradually became milder. The days became longer, allowing a freshness in the air. In March, you can expect occasional snowfall in Kyiv, but it quickly melts away as the sun gains strength. The iconic Dnipro River, flowing through the heart of the city, starts to melt, and the banks become more accessible for walks.

For the second time in a week, we were back at the *Lybidska* recording studios. Misha was tired after his successful televised concert at the Opera House; he always referred to it as *his* house, he spent so much time there.

He and I resumed our same positions in the tracking studio as before. Oksana was sitting in the control room with 'Dave' and we were working our way through the verses. Misha was singing the first verse almost perfectly, although he still stumbled on the *'the Night'* singing it as *'za N-eye-t'*. Standing opposite him, I demonstrated, like a primary school phonics teacher, how to stick his tongue out to do the *'th'* sound properly. Everything else was improving through each round of singing, but he had to get the name of the song correct.

Four hours later and we had it, albeit tentatively. Every time Misha sang *'the Night'*, he had to look at my 'naughty clown' impression: me overemphasizing the *'th'*, sticking my tongue out. Time was running out. The concert was in ten days.

"Misha will be ready, I'm sure of it, thanks to you Richard," Oksana beamed. To me, he was miles away but I just hoped he'd carry on improving the way he had in a week.

"He needs to give his throat a rest, doesn't he?" I said, feigning authority on the voice of a professional singer.

"Misha is happy, Richard, I wouldn't worry. He knows what he is doing," Oksana replied. Of course, she was right, he was a professional and would know how to rest and test his voice.

Before we left the recording studio, 'Dave' produced a compact disc with the last and best version of Misha's *Strangers in the Night*. It sounded good when it was played with all the editing complete. I could still hear the '*z's* instead of the '*th's*.

When the weekend came around, I was ready for a catch up with the usual *Rock Café* crowd. I needed some grounding. As usual, Greg was there with all the other *TEFL* teachers, supping their bottles of *Obolon*. He was eager to know what I had been up to.

"I spent four hours in a recording studio."

This tapped into an inner desire that Greg nurtured. He wanted to know more; he wanted to know about the singer and about the concert. He "wanted to rock."

"Misha is performing in concert on 11th March at *Palats Sportu*, I'll try and get you all tickets if you want. No promises," I said.

"That would be bloody amazing!" Sitting next to Greg was a new teacher I hadn't met before.

"Rich, this is Chris – Chris, Rich," Greg introduced us. Greg enjoyed being at the heart of the social group. He was a good leader. A natural leader. I trusted him. Chris was on a 'gap' year, as were many teachers. Tom had been the same.

"Pleased to meet you Chris," I said. It was always good to see a new face at the *Rock Café*. I was delighted to see Eugene With Pipe arriving too; he was always a good conversationalist. We had several beers that evening: games of pool and some dancing with Ukrainian girls. Unlike British guys, Ukrainian girls were good dancers, as we demonstrated. It was a weekend of two halves. The rest of the weekend was spent writing as I prepared my first draft paper and some Russian language with Natasha, *Colloquial Russian* Chapter Seven.

On the Monday, Natasha invited me to visit her place of work, which was the Central Universal Department Store, or *TSUM* for short, on *Kreshchatik*. It had been a department store during Soviet times. I was quite overwhelmed by how large it was and it served as a one-stop-shop; it had everything. The layout of the department store was vast, with multiple floors and sections dedicated to different types of products. From clothing and footwear to household appliances, electronics, and even groceries, these stores aimed to provide a comprehensive range of goods for the Soviet population.

As we walked through the department store, every member of staff behind the counters greeted us. Natasha was popular at work, and they all knew that she had an Englishman staying with her. She introduced me to so many of her colleagues that I stopped trying to remember all their names. We headed to the staff canteen, grabbed a coffee, and sat down near some of her colleagues. It was a friendly atmosphere and I noticed there wasn't a single man amongst them. *It was another women-only world.* Later, I learned that many of the women were glad to get to work, away from the abusive homes they belonged to. *This made me suddenly think, where was Natasha's husband? Ivan's father? I had never thought to ask.*

6th March 1997

Thursday. After the beautiful blue skies of the last week, it snowed. Natasha at work, I had to make my own breakfast which consisted of fried *kasha,* a dried porridge. By itself, grim, but with a fresh coffee, it was a good start to the day. I was sitting on the balcony, watching the snow fall with my coffee and this week's *Kyiv Post,* when the telephone rang. As expected, it was Oksana and she sounded very excited.

"Richard, good morning. Are you sitting down?" she said excitedly. Oksana only had two different moods: good or excited. She was one of life's optimists. I could relate to that, which is why whatever working relationship we had was working. I could always tell what mood she was in.

"I *was* sitting down until the phone rang," I said sarcastically.

"We have got tickets to the Presidential Performance of *Nabucco* in the Opera House tomorrow night!"

"I'm thinking that's a good thing," still toying with her. I sensed she hadn't picked up the sarcasm in my voice.

"Yes, of course. It is a big occasion. The President and his wife will be attending," Oksana said, selling it to me. I conceded and started taking it seriously.

"Why are we invited?" I enquired, still picking the coffee-flavoured kasha out of my teeth.

"Misha is very thankful for your help with the song recording and he wants to invite you to the Opera House at its best...as a thank you," she mused. It was true that Misha had expressed huge gratitude for the coaching I had given him.

"Amazing! Please thank Misha from me, it really was my pleasure," I said. And then taking the opportunity as it presented itself, "Do you think he would let me have a few tickets for the *Palats Sportu* concert next week?"

"Yes, I'm sure that would be fine. Who are they for?" she enquired.

"Some of the new English teachers that arrived in Kyiv; it would be great to get them into an event like this, show them a bit of culture," I said, over-elaborating.

"Super. I will ask for five tickets. Will that be enough?" Not really knowing how many of the *Rock Café* crew would attend, I had no idea.

"Perfect!" I said.

153

"Great! I'll do that for you. Oh, one more thing. Korolyuk, how did you say, *'demolished'* another visiting professor yesterday. Are you scared of him now?" Oksana attempted a joke.

"I think I'm more scared of you than Professor Korolyuk," I retorted before Oksana said goodbye and put the phone down. Maybe there was reason to be scared of Korolyuk, but I didn't feel it. My life in Kyiv was beginning to get busy, primarily with my growing involvement in the Mathematics Institute. Also, the extra-curricular activities like concerts, recording studios, liaisons with the British Embassy; just absorbing the Kyiv buzz kept me from thinking about being scared.

7th March 1997

President Kuchma exited the black limousine, followed by the First Lady. The Opera House looked amazing and the whole event felt truly special. Oksana and I stood to the side of the main entrance to watch as the president and his wife arrived, greeting the Opera House dignitaries. As they passed through the entrance, we scurried back through the stage door where I had met with Oksana a few weeks ago.

We made our way through the various tunnels and corridors to exit through the orchestra pit and up the steps into the front row. The audience rose and began applauding as the President and First Lady appeared on the Tsar's Balcony. Also known as the Imperial Box, this was a prominent feature of the theatre. It was a specially designed balcony, reserved for the Russian Tsar and his family during their visits to Kyiv. The balcony was in a prime position, providing an excellent view of the stage. Nowadays, while the Opera House no longer serves as a royal theatre, the Tsar's Balcony remains a symbol of the historical connection between Ukraine and Russia. It is often used for special guests and dignitaries during performances, adding a touch of grandeur and prestige.

The lights dimmed and the buzz of the audience calmed as the orchestra began playing. The curtains were raised to the opening scene where *Nabucco,* imprisoned in his own palace, suddenly awakens after the horrors of his nightmare. The whole occasion was thrilling. Oksana told me that the works of Verdi are Misha's speciality. He hoped to one day perform at *La Scala* in Milan where *Nabucco* was first performed in 1842.

After several cries of *"Bravo! Bravo!"* at the end, the curtains came down and the President was the first to depart. One hundred and fifty-five years and three hours after the first performance in Milan, we left the Opera House feeling honoured to have been there on this night.

The following day was *Women's Day* in Ukraine. I left the flat before breakfast and jogged over to one of the local kiosks to get a bunch of flowers for Natasha. I was spoilt for choice as all the kiosks seemed to turn into florists on this day. The currency had changed from the old *kupon* since last winter, it was now the *hryvnia*. Each time I went into a different kiosk to see what flowers I could buy for ten hryvnia, the shop assistants would shriek,

"It's the Englishman, what would you like Englishman?" I had most definitely turned into the token neighbourhood Englishman – I was like a minor local celebrity. I found a bunch of flowers for thirty hryvnia, approximately ten pounds sterling, and managed to get it back to the flat in time to see Natasha coming out of her bedroom.

"Happy Women's Day, Natasha!" I didn't expect her first reaction to this would be to start crying.

"Thank you so much, Richard. My delight," she responded. This was a frequently used term of affection from a Ukrainian woman. *I was a delight, indeed!* The main celebration took place at *Koncha Zaspa,* to include old-Natasha, with more bunches of flowers, lots of Ukrainian food, toasts to all the women and invariably the Colonel's home distilled vodka.

11th *March 1997*

Project Frank day had arrived. Greg, Chris, a few other English teachers and I arrived at the steps of *Palats Sportu* on the dot of 7pm in anticipation of the concert, which included many of Ukraine's pop stars and singers. Oksana met us and gave us our complimentary concert tickets.

"Enjoy the show!" Oksana handed out the last ticket.

"Best of luck to Misha and Frank," I said to Oksana, knowing she was going straight to the stage door to keep Misha focussed.

"Thank you. Come to the stage after the concert is finished and we will go for a drink," Oksana replied.

"And remember it is *'th'* and not *'z',*" I poked my tongue through my front teeth to Oksana. She laughed and disappeared into the oncoming crowd.

Palats Sportu, also known as the *Palace of Sport,* had become a popular multi-purpose indoor arena, located next to *Respublikanski Stadium*. It was a prominent venue for sports events, concerts, exhibitions and other entertainment. We climbed the steps and showed our tickets at the main entrance. The concert security waved us through, and we entered the ten thousand seat arena. Greg, especially, couldn't contain his excitement and started dancing before the music started. It was already filling up with students, mostly in their twenties, but also some families with younger teens.

The cavernous arena had hosted numerous international sports competitions, including basketball, volleyball, boxing, and figure skating. It had also been a stage for concerts by renowned artists and bands from all over the world. This evening, it was lit up for a major concert. The lights dimmed and Iryna Bilyk appeared on stage to a huge roar from the hall. Bilyk was currently hot pop property in Ukraine; she famously performed for US President Bill Clinton two years earlier but now she opened the concert with her latest hit.

After two hours of non-stop Ukrainian artists, the time came for Misha to come on stage and sing *Strangers in the Night*. He must have been nervous because it was not quite the Opera House with its classical opera and orchestras. I was feeling nervous for him. "Good luck, Misha," I thought. The music started and he began singing. Was it going to be a *'th'* or a *'z'*? It was a stunning *'th'*. He did it! We did it; he was Frank Sinatra. The nerves disappeared. I imagined Oksana's nerves would be shredded too; Misha sang the song brilliantly. The crowd gave a huge roar of appreciation. We had done, what I felt three weeks before, was impossible. His was the penultimate song as Iryna Bilyk came back on stage for the last slot. She and Misha must have been good friends already because she beckoned him out onto the stage to sing with her. The hall gave an even bigger roar as the last song ended and the artists left the stage.

The crowd moved towards the exit, and we slowly manoeuvred ourselves towards the side of the stage. Everyone had enjoyed it. Greg was singing *Strangers in the Night* John Travolta style and loving it. The hall emptied and we waited. When Oksana and Misha appeared, we congratulated him on his first success as a pop-singer.

We exited *Palats Sportu* towards the metro station. As we all walked onto the escalator to take us down to the platform, Greg broke out into another burst of *Strangers in the Night,* entertaining the Ukrainian passengers who had never experienced a character like Greg before.

"I'm very, very impressed with this stranger in the night," Misha joked as we reached the platform. The champagne was on the *Mouse* that night and we all felt part of his success.

Chapter 14. Podil and the Golden Gate

13th March 1997

Two days later, I woke up with a stinking cold. I could have picked it up from anywhere: the underground, the opera, the concert or the recording studio. My bet was the recording studio. The scary thing in Ukraine was that it was easy for colds to turn into flu, flu into pneumonia or even diphtheria. Many people had died of diphtheria over the winter in Kyiv. *One thing for sure was that I wouldn't be sitting in the same room as Misha for a while.*

By the weekend, I had already begun to recover from my cold, so it probably wasn't pneumonia. Natasha and I had breakfast then a Russian lesson *Colloquial Russian* Chapter Eight. She suggested that we go to the covered market at *Kontraktova Square* because I wanted to get a pair of trainers. I was keen to start track running around *Respublikanski Stadium,* a freely available sports facility and convenient to *Druzhbi Narodiv.* I wanted to get fit after my cold and the the winter in which I'd done no proper exercise and my diet had deteriorated to carbohydrates and vodka.

The market was three stations north on the blue line from *Palats Sportu.* Natasha and I got there by midday and had a concentrated coffee inside the covered market cafe. It reminded me of the covered market at Covent Garden which is about the same age. It was snowing again but not settling. The pavements around the market and floors inside were covered in wet, black, mushy snow.

Kontraktova Square is a historic square located in the old city, known as the *Podil* district. It is one of the oldest squares in the city, named after *Kontraktova House*, which used to be a centre for trade and commerce in the 18th century. *Kontraktova Square* is surrounded by beautiful architectural landmarks, including the *Kyiv-Mohyla*

Academy, one of Ukraine's oldest educational institutions. The square also features a monument of *Petro Mohyla*, a prominent figure in Ukrainian history and the founder of the academy in his name.

After coffee and finding a suitable pair of running trainers, we bumped into Luda and her girlfriend. They were both distinct in a crowd, especially when together. Both were as platinum blonde as *Marilyn Monroe*. They invited me to a nightclub, called *Dynamo Club,* located at the *Dynamo Kyiv* football stadium. Now that my cold was getting better, I happily agreed.

We met at the gates to the Dynamo stadium, and the path to the club entrance. At this point, I realised how tight knit our Kyiv community had become; Greg and the *TEFL* teachers with Veronica all arrived. The numbers had swollen since our last evening at the *Rock Café*. This was how I could gauge who had arrived and who had left Kyiv. Everyone seemed to be enjoying themselves until Greg had his camera stolen in the Dynamo Club, leaving him distraught for days. I tried to console him, a few days later, with a drink at the new *Zodiac Bar,* which had opened on *Kreshchatik,* and he seemed to be happier. We foreigners abroad had no choice but to lean on each other, to recognise that we were still young. The group was aged between eighteen and twenty-four years. No parents around, and frankly no safety net if anyone got hurt or depressed. We had to deal with it ourselves as no-one wanted to go home just yet.

17th March 1997

It was St Patrick's Day, and this was an occasion that brightened everybody up. In the morning, after breakfast, I spoke to Oksana and told her that I would be in O'Brien's pub after lunch, we should meet for a pint of Guinness. She had never tasted Guinness before. Before departing for *Independence Square,* I spent three hours writing the initial draft of my first paper. The good progress and near completion gave me the green light to spend the rest of the day celebrating.

We arranged to get to the pub by lunchtime and spend the rest of the day there drinking Guinness, playing pool and enjoying the *craic*. The usual crowd were there. Of course, Greg led the way with the Guinness consumption.

After we drank at least four pints of Guinness each, Oksana arrived to an atmosphere that seemed entirely alien to her. The pub was loud, and generally full of Irish and British people dancing, singing and laughing. She entered with a big smile on her face and walked straight over to the bar, where I bought her a pint of the black stuff.

"Happy St. Patrick's Day!" I said to her, attempting to raise my voice above the background buzz.

"Happy St. Patrick to you too!" Then, thinking she was going to take a quaint sip of Guinness, I watched as she downed the whole pint. A great cheer went up from around the bar. I couldn't believe what I had just seen. That out of the way, it was back to business. Apparently, Misha had invited me to a concert that evening at the National Philharmonic Concert Hall on *Europa Square.* It was last minute, but Misha really wanted me to attend.

"The concert starts at 7pm. Be there at 6:30pm."

"It's 5pm now. It will be a tight making 6:30. I need to go home and get changed, then come all the way back," I said, trying to subtly let her down. *I needed to flush four pints of Guinness out of my system.*

"No problem, we'll see you there.", Oksana put her empty pint glass back on the bar. Oksana smiled and turned to fight her way back out of the bar. *What sort of an animal was she?*

My first thought was this was beginning to be 'concert crazy'. I was attending a different concert every week, sometimes two. What was Oksana trying to achieve? I decided, through the Guinness and the sweat, that I should attend. For some reason I felt committed to Misha and his positive energy. Misha was trying to achieve something special, and he wanted to take me with him.

"You off already?", Greg shouted, half full pint glass in hand.

"Yes, see you mid-week in *Bacchus,*" I called over the top of half a dozen people. I put down my fifth pint glass, grabbed my coat and dashed out into the cold afternoon.

By mid-week, I finished the initial draft of my first research paper which needed to be approved by Korolyuk before presentation to an audience of my peers. *It was important to celebrate small achievements in this challenging environment.* I invited Greg, Rory, Chris, Luda, Veronica, and some other teachers to mark the occasion in *Bacchus* at *Poshtova Ploshcha.* The bar was inspired by the ancient Roman god of wine, Bacchus, and offered a wide selection of drinks, including beer, cocktails and vodka except wine. My quiet celebratory drink turned into a game of *'Sixty Russian Verbs',* simple rules to correctly say an understandable Russian verb, in order to avoid drinking a glass of vodka. Fortunately, I had learnt verbs with Natasha the previous week and so ended up winning this game without drinking a drop of vodka. I later told Natasha about this, and she expressed her delight.

"Super! It's good to know that our Russian lessons are not going to waste," she joked sarcastically.

After *Bacchus,* we hopped around the corner to the *Arizona* for a beer and five minutes of western culture, which included Luda getting two proposals of marriage. Also, Rory and Chris were fined fifty hryvnia each for loitering outside a bar, which was a common made-up crime in Kyiv at this time. Chris saw the funny side of it. However, this was the last fifty hryvnia in Rory's pocket and the confrontation caused him to feel very homesick.

The next day, I visited the consular to speak with Inna about the incident. She confirmed what we had suspected. The charges could be dismissed straightaway as they were unfounded. After this, I met up with Chris and Rory at the British Embassy, to support their story as a witness, just in case the penalty charges were not dropped. Fraser was the friendly face representing on behalf of the embassy and thanked me for supporting them.

Afterwards, we used the opportunity, given the location of the embassy to take an excursion down *Andriyivski Uzviz*. The *Uzviz*, or 'descent', is a picturesque street in the *Podil*; it is known for its charming atmosphere and rich cultural heritage. Veronica, with a few of her Ukrainian and Dutch friends, met us outside the embassy. We walked the short distance to *St. Andrew's Church* which sat at the top of the *Uzviz*. One of her Dutch friends, Jaap, was continually talking and had an opinion on everything. He described the church, which is one of the most eye-catching in Kyiv, as looking 'like a big cake', humouring no-one but himself.

Veronica, now acting as tour guide, informed us that "the church was constructed in the 18th century, designed by the renowned Italian architect *Bartolomeo Rastrelli.*" It stood on a hill overlooking the Dnipro River. According to Jaap, it was 'Bartholemew Raspberry'. It's distinctive green and white façade, 'marzipan and cream', adorned with intricate sculptures and ornate details, 'candles', makes it a stunning sight, 'cake', to behold, for any 'occasion'. Veronica finished by saying that the church is named after the apostle St. Andrew, believed to have visited the hills of Kyiv and prophesized the foundation of a great city.

We continued down the descent which started at the upper part of the *Podil* and wound its way down to the Dnipro River. It was a pedestrian-friendly street, adorned with cobblestones, lined with colourful buildings, art galleries, cafes, and souvenir shops. About halfway down, on the right-hand side, was the museum house of *Mikhail Bulgakov*. Veronica had got us a group ticket. *Bulgakov*, a Russian writer, lived in the house until 1919 leading up to the Russian revolution. It played a significant role in *Bulgakov's* life and literary career, serving as the inspiration for the setting of his novel *The White Guard* about the turbulent times of the Revolution in Kyiv.

The museum was interesting, but after an hour we were ready to grab a coffee. I promised myself that I would read *The White Guard* so I could say that I'd been in the house depicted. The visit inspired me to delve into the Ukrainian psyche. We stepped out on the cobbled street and ambled to the café opposite, Veronica's idea. All the cafes on the descent looked like they were hanging on by a thread. Some were old wood cabins, others were modern prefabs, in keeping with the surrounding character of the *Podil*. Although Spring was coming, it was chilly when the sun went down, and the east-facing hill went into shadow. We camped under the café's huge, covered balcony with heater fans, ordering hot chocolates and coffees.

After discussing our opinions on *Bulgarkov's* house and his works, the subject moved onto the Russian Revolution. It was interesting to hear the varied opinions on this subject. The discussion, aided by hot chocolate in our cosy alpine setting, quickly got on to Ukraine's place in Europe. Had this been a revolution? It was only six short years since the end of the Soviet Union; Ukraine, although seat of the ancient Kyiv Rus, was a young independent country. Unlike the bloody revolution depicted in *Bulgarkov's* book, which put an end to the *White Guard*, Ukraine had side-stepped a bloody revolution. The consensus from everyone seemed to be that Ukraine's rightful place should be part of an expanded European Union.

"Ukraine should somehow bounce out of one union into another," Jaap said. Is this what Ukrainians really wanted? This is what young Ukrainians wanted; they had their whole lives ahead of them and could see opportunities to travel freely. They would also worry that Ukraine could fall back into the old oppressive Soviet Union. Young Ukrainians wanted Ukraine to exist as an independent state before committing to the new and ever-expanding European Union. Ukraine standing knee deep in *No Mans Land*, between two giant economic and political blocks, may not be sustainable for the longer term, but we agreed European membership could happen within a generation. Our quick drink turned into four hours of discussion about Ukraine's past, present and future. In contrast, the older generation in Ukraine had fond memories of life under the Soviet Union. The generation in between, Natasha's generation, were undecided but open to living the second half of their lives in a different jurisdiction.

It was dark when we left the comfort of our alpine café and meandered down the remainder of *Andriyivski's Uzviz*. We jumped on the underground at *Kontraktova Ploshcha* and headed towards our respective homes, having turned a day of consular activity into a pleasant tour of the *Podil*. Even Rory was feeling less depressed and homesick about his fine.

Natasha greeted me in the usual way as I entered the flat. The moment I stepped in, the phone rang. Natasha picked up as normal.

"Mama." Natasha recognised my mother's voice and was happy to say hello in English. Passing the receiver to me, this was Natasha's linguistic limit for now. My mother told me that she had booked a flight over to visit me in Kyiv, landing at *Borispil* airport on the 13th April, about three weeks away. *This made me very nervous.*

26th March 1997

It was mid-week, and I had an appointment with Korolyuk at his apartment to review my initial draft. I hadn't been to Korolyuk's apartment before. Oksana called after breakfast to make sure that I was clear with the address.

"Do you remember which metro station you need to go to?"

"Golden Gate,", I said confidently, holding the notes in front of me. "Then round the back of the apartment block, third door and first floor."

"Yes right. 1pm. Don't be early," Oksana confirmed. Korolyuk never liked anyone arriving early; there may be someone leaving from the previous appointment who he didn't want you to see. He preferred late to early.

"I'll let you know how it goes," I said, replacing the receiver.

After the call, Natasha and I had a Russian lesson *Colloquial Russian* Chapter Nine. Later, I unhooked a calendar off the kitchen wall which I had given to Natasha when I had arrived in January. The calendar showed the sights of Oxford which was mainly university buildings. I placed it in my folder to show Korolyuk if he was interested.

Before I left, I had a *Vermicelli Pavlovski* lunch then I made my way to *Golden Gate* on the green line. This was convenient as I could get to Korolyuk's apartment without changing trains, within twenty minutes door-to-door. Arriving at *Golden Gate*, it was a wonder to step out and view the historic monument after which the metro station is named. An ancient fortification that dates to the 11th century, once the main entrance to the city, it served as a symbol of Kyiv's grandeur and power.

I checked my watch to make sure I wouldn't be early; it was 1pm. Perfect. I looped around the other side of the apartment block which overlooked the Opera House. Never appreciating the layout of this neighbourhood before, I saw that Korolyuk's apartment sat between the Opera House and the Golden Gate monument. This was prime location for an apartment in Kyiv. I entered the outer door to the building and climbed the steps which were cleaner and grander than the steps in my block. A door closed above. A man passed me coming down and smiled. I returned the smile with a *"Dobry Den"*, meaning 'Good day'. Reaching the second floor, I went to the door instructed by Oksana. It could have been the door I heard closing some moments ago. I rang the bell, and, within three seconds, a lady opened the door. Before I could enquire whether this was the apartment of Professor Korolyuk, she greeted me.

"Richard, welcome, do come in," she said with a welcoming smile. She proceeded to find the customary pair of slippers so that I could take off my muddy shoes. Ukrainians were exceptionally house proud and never wear their shoes indoors. I put the slippers on; they were slightly too big.

"Thank you, I'm very pleased to meet you. Is Professor Korolyuk busy? I do hope I'm not too early," I said.

"Please call me Nina," she said delightfully, directing me towards a room leading off the hallway. "Please, go through. Professor Korolyuk is waiting for you in his study." The apartment was more spacious than my apartment. The soaring ceilings were adorned with intricate mouldings and ornate decoration. Walking past the entrance to the living room, I saw how spacious and inviting it all was. The living room was filled with plush furniture and antique pieces, another touch of luxury. Large windows allowed natural light to flood the room, offering breathtaking views of the Golden Gate.

"Thank you, Nina." I assumed she was Professor Korolyuk's housekeeper. Feeling like Donald Duck, I shuffled across the floor in my big slippers towards Korolyuk's study, knocking on the slightly ajar door.

"Richard, welcome to my home," Korolyuk stood up and welcomed me with outstretched hand. In Ukraine, it was customary to shake any other man by the hand, every time you met them. It could be in the street, in an office, anywhere.

"Thank you for inviting me and it is a very nice home," I replied.

"Nina, would you bring us some tea please?" Korolyuk called out as he closed his study door.

"So, how are you today? How is your hostess? Is she looking after you?" Korolyuk asked. He was always interested in me as a person before talking business. I sensed his humanity. I think he was fascinated how I, as an Englishman, was adapting to life in Kyiv.

"I'm very well thank you and Natasha is a very good hostess," I replied. "She is teaching me Russian too."

"Yes, very good, Oksana told me. This will make your life easier here, especially when presenting your papers," he said smiling. *I slowly registered what he'd said.* 'Presenting' papers in Russian, sounded scary. I thought it a good time to pull out the Oxford calendar to show Korolyuk.

"What do we have here?" he asked. I opened on the month of January and explained that it was a calendar of sights in my home city of Oxford, mostly college buildings. The photo of the *Bodleian Library* fascinated Korolyuk.

"This is Oxford?" he asked with a sense of incredulity. I confirmed that it was. "And all the buildings are like this in Oxford?" he said beginning to shuffle through all the different months.

"Most of them," I said, "especially around the university."

"Wonderful. I have never seen photos of Oxford university. It is truly a beautiful place." Korolyuk marvelled at the photos then looked up and asked, "This is for me?" It had been a gift for Natasha but how could I take this away from Korolyuk, given it was obvious how much he appreciated it?

"Yes, it is a gift from Oxford to you." Thinking quickly, I would get Mum to bring a replacement calendar for Natasha when she visited in a couple of weeks.

"Thank you, that's a wonderful gift," Korolyuk said, still holding it in both hands. There was a light tap on the door; it was Nina with a tray of tea. She entered the study and placed the tray on a low table. I suddenly thought of Eugene and how much he would enjoy this cultured moment.

"Thank you, Nina. Please could you hang our new calendar up in the living room," he said. I found this quite amusing as it would surely not fit in with the ornate wall-to-wall paintings.

"Let's work," Korolyuk turned to me. I pulled the neat twelve-page draft out of my folder and presented it to Korolyuk. Over the next three hours, we checked the logic and references. He asked questions about the peripheral boundaries of the equations. Korolyuk always asked a question sympathetically, in a way which made the answer obvious. I enjoyed his company. He was young at heart, even though he was over seventy years old. I knew this because Oksana was compiling a book about Korolyuk at seventy. It would be presented to him upon publication. I assumed it was a secret, so I said nothing about it. It was yet another project in which Oksana was involved.

"I approve," Korolyuk said after three hours. This was fantastic and an enormous sense of relief. My first paper written in conjunction with Professor Korolyuk had passed the test. If I had not been so tired, I would have jumped in excitement.

Korolyuk invited me into the living room. He took out a bottle of vodka and two glasses from a secret door in one of his antique sideboards.

"To celebrate our achievement," he said as he began pouring. He passed me a glass of vodka.

"*Budmo*," I said knowing he would appreciate the Ukrainian toast.

"*Budmo!*" he smiled cheerily. Nina entered the living room.

"Congratulations," she said, realizing that we had achieved something.

"My wife is also a professor," said Korolyuk. Nina was his *wife* not his housekeeper. I tried to conceal my embarrassment though they couldn't possibly have detected my misunderstanding.

"Wow, that's incredible," is all I could say. "A professor of what?"

"Music," replied the other Professor Korolyuk. "In the Chorus of the Conservatoire." I wasn't too sure what that meant. Oksana told me later that she was a key member of the Musical Conservatoire in Kyiv. She was as powerful in the Opera House as her husband was in the Mathematical Institute. *Good people to have on my side in Kyiv.* The experience at the Korolyuks' apartment that day was pivotal to the events in my life moving forward.

Chapter 15. Rigoletto and the Lecture

Greg invited me out to the Opera House. This was unexpected from a man from the Northeast of England, but he'd met a Ukrainian girl who he had invited to the ballet *Swan Lake*. She insisted on bringing her girlfriend, a kind of chaperone, so Greg invited me to balance things out and for a bit of moral support. We were on a double date. Our seats were in the stalls, high up in the gods. Everyone enjoyed the ballet, but my mind wandered off into the intricacies of the people that made things happen in Kyiv: Oksana was one of them; so were both professors Korolyuk; so was Misha. *How and why, they had all come together as such a powerful force?* They all seemed to be connected somehow. The ballet passed well, and we finished off with a couple of drinks in the *House* bar. Greg and I would catch up at the *Rock Café*, on Friday, to discuss how well this evening had gone. But it was the next visit to the Opera House that was to be the most curious.

28th *March 1997*

It was a Friday, *Rock Café* night, and I had promised to meet Greg and Chris for two reasons: firstly, to catch up with Greg about the *Swan Lake* double date; secondly because it was Chris' twentieth birthday. At least, this was the plan before I received the usual breakfast call from Oksana.

"Richard. Good morning. How was Professor Korolyuk?"

"Good morning, Oksana. Which one?" I replied, referring to the two Professors Korolyuk that I knew about.

"So, you met Korolyuk's wife?" Oksana would be good in the secret police.

"Yes, she was very hospitable and even brought us tea. I thought she was Korolyuk's housekeeper to begin with as she opened the door for me and gave me a pair of slippers. Does she always refer to Korolyuk by his formal title?" Oksana found this amusing.

"Nina Korolyuk is one of the great music directors in Kyiv. She oversees the Choral Conducting Chair which means that what she says goes," Oksana confirmed. And yes, she always refers to him formally whenever any of his students, like you, visit."

"Korolyuk approved my draft paper," I mentioned.

"That's excellent! Well done." Oksana was genuinely delighted. "Did he bring out the vodka from his secret cabinet?"

"Yes, he did, clearly not that secret", I joked.

"Now you'll need to present your paper to the Institute so it can be approved for publication," she said. The thought of this made me somewhat ill. I'd have to present the paper in Russian, still the formal language of the Institute.

"Anyway, I also called you to let you know that Misha is appearing in the Evening Premier of *Rigoletto* this evening. This is a big deal as it is another opera by *Verdi*."

"That's great, I assume you will be there?"

"Yes, I will be. Misha has also invited Professor Korolyuk and Mrs Korolyuk. I have a spare ticket which I want you to have," she said excitedly. It sounded like I was going on another double date, albeit upgraded to an evening premier.

"Of course. I'll meet you there at 7pm." I was getting very familiar with how things worked in the Opera House. In fact, for Oksana, I was beginning to understand that it wasn't so much the content of what was on stage, but who was in the audience that mattered. She was a socialite behind the scenes. "Dress smartly," were her parting words.

This new event conflicted with my Friday night at the *Rock Café* but I knew I could go there afterwards as the opera usually finished by

10pm. It was a quick one-stop-hop from *Teatralna* to *Kreshchatik* so that would work. I relied upon the weekly connect-ups with Greg and the other teachers; without them, I would need to be overly self-reliant across a long period of time and this was not sustainable. I found the Friday nights kept me grounded. I was here to work with Korolyuk on serious research, but I recognized the right life balance needed to be struck.

Natasha had gone to work before I woke up but left a freshly cooked breakfast on the stove. *Dumplings, my favourite.* After the conversation with Oksana, I spent the rest of the day in the apartment learning Russian words that could be useful for presenting maths papers. This sounded harder than it was. I learnt there were only about ten different expressions that were necessary for the presentation of a maths paper, ones that linked mathematical equations together. For example, 'therefore', 'as such', 'this means' and 'etcetera'. I listed them down and learned them in Russian. I was still waiting for confirmation for the imminent presentation of my paper by Korolyuk, and Galina, in the Institute.

It was 7pm and I was waiting outside the Opera House for Oksana. I was dressed in the smartest evening wear that I could scrape together; none of it really matched but was good enough. The evening was cool but not cold and the sky was clear, full of stars. *Perfect for a night like tonight.* Many people were arriving, dressed for an evening premier, and making the most of their entry through the grand main door. Oksana appeared from the side of the building. She must have been giving Misha some moral support ahead of this premier as she'd come from *the side door*. She looked nervous.

"Misha is very nervous tonight," Oksana said.

"I'm sure he will be fine, if he knows his words. He'll be OK," I said displaying my usual opera naivety.

"He has a sore throat and has been taking throat sprays, lozenges and *vodka scarves* all day. Come on, let's go inside." We entered the great building into the main corridor that curved around the whole auditorium. Then we headed to the grand staircase on the right. At the top, we headed towards a door that was being guarded by two ushers. Oksana showed them the tickets. They smiled and opened the door for us. We walked onto the Tsar's Balcony.

"We're on the *Tsar's Balcony*," I exclaimed to Oksana, who probably already knew. The President and his wife sat in the same spot only three short weeks before.

"Yes, the President and his wife sat here and here," she indicated two seats to the right of us. We settled into our seats as the lights dimmed, the two seats to the right of us still unoccupied. I was about to suggest to Oksana that we shuffle along two seats, when the door at the back of the balcony opened.

"Good evening, Professors Korolyuk," Oksana timed her greeting to perfection as both Professor Korolyuk and Nina took their seats. I shook Korolyuk by the hand and he gave me a relaxed nod. The *Tsar's Balcony* was fully occupied, although I didn't recognize any of the other occupants. The curtain came up and the first act of Verdi's *Rigoletto* started. *Rigoletto* is a tragic tale of jealousy and betrayal. It is a dramatic opera that revolves around *Rigoletto*, a hunchbacked jester for the *Duke of Mantua,* a morally corrupt ruler known for his womanising ways. The opening scene depicts a party in the palace of the Duke who is boasting of his way with women before dancing with the *Countess Ceprano.* His hunchbacked jester, *Rigoletto,* mocks the countess' enraged husband. Misha was playing the *Duke of Mantua* and there was an excited buzz in the auditorium.

"His voice sounds good," Oksana whispered to me in relief. "I hope he's not in too much pain." I gave her a thumbs up, not wanting to say something stupid. Nina was fixed on the scene while Korolyuk only looked mildly interested. He'd probably been dragged to the opera many times since getting married.

As the curtain fell after Act One, there was a huge round of applause. The audience approved; Misha should be pleased. Oksana stood as the applause was replaced by a hum of chatter and laughter from the whole auditorium.

"I'm going to see Misha," Oksana said. "I'll be back before the start of Act Two." As she departed, I hopped into the seat next to Nina and Korolyuk. I turned to address both professors.

"Are you enjoying the opera?"

"Very much so," Korolyuk smiled. Korolyuk always had fun in his responses.

"I think the Duke has a sore throat," Nina said. As the choral supremo in Kyiv, nothing escaped her. She could hear and probably distinguish Misha's voice when he didn't have a sore throat. "But it is a wonderful opera," she continued. "What do you think?" Generally, this wasn't a question I wanted to hear from a choral supremo. I knew I needed to answer it in the least clumsy way possible, especially with my professor Koroyluk listening.

"It's quite the performance. The Duke reminds me of our Prince Andrew, Duke of York, in England," I said, instantly regretting it.

"Why?" asked Nina not understanding the reference.

"Because he has a lot of girlfriends too," I blustered. Had a tumbleweed rolled by, I would have stood up and walked off the balcony. Korolyuk howled with laughter.

"Does Prince Andrew sing?" Nina asked, slightly off the mark which Korolyuk had bull's eyed.

"Only when he gets caught," I said, causing Korolyuk to laugh even more. Nina smiled and acknowledged it was more a joke between Korolyuk and me.

"I may not have understood," Nina smiled. "His English is better than mine."

Oksana returned to the balcony out of breath. I shuffled back to my own seat, and she sat down in hers.

"Everything OK?" I enquired quietly. "The audience loved Act One."

"Yes, all good, he's putting some more spray on his throat now," she said, breathing normally. The lights dimmed and the audience settled for Act Two. The curtains rose upwards to reveal a room in the Ducal Palace. There were doors on both sides. By a larger door at the far end, hung full length portraits of the Duke and his wife. A singular high-backed chair covered with velvet was next to a table.

Oksana and Nina waited for Misha's next singing part. He began and Nina leaned over to Oksana to make a comment about his voice. Both sat back and listened intently. As far as I was concerned, his voice was excellent. I would never have known there was a problem. Act Two came and went, with even louder applause. Oksana stood up again, making her way to the balcony door. I took this opportunity to pop out to the loo.

Returning, I saw Oksana rushing back to take her seat for Act Three, the final act. She looked frantic with worry. She'd been to Misha's dressing room again. We entered the Tsar's Balcony door at the same time from opposite directions.

"How is he?" I asked, noticing that the lights were dimmed and the audience hushing.

"He is suffering. He is so brave." She was likely to be a mess until the final curtain came down at the end. We took our seats and waited. The curtains rose to a scene in a taverna at night. Two rooms were open to the audience. This scene was the hardest for Misha's voice and Oksana knew it. The Duke's voice, Misha's voice, could be heard from inside, singing *La Donna e Mobile.*

"The strain on Misha's voice was at its maximum during this aria," she insisted. We waited with bated breath. After what seemed like a lifetime, the aria ended. The audience erupted. Misha had done it. He only had the rest of Act Three to complete then he could rest his voice.

"He's done it. I'm so relieved," Oksana whispered. Oksana leaned the other way to listen to a comment from Nina. Thirty minutes later, Misha had sung his finale and the curtains dropped.

The auditorium rose as one, erupting in loud applause. Cries of *"Bravo! Bravo!"* rang out around the Opera House. It was a stunning success for the premier and for Misha in the leading role. Oksana was in tears. Nina was applauding and smiling. Korolyuk was just happy that it had finished. I was delighted to have witnessed a performance of a lifetime from someone I had not only worked with, but now knew as a friend. We hugged each other and exited the Tsar's Balcony, knowing that we had experienced something very special. Oksana, a nervous wreck an hour ago, was smiling and relaxed. Whatever she had done in that dressing room worked.

Thirty minutes later, I emerged from the *Kreshchatik* metro station, towards the Rock Café. By 10pm, Chris' twentieth birthday proceedings were well under way. Everyone had an *Obolon* in hand and were chatting or playing pool. Greg held up his hands when he saw me come around the corner into the square. To be honest, it was never hard to identify where the usual gang were in the Rock Cafe; numbering about twenty people, it was by far the biggest - Greg sitting in the middle. He was a natural entertainer as well as a natural leader.

The size and sound of our group attracted other groups of foreigners living and working in Kyiv. On this night, a group from the *French Embassy* and a French bank were out together. Naturally, we were all fascinated to understand who they were in Kyiv. We noticed how much beer they drank, and we enjoyed each other's company as ex-pats. For some unsubstantiated reason, they were known thereafter as the 'crazy Frenchmen'. None spoke much English except Thibaut who was fluent and handsome. He worked in one of the French banks that established an office in the country since independence. By the end of the evening, we were all on our way to *New York*, the night club, that is, to make sure Chris had a birthday to remember. Thus grew our European community in Kyiv, a microcosm found at the Rock Café every Friday night.

31st March 1997

The start of a new week and the weather was spring-like. I met Oksana in *Teatralna* prior to going into the Institute. My first stop was to visit Galina in the Administrators' office. I was eager to find out the date of the lecture on my research paper so I could prepare for it. I knew the paper well and could recite it in my sleep.

"I think you are allowed to go in there unaccompanied," Oksana said. "I'll come back and meet you in thirty minutes." Oksana left me while she went to visit another professor.

"No problem, I'll just ask Galina when and where my presentation will be." As Oksana disappeared down the corridor, I entered the office. The two secretaries sat quietly behind their desks typing. Galina was sitting behind her computer at the far end.

"Good morning," I smiled to the whole office. The two secretaries both looked up from their screens.

"Good morning, Richard," they both said in unison. It sounded like stereo as I stood between their desks. Galina didn't acknowledge me, so I edged closer towards her desk.

"Good morning, Galina, how are you?" I asked, asserting my presence. At last, she looked up and glanced over her glasses without smiling.

"Good morning, Richard. Why do you want to know how I am? How can we help you today?" she asked.

"I'd like to know if I have a lecture room booked for the presentation of my paper with Professor Korolyuk" I replied, ignoring her rudeness, knowing it would probably antagonize her. It was a Monday morning and she seemed particularly cold today.

"Ah yes, Professor Korolyuk booked it on Friday," she said, checking her register. They hadn't fully transitioned to computer records yet. "Lecture Room Two, third floor."

"Thank you," I said, relieved that it had been booked. I turned to leave.

"Do you not want to know when it is?" It wasn't a friendly tone. "2pm on the 10th April," she confirmed. The date sounded familiar, but I couldn't remember why.

"Thank you, I'll see you all then," I said, getting a nice smile from the two secretaries and a glare from Galina, presumably annoyed that I was being too familiar with her staff. The two secretaries stared back at their screens straightaway, aware of Galina's cold stare now at them.

I returned into the hallway, but Oksana had not yet arrived. I wondered why there weren't ever any lights on in the hallways. Feeling uncomfortable loitering outside Galina's office, I wandered down the corridor. Maybe I would catch Oksana as she came out of one of the rooms. I walked to the end of the second-floor corridor and came to another marble staircase, curiously leading only upwards. The lecture room I had been given was on the third floor; there wouldn't be any harm if I just had a look to familiarise myself where it was and what it looked like. There weren't many people around that day. I slowly walked up the steps; the first flight towards a window, then a second flight returning on itself to the third-floor corridor. I remembered what Oksana had said about not going to the third and fourth floors unaccompanied but there was no-one about. I would only be a couple of minutes. I walked down the dark third floor corridor checking the labels on the doors, almost tiptoeing. As it was dark, I had to get quite close to read what they said. I went down one side and didn't see any lecture rooms. I thought one of the rooms was where I first met Korolyuk, but I couldn't be sure. It all looked the same. The doors were all identical.

I turned to the other side of the corridor and passed two more doors before I saw 'Lecture Room Two'. This was it. I found it. Checking the handle of the door was open, I gently pushed forward. The room opened into a sizeable lecture theatre with sloping seats to the left, a series of sliding greenboards to my right. That's where I would be presenting my paper. I felt reassured that I could visualize my presentation setting. Then I suddenly remembered about the 10th April! This was the day my *Mum* was flying to Ukraine. *She would be landing at Borispil airport around 4pm*. That didn't give me much time to get there after the presentation. I would be under pressure.

Having seen enough, I edged backwards out of the lecture room, still holding the door handle. The door clicked. I turned around to see Galina staring back at me.

"Lost something?" she asked, her tone sarcastic.

"No, I was just checking out the lecture room in preparation," I said truthfully.

"Did Oksana tell you that you should not be on this floor without being accompanied?" She began interrogating me.

"Yes, she did. To be honest, I forgot that this is the third floor. In England, this would only be the second floor." I gave the weakest reason I could as to why I was here. Incredibly, it worked.

"OK well you know now. Please go back down the stairs and don't come up to this level without being accompanied again." Feeling like an admonished schoolboy, I headed towards the stairwell while she watched me. When I turned back, she had disappeared as if by magic.

I retuned back to the Administrators' office entrance as Oksana came down the corridor.

"I hope you haven't been waiting long?"

"No, just a couple of minutes." I didn't want to lie to Oksana, but I failed to mention my little trip up to Lecture Room Three.

"Did you find out your lecture room?" she asked.

"Yes, Lecture Room Two. 2pm on 10th April," I confirmed.

"OK great, let's go and get some lunch." I couldn't get out of there quick enough; I hadn't done anything wrong, but Galina made me feel awkward. Should I tell Oksana, or even Korolyuk, what had happened? Was it just a storm in a teacup? Of course, the longer I didn't mention anything, the more it festered. Would Galina say something to someone to cause trouble? My suspicion that she didn't like me being in the Institute were starting to crystallize.

1st April 1997

The weather was improving and there was more football being played at *Respublikanski Stadium*. Ukraine was playing Northern Ireland the following night in a World Cup qualifier, and I felt it my duty to support a fellow UK nation. The World Cup would be hosted by France next year, notably they had never won the trophy.

I arrived at the ground ahead of training to see the players coming out on the pitch. I couldn't believe how close I was able to get to the players. There was no security or even anyone to say, "stay behind the barriers". I walked through the pitch-side gate of the hundred-thousand-seater stadium and sat on one of the benches, hoping to bump into the players training. Iain Dowie, a striker for Northern Ireland and West Ham, was out so I started to chat with him as he warmed up.

"Are you going score tomorrow night Iain?" I asked from pitch side. He looked up, surprised to hear an English voice. Maybe he assumed I was Ukrainian, but he smiled.

"What are you doing here in this god-forsaken place?" Iain Dowie wasn't known for mincing his words.

"I live here. Good luck tomorrow night," trying to keep the chat as brief and fast moving as possible. He started to warm up. Other Northern Irish players came onto the pitch and started warming up.

"Is this an April Fool? Are you coming to watch the match?" Iain asked as the squad started to huddle.

"Yes, the atmosphere is crazy here when the stadium is full and Ukraine score," I said. He looked up at me with his massive eyes.

"Hopefully they won't," he said.

"Andriy Shevchenko will score, for sure," was the last thing I said to him as the squad ran off around the pitch to warm up.

The coach walked onto the field and invited me to stay pitch-side. I stayed for most of the session, fetching balls back off the running track and picking balls out of the front seats. When I got cold, I thanked the coach and headed back to *Druzhbi Narodiv*. I felt thrilled to have been at a training session for a UK team so far from home.

The next evening, I went to the game with Greg, Chris and Rory. We watched Shevchenko score the winner after an Iain Dowie penalty pulled them level, at one all. I was proud of Northern Ireland. We had enjoyed the atmosphere in one of the biggest stadiums of the world. Afterwards, we went to the Rock Café to celebrate Jaap's birthday. Rock Café was subdued mid-week, but we celebrated with Jaap as if it was a Friday.

5th April 1997

On Saturday, we decided to get out of the usual routine and explore. Greg, Rory and I all met up with a new English teacher, Lucy, at *Hydropark* metro station on the red line. This was a desolate place at this time of the year, but I could imagine how pleasant it could be in the summer months. The whole park was spread across two islands with a connecting Venetian bridge. It was created as an entertainment complex with beaches, boating and other water attractions. However, the reason why we were there that day was for moral support; Lucy, had been attacked in *Minska* the previous night. *Minska* was at the end of the blue line right in the northern suburbs of Kyiv and this is where her host family lived. Understandably, Lucy was worried about living there and wanted to change her host family. Naturally, Greg, Rory and I tried our best to support and be there for her.

7th April 1997

A week had passed since the *third-floor* episode in the Institute, and I hadn't mentioned it to anyone. As I emerged from my bedroom for breakfast, Natasha was in the kitchen.

"Good morning. Where did our calendar go?" asked Natasha. I had completely forgotten to tell Natasha that the calendar had stayed with Korolyuk when I had visited his apartment. I came clean.

"I showed it to Korolyuk for interest. He liked it so much, he asked if he could keep it," I said hoping that she wouldn't be upset. "My mum is bringing a new one next week."

"Oh OK, so I get a new one," she smiled jokingly.

The phone rang. It was Oksana.

"Do you have a spare hour this afternoon?" she asked.

"I have *two* spare hours if you need them," I responded.

"Could you teach some children English at a school not far from you? It's just a few children at a school sponsored by the UN."

"UN as in United Nations?" I enquired. Usually, projects like this were sponsored by the European Commission, but they had not yet fully established themselves in Kyiv.

"Yes. It's part of an educational project across Ukraine. They have been let down at the last minute by another English teacher. I said you might do it. It would be good preparation for your presentation next week. Have you got a pen and paper?" She had a good point. I could use this to prepare my technique in front of an audience and it was only a class. It would be like the occasion when Taras took me into his school to meet his class. That was good fun and not too difficult.

"Yes, no problem, that's a good idea," I said.

"Great, can you be at *Lukiyanivska* metro at 1pm?" Of course, I could.

In the time it took to enter *Druzhbi Narodiv* metro and arrive at *Lukiyanivska,* the weather turned from spring sunshine to winter snow. I looked at the directions on the paper Oksana had given me over the telephone. The snow didn't help as I was trying to get my bearings. She had told me several street names, but the snow obscured all the street signage. I had no idea which street to try first.

I noticed an old *babushka* sitting on a bench, selling a couple of loaves of bread and some milk, having probably travelled in from her dacha. She just sat there as the snow accumulated around her. She appeared as though she had frozen to death. I felt sorry for her and wished I could help her.

"Are you alright?" I asked the babushka. I asked several times before I get any response.

"Yes, why?" she responded belligerently.

"I just wanted to make sure you were…," I wanted to say 'still with us' but I didn't, "…alright, sitting there in the snow." I finished, still surprised by the babushka's response. She didn't even ask if I wanted to buy her bread and milk.

"How much for the bread?"

"A rouble," came the reply. Older citizens still referred to their beloved rouble from Soviet days. They meant a Ukrainian hryvnia. I had a twenty hryvnia note in my pocket, so I wasn't going to give that for a one-hryvnia loaf of bread however frozen she looked. I was wasting time so, to change the subject, I asked,

"I'm looking for the United Nations school." I thought I would just get a 'why do you want to know?' To my surprise, she raised her right arm and pointed down the road to the right-hand side. In fact, looking where she had pointed, I could now see a blue UN flag.

"Thank you so much," I said, still surprised at this fascinating character. I was so thankful. Without her I wouldn't have seen the school. I pulled the twenty hryvnia note out of my pocket and put it in her hand.

"Ow, how many loaves do you want?" she suddenly said with expression on her face.

"None. Keep the change!" I crossed the road and headed with purpose towards the UN school.

I skipped up the steps of the school and entered the double doors into the warm reception area. As I approached the desk, a lady approached me.

"Are you Richard?" she asked.

"Yes, that's me. I'm sorry if I'm late." I wasn't late at all. The conversation with the snow babushka had only been five minutes.

"Good! Nice to meet you. My name is Sylvia." *Was that even a Ukrainian name?* "Follow me." I thought I would have a few minutes to prepare something for the class, but I was going to be taken straight in. I followed her down a corridor and up some steps. We approached some wooden double doors. She pulled one side and gestured me to enter first.

I hadn't noticed straightway that the entire school of five hundred students was in the hall. I shook hands with several teachers as I arrived on the stage. There was an audible gasp as I entered, as if the late Freddie Mercury had just turned up with his piano. I could easily have apologised, turned around and left, thinking there had been a mistake. But I didn't, instead I thought what the heck. With Freddie Mercury still in mind,

"Hello, Kyiv!" came out of my mouth. The audience gasped again, even louder this time.

"This is Richard," Sylvia announced as if I was the new boy in class. "He is from England." There was another gasp and applause. I was beginning to think these children had never seen the light of day. *What had they been expecting from the person that cancelled?* Oksana had told me that I should stay for around thirty minutes. So, I quickly thought about what I needed to tell them. My mind returned to the wedding speech: just say anything.

"Thank you. My name is Richard and I am from a city called Oxford, in England," I said, speaking slowly but trying not to sound patronising. There was another gasp. I was getting to understand the relationship with the audience now. It didn't bother me in the slightest that the school hall was full to the rafters.

"Who has got a question for me?" I just threw it out there as I had not prepared any script. Twenty hands went straight up across the hall. I pointed towards a girl at the back of the hall.

"What do you like about Ukraine?" came the question in heavily accented English. Given that this was the UN school, I knew I had better be diplomatic.

"That's a very good question," I began. "Before I came here, I liked the Ukrainian flag. How it represents endless fields of wheat and the blue summer skies." I paused for effect. "But now that I'm here, the *vodka* is pretty good." I could not have imagined the response being a round of applause from the hall, including the teachers and staff on the stage. This was an easy audience and I was just warming up. I pointed to a boy with his hand up near the front.

"Do you know the Queen?" he asked seriously. I thought about this and wondered what I would need to say to get an even bigger round of applause than the last answer.

"Everyone knows the Queen. In England she is everyone's grandmother." My mind suddenly thought of the snow babushka, freezing cold outside. I continued, "Make sure you all look after your grandmothers." Applause. More hands went up. I pointed to a girl in the middle of the hall.

"Do you have a girlfriend in Kyiv?" she said. It was the one question I dreaded.

"No, they are all too beautiful for me." This got a huge laugh. What a great audience; standup comedians would die for this audience. I pointed to a boy at the back.

"Why are you here?", he asked. The tone was confrontational, and I wouldn't get any laugh with this one. I thought about it and responded,

"Because I can." I continued. "When I was growing up, Ukraine was just a part of the Soviet Union. No-one could visit you and none of you could visit us." Silence. "What better place to visit than one I had thought that I could never visit, ever. When the chance came, it was top of my list." Applause and cheering this time. The next question came from a young girl to my left. It baffled me for its sheer audacity.

"Have you seen the *Loch Ness* monster?" There was a murmur from the audience as if to say, 'that was a stupid question'. I turned to the big blackboard which reached across the stage, picked up a stick of chalk from the tray, and started drawing. This is a drawing that everyone has done of the Loch Ness monster as an 'm' shape going in and out of the water. As a boy, I would trace *Asterix the Gaul* characters, then draw them myself until I became quite good. Having drawn the body of the Loch Ness monster, I drew a face of *Asterix* on it. I turned back to the girl.

"This is what I saw!" I smiled at her. Standing ovation. Applause. Laughing.

Sylvia approached me. My half hour was already over. I didn't want it to stop, I was having more fun here than anywhere I had been in Kyiv.

"Thank you so much. That was wonderful," she said with a wide smile, revealing a gold-capped tooth in her right molar. She turned to the hall.

"I want everyone to show Richard a *big* Ukrainian thank you," she hailed.

"*Dyakuyu!*" Responded the hall in Ukrainian. A wall of sound from each and every member of the hall. Sylvia led me back out of the side stage door into the corridor.

"Thank you again!" Sylvia said. "That was just wonderful. The children loved it."

"It was an absolute pleasure, I enjoyed it."

"Please come again," she said as we walked back down the stairs, towards the door. I shook Sylvia's hand and headed back out of the school towards the *Lukiyanivska* metro. The snow had stopped falling and the sunshine returned.

I looked to the bench where the 'snow babushka' had sat. She and the snow were both gone, almost as if she had melted. *I hoped she would be alright.*

Chapter 16. The English Lady and the Memorial

10th April 1997

I made sure I was at the Institute in good time ahead of the presentation of my *first* paper. Oksana was very encouraging as usual.

"You'll be great," she said with an encouraging smile. Oksana knew she had started the process of me being there. We had come a long way, achieving a lot. But there was still a long road ahead.

"I'm not worried about the presentation. It's the questions I'm worried about," I said, revealing some nerves.

"Korolyuk will support you if there are any difficult questions, or difficult people. He wants you to succeed."

"No problem. I hope there won't be too many questions. I need to be out promptly to get up to *Borispil* airport to meet Mum," I said, changing the subject.

"Oh yes. I'm so excited to see your mother, Diana, in Ukraine," she said excitedly. "A real English lady here in Kyiv. You will have to introduce her to both Professors Korolyuk." She said *'mother, Diana'* as *'Mother Diana'* like she was some British colleague of Mother Teresa.

"I suppose that depends how today goes," I semi-joked.

It was 2pm. I stood at the front of Lecture Room Two. Students and lecturers were taking their seats. Korolyuk was sitting in the centre of the front row. He was smiling and relaxed. I really didn't want to do anything to change that. The lecture room was half full, about fifty percent more than I had anticipated, or wanted. Having sat in several of these presentations before, I knew that niceties were not considered appropriate; one should dive straight into the maths.

I waited for Korolyuk to give me the nod to commence. When he did, I started. I had been around the Institute long enough to assess the average English language skills of the general students and lecturers and it was quite high. As such, I walked through my paper presentation in a mixture of English and Russian. The ten useful Russian phrases I had learned *off by heart* proved to be useful; as anticipated, the simplicity of the formulae structure didn't require much more. Any concepts not adequately covered by my rehearsed phrases would be stated in English. If anyone had any objections in the hall, Korolyuk was there to clarify. As such, the presentation went smoothly. There was one simple question at the end about conditions which I was happy to answer myself. *Why weren't there more questions?* Maybe all the students knew how devastating Professor Korolyuk could be when challenged. Once the presentation was over, I received a ripple of applause and a confirmational nod from Korolyuk meaning 'job done'. The whole thing was done and dusted in under an hour. I felt the protective wing of Korolyuk that day.

Oksana was outside in the corridor waiting for me as Korolyuk and I came out of the lecture room together.

"Sounds like everything was good?" Oksana enquired to both of us. I respectfully waited for Korolyuk's response.

"Richard demonstrated that 'where there's a will there's a way' and 'you can't make an omelette without breaking a few eggs'" I had no idea what he meant but I knew he loved practising his English proverbs. Oksana smiled as if she did.

"I enjoyed it very much," I said with less proverbial eloquence. I looked at my watch. It was already past 3pm. My mum was due to land at 4pm so I had about an hour to get to the airport in a taxi to meet her.

"Well done to you both!" Oksana said.

"I must dash. I have an important appointment about a trivial matter," Korolyuk said as he left us and headed towards the stairs.

"I'll walk out with you on to *Kreshchatik* where you can get a taxi," said Oksana. I left the Institute exhilarated that I had banked my first real achievement.

I arrived at *Borispil* airport in good time. In fact, I was early. Mum's plane hadn't landed yet; she then took thirty minutes getting through Passport Control and Baggage Reclaim. I had time to relax with a coffee in Arrivals. As I sat with my coffee, I noticed an English newspaper stand in the adjacent kiosk. Tony Blair was on the front page; they were tipping him to be the next prime minister. I bought a copy of the *Daily Telegraph*. The only other option was *The Sun*, which was typically a whole week out of date by the time it had reached Kyiv. I had read it from cover to cover before *Mother Diana* appeared at arrivals.

Mum greeted son after four months and she immediately commented that I looked thinner. I commented that this was not possible given my strict new diet of carbohydrates, salo and alcohol. Had it really been four months since returning to Ukraine? The time had flown much quicker than the previous winter for the simple reason that I was constantly occupied with both work and play. Life was good in Kyiv, and I no longer had a feeling that this was somewhere foreign to me, but a home from home. Mum's arrival that day crystallised the feeling. We arrived at *Druzhbi Narodiv* early evening, so Mum was ready to rest after a day of travelling.

"Welcome Diana!" Natasha greeted her in her best English at the door of the apartment.

"I'm very pleased to meet you," was Mum's response in her very best English. For the next few days, I acted as translator, making me appreciate how far I had come with my Russian. It was functional with a degree of fluency for the more basic expressions. Natasha had done a great job as teacher. Mum's visit also meant a temporary change in sleeping arrangements. She was in my bedroom, I slept in Natasha's room and Natasha went next door to her sister's flat.

The next day was relaxed after the tense day before. Natasha was at work. Mum was in no rush to get out and about in Kyiv, preferring to have a leisurely breakfast with a catch up of the last four months. After lunch, I showed her Kreshchatik, including the central post office where she sent a postcard to Dad. *We avoided kiosk number nine!* I pointed her to the sunflower postcards I'd sent that first visit to Kyiv. We had tea in the *Podil* then took a metro over to visit Korolyuk at his Golden Gate apartment. Nina answered the door.

"Welcome to Ukraine" she hailed; then showed us into the living room where Professor Korolyuk greeted my mother. Mum now also wearing a pair of oversized *Donald Duck* slippers. I noticed how interesting it was for them to acquaint an English lady of a certain age in Kyiv, a contemporary from a foreign land, previously off-limits. At sixty-two years old, honestly Mum was youthful in appearance compared to her Ukrainian contemporaries. In addition, Ukrainians changed their behaviour around her; there seemed to be an unusual deference just because she was an English lady from a certain generation. It was amusing to watch. Suddenly, it seemed, both professors were subservient, sympathetic to the fact that they had never had an English lady for tea. Maybe they thought she would report back to the *Queen* about how good or bad their manners were; how well they had brewed the tea; how fresh the cucumber sandwiches were. Added to this list would also be how chewy the *salo* was. Given that it was being served on the tea tray, I must have mentioned how much I liked it to Korolyuk on a previous occasion. The sentiment was well-meaning, but I wasn't quite sure if salo had been served with tea and cakes before.

Mum had a nibble at one piece then politely held onto it in her left hand, refusing to put it back down as if to avoid any cultural offence. Korolyuk was fascinated by my mother's etiquette; she wasn't aware, but I could see him watching her behaviour. She may as well have been a chimp at a chimps' tea-party. After tea, Nina reached over to one of her China-filled cabinets and took out a large porcelain sculpture of a traditional Ukrainian goat herder with some goats. She handed it to Mum, sitting on the sofa, still holding the salo in her left hand, or more accurately delicately between index finger and thumb.

"Mum keeps a herd of goats at home in the Cotswolds; she makes her own goats' cheese and ice-cream, often winning prizes at national cheese shows," I had previously told Nina. She was attempting to bond with Mum at the *goat herder* level, but Mum now found that she was balanced on the edge of the sofa, wearing Donald Duck slippers with an expensive porcelain figurine in one hand and slightly chewed pig fat in the other. Even in this awkward position, Mum managed to engage in the conversation without breaking a sweat.

"This is lovely," Mum said of the figurine attempting to hand it back, needing a spare hand before sliding off the sofa edge.

"Diana, this is for you," Nina said insistently. Mum looked at the salo and put it in her mouth to free up the other hand.

"She meant the figurine," I said in case Mum thought that Nina was insisting she eat the salo. Then, Mum understood she was receiving a thoughtful gift from Nina.

"*Bolshoye spasibo*," Mum was extremely grateful and used the only Russian she had been practicing for weeks, then the gift was wrapped in newspaper and placed in a box. I worried it wouldn't survive the journey home to *Druzhbi Narodiv,* let alone the Cotswolds. The tea was a wonderful gesture by the Professors Korolyuk and a real highlight of Mum's trip. Before we left, Korolyuk pulled out his secret vodka bottle and offered it to Mum. This was the last thing she wanted as part of her salo-tea experience, and she politely declined. I, on the other hand, graciously accepted so as not to cause any cultural offence, indeed.

The porcelain goat herders in hand, we thanked both Nina and Korolyuk before heading out of the apartment building towards the

Opera House opposite. I told Mum about the times already spent there and was sure there would be many more to come. That night, the Opera House was showing a concert called *Around the World*. I had bought tickets earlier in the week as part of Mum's action-packed tour. However, she declined, stating overtiredness and digestive issues due to excessive salo consumption as her reasons for an early night.

"Invite Natasha out for the concert. She will enjoy it," Mum insisted.

So, I did, and we had a great time at an amazing concert. The National Philharmonic orchestra played different samples of music from *around the world*. Coincidentally, we bumped into Nina and I was able to introduce Natasha to her for the first time. It wasn't clear whether Nina was working or visiting for enjoyment.

"Are you both enjoying my concert?" Nina asked, giving a strong hint that she'd something to do with it. We both replied that we were having a great time.

"Where is your mother?" she enquired, almost slightly annoyed that I had brought Natasha to the concert instead of Mum.

"She had to take an important telephone call with my Dad," I replied, making an excuse that didn't offend and couldn't be contested. Nina smiled and said she had to dash backstage. Natasha loved her evening at the concert; I sensed that she didn't often go out to the theatre.

After the concert in the Opera House the night before to thank Natasha for hosting my mother, Natasha insisted on her visiting *Koncha Zaspa* as a thank you, for taking her place at the concert the night before. Mum had recovered from the previous day's antics, and she was happy the goat herder figurine had made it safely back to the flat unscathed.

We arrived at the *Koncha Zaspa* bus stop and crossed the road to the forested side. There, waiting in his *Zaporozhets,* was the Colonel with flat cap, raincoat and driving gloves. He looked like he was ready for the *London to Brighton Rally*. Mum sat in the front passenger seat while Natasha and I bundled into the back.

"I would advise you to hold on tight," I said to Mum as the Colonel swung the car around off the lay-by onto the forest track. He drove through the same part of the forest that Natasha and I had walked through under snow a couple of months before. The forest felt different now. As the winter frost melted, the forest came alive with vibrant colours and renewed energy. We didn't stop at the apartment; instead, we drove straight down the forest track to the dacha. Trees, once bare and dormant, began to sprout fresh green leaves, creating a lushness. The garden behind the dacha had started to turn from brown to green, although not yet a place of growth and abundance. Vegetable patches had been carefully tended and seeded, with rows of young plants emerging from the soil. Herbs such as dill and parsley were beginning to appear.

Old Natasha had prepared a full Ukrainian table which was gratefully received as it was another *welcome* for mum. The Colonel ensured I sat on his right, as usual, and Mum sat on my right. Sitting on the right of the person at the head of the table was an honour. In the army, a Ukrainian officer would only keep his most trusted comrade on the right hand as it was the same side as his gun. On this day, at least, there were no guns and the seat on the right merely meant that I drank whenever he drank. The ladies compared ages again. Old Natasha was the same age as Mum but she had to concede that Mum looked ten years younger. She was turning into a role model for the *sixty-two-year-olds* and a minor celebrity for her anti-aging looks.

After lunch, and a couple of vodkas, we all got back into the *Zaporozhets* and drove down another forest track. The track started winding and became more winding, eventually disappearing as we approached a black granite monument in the middle of the forest.

The five of us extricated ourselves out of the *Zaporozhets*. We had arrived at a line of ditches.

"These were trenches from the front line in the Battle of Kyiv in 1941," Natasha explained. The Colonel led us to the monument and described how this place was a decisive area of the German army's encirclement and the Soviet army's defence. We walked a hundred yards from the monument to a bend in the trenches; the Colonel stopped abruptly. We stopped abruptly behind him.

"This is where I stood and fought," he said, pointing to a very specific place in the trench. The trenches were two metres deep but likely to have been much deeper during the battle. I jumped in to see how it might have felt. My height allowed me to see over the top, but this wouldn't have been the case in 1941.

"We stayed in these trenches for weeks," he said, "until there were either none of us left, or the Germans took over the line." His tone turned from his usual jolliness to a solemness as his memories flooded back.

"They came from over there," he said, pointing his finger due south of the trench. "We held them off until the tanks came, then we had no chance." I could hear the fear in his voice even then. Their bravery must have been astonishing. He named several of his friends who had died in the same section of the trench, inviting me to take a photo with him, which I was honoured to do.

"Let's go back now," he wiped away a tear as the memories of his friends became too real. This was a difficult place to return to for him, but he had wanted to show Mum. We walked back along the line of the trench while translating everything for her. She was fascinated by the man and the place.

"I can remember the German *Luftwaffe* flying over the Liverpool docks in 1941," she said, indicating in a way that I should translate her words for the Colonel. She continued, "I remember the silhouette of the barrage balloons as the fires lit everything up." Mum would have been about seven years old, but the memories were as clear and as vivid as the Colonel's memories of the trenches. The Colonel was fascinated to hear about Mum's childhood experience in the same year of the war, in another world. We arrived back at the granite monument and took a couple of photos of Mum with the Colonel before climbing back into the *Zaporozhets*. After a short tea stop back at the dacha, we headed back home to *Druzhbi Narodiv*.

We returned to the flat and Mum immediately went for a lie down to recover from the day's exertions. Greg phoned and reminded me that, being Saturday night, it would be rude not to get out to the *Rock Café*. After dinner, that's where I headed.

It would have been like any other Saturday night out at the *Rock Café* had I not met *her*. Yulia was an exceptionally bright first-year law student at *Kyiv-Mohyla Academy*. Not only was she smart, but she was also beautiful and elegant in an understated way. She had silky brown hair, clear skin and an amazing smile. She was the first and only girl I'd met in the Ukraine that turned my head.

Greg, seeing the two of us getting on so well, suggested that we all go to the *New York* nightclub for a bit of a *groove*. I took Greg to one side of the bar and told him I would love to go but that, with my Mum in town, it would be awkward to be out until late. His advice to me was clear and decisive.

"Would James Bond ask his mum before going out with a beautiful girl?" His argument was compelling, so I stayed out. Yulia didn't disappoint and let's just say, I felt like James Bond in her company.

I called Natasha to let her know that I was out with the usual crowd and would be home late. Natasha was always concerned when I was out late, for security reasons, but she knew that I was becoming very confident about what and what *not* do in Kyiv. We all had a *groove* in *New York* and got home before sunrise. Before anyone had woken up. That night was the beginning of a love affair which made sure I stayed in Kyiv. I was immediately under Yulia's spell. Greg was thrilled with his advice to me which solidified him as a most trusted friend.

The next morning, I was feeling tired but happy that I had met Yulia the night before. I mooned around the flat thinking about how Yulia looked on the dance floor and what that first kiss felt like. I wondered how I would contact her to see her again.

Satisfied that there had been no inquest from anyone, Natasha, Mum and I settled our Sunday plan to visit the *Percherska Lavra*. The *Percherska Lavra* is a historic Orthodox Christian monastery, located next to the Botanical Gardens we had visited with *Funtik* the dog. It is one of the most important religious and cultural landmarks in the country and the only place in Ukraine Mum had ever heard of. The one metro station journey was simple that morning; we quickly arrived at the famous entrance.

The *Lavra* was founded in the 11th century by a group of monks known as the 'Caves Monks' and consisted of two parts: the *Upper Lavra* and the *Lower Lavra*. The *Upper Lavra* is the administrative and religious centre, while the *Lower Lavra* is home to the famous *Caves*.

We began by wandering around the *Upper Lavra*. In an hour we had entered several churches and bell towers, including the original *Dormition Cathedral*. This was the main church and housed the relics of many saints. Mum was fascinated to climb the *Great Lavra Bell Tower* with its gilded dome, standing nearly one hundred metres tall, offering panoramic views of Kyiv. The clock on the tower had replaced the older 18th century clock which had only stopped once during its existence; this was in September 1941 when the *Dormition Cathedral* had been blown up by the Germans during the Battle of Kyiv.

By the time we got back down to the ground, Mum decided that she needed a coffee. There was a small café, consisting of two tables, on the inside of the main entrance. The lady brought us our coffees and Mum promptly picked up the salt pot, thinking it was sugar.

"I don't think much of this coffee." Until I pointed out what she'd done, I think she thought this is what coffee tasted like in Ukraine. Natasha especially saw the funny side and laughed at Mum's latest social faux pas. Natasha was impressed that rather than spitting it out, Mum just swallowed it, making a polite understated comment.

Natasha said smiling, "A very English lady."

Soon after, we entered the caves, one of the *Lavra's* most unique and revered features. These underground labyrinths consist of narrow tunnels and chambers housing the remains of monks. Pilgrims visit the caves to pray and seek spiritual solace. By the end of the excursion through the caves, Mum was ready to collapse so we made our way back to the metro.

Natasha explained "To the Ukrainian people, the Lavra and caves are another symbol of national identity, struggles and triumphs throughout our history, it has survived numerous invasions, wars, and political changes, making it another symbol of our resilience." She spoke with immense pride.

Monday was Mum's last day before flying back. It went according to plan, mostly. I went to visit Professor Korolyuk in the morning to discuss some new calculations, while mum went to the Botanical Gardens with Natasha. After lunch, we had a well-planned walk, starting at *Shevchenko Park*, opposite the red *Shevchenko University* building, up *Shevchenko Boulevard* to the cathedral then a quick metro to the *Dynamo Stadium* and *Mariinsky Palace*. By the end of the walk, Mum could walk no more, having successfully walked several kilometres every day. We all returned to *Druzhbi Narodiv* where she went to her bedroom to rest, locking the door behind her.

An hour later, Natasha and I were in the kitchen.

"Help!" came a faint call from somewhere. We both entered the living room. "Help!" called Mum from the bedroom. The door was locked. Firmly locked.

"Can you unlock the door?" I asked, not yet realizing the seriousness of the situation.

"I can't" came the response. Indeed, the lock appeared to be completely stuck.

Another hour passed; Mum was getting hungry, so we began passing food under the door. Thin slices of meat and cheese were ideal for passing under the door to a helpless, and now hungry, English lady. For Mum and I, this was hilarious, but for Natasha this was a domestic disaster. Neighbours were starting to appear at the front door, saying that they could hear someone in distress calling for help. Before the whole block became alarmed, that an English lady was trapped inside the bedroom, Natasha felt that she needed to act. And fast. She opened the balcony door and pulled a long thin rope out of the balcony storage container. Appearing to know exactly what she was doing; she came back into the living room and gave me one end of the rope to hold. Natasha returned to the balcony and asked me to tell Mum to open the near bedroom window.

"Open the bedroom window!" I called, sensing the growing urgency with Natasha's actions.

"How far?" came Mum's response. More neighbours arrived at the front door; word was getting around that an English lady was trapped in the building.

"As far as you can!" I responded.

Natasha lobbed the length of the rope through the bedroom window from the balcony.

"Tell Diana to pass the rope under the bedroom door," she said urgently. I did this and the end of the rope suddenly appeared. I pulled it through, still holding the other end of the rope. Natasha came in from the balcony and tied the ends of the rope together, making a closed loop that ran through the living room and bedroom. Natasha returned to the balcony and began to climb over the edge. With rope under each arm, she skilfully manoeuvred across to the outside of the bedroom and levered herself up in through the open window. This was textbook *Special Forces*. Natasha entered the bedroom through the window, asked Mum if she was OK – *why wouldn't she be?* – and then unlocked the door. Within five minutes of grabbing the rope from the balcony, the door was unlocked, and Mum was rescued. Rescued, it must be said, before the neighbours claimed that the English lady had been kidnapped. For Mum, this was a hysterically funny, albeit embarrassing, episode, and the final social faux pas of her trip. Indeed, the message went out to the neighbours that the English lady had been freed from her ordeal without a ransom being paid.

15th April 1997

Today was the day that *Mother Diana* departed Kyiv. She insisted I go out in the morning to buy a nice pot plant for Natasha for rescuing her. I did this before breakfast. We then popped into the *SwissAir* office, on *Shevchenko Boulevard,* to confirm her return flight. I noticed *SwissAir* was next to the *Naftogaz* office, the national oil company. We then had time for a quick tour of the *Motherland Statue* near the *Percherska* metro, before booking a taxi to *Borispil* airport. Natasha and I escorted Mum to the airport, not forgetting the porcelain goat herder. We arrived just in time for Mum's boarding. Mum thanked Natasha for her hospitality.

"See you in June," I said, knowing that I would be returning for the summer at around that time. It had been an eventful, few days which ultimately had been successful. Although stressful, my Ukrainian *family* had done all they could to make her feel welcome.

The following day I stayed at the flat with Natasha and had a Russian lesson: *Colloquial Russian* Chapter Ten. Oksana had invited me to see *Rigoletto* again that evening but, with Natasha's insistence, she said that I should have an early night. This was the right call, which Oksana was unhappy about. Natasha knew my limits and strongly advised that I *recharge my batteries.*

It should have been an uneventful, relaxing Thursday but I woke up to discover that my visa was not registered with the local police station. I needed a police stamp. I had checked my passport only because I'd heard, by chance, a commotion at *Borispil* the day of mum's departure, that somebody else hadn't had the correct visa. This was a big deal in Ukraine, and I needed to find a way of getting my visa registered properly at the police station. If caught without it, I could be sent home on the first flight out of *Borispil* airport. I phoned Oksana and told her of my visa status.

"OK stay at home until we have this sorted out," she said reassuringly. "The police can arrest you on the spot if they ask to see your passport and you don't have a valid police stamp."

I accepted that I would stay at home which was more difficult than it sounded. Natasha was already out at work, and I needed some bread for a sandwich. I thought that I would be alright if I just pop over to the local kiosk for some bread. I had never seen any police around here. I decided to go for it, as the chances of seeing a *militsia* were slim to zero.

I exited the building, carrying my passport as usual, suddenly conscious of the lack of freedom I found myself watching for *militsia* around every corner. This inevitably garnered the suspicious behaviour I was trying to avoid. It was likely to attract any suspecting *militsia* if there were one, so I tried to behave as normally as possible. I was, for the moment, an illegal immigrant.

I crossed the street and entered the bakery kiosk selling fresh bread, standing in the middle of about five other kiosks. No *militsia*. All good.

"Good morning, Englishman!" the girl behind the counter greeted me. I should have expected this. Fortunately, the kiosk was empty except for me.

"How can I help you?", she asked.

"Just a loaf of white bread, please," I asked, not seeing two *militsia* wandering down the street, just outside the bakery kiosk door. They stopped and lit up a cigarette. I paid the girl and turned to leave. I couldn't believe it, not today. I needed to stay in the kiosk until they had finished their cigarette, so I began chatting to the girl about some made up subject to stall for time.

"Have you been working here for long?" I asked. I couldn't think of anything else.

"No not long, ever since leaving school last year," she replied, having taken off her gloves, fully engaged with what I was saying. I hoped she didn't think I was chatting her up, I was not in the mood for small talk. I was still the only customer in the kiosk and the *militsia* were still outside. *How long to smoke a cigarette?*

"How do you like Kyiv?" she asked. She *must* have felt that I was completely distracted by the *militsia* outside. Or chatting her up.

"Great," I said. "I really like the bread here." She laughed. I was now unintentionally entering small talk territory, and she would surely start to make the connection between my pathetic conversation and the *militsia* standing outside. As I was just about to say something even more stupid, the police dropped their cigarettes and moved down the row of kiosks. This was my opportunity.

"Goodbye!" I said to the girl.

"Nice to chat. See you soon Englishman!" she said as I left the kiosk. Without looking down the street, I crossed back over to the apartment building. I was back in the flat with my loaf. I stayed there for the rest of the day, feeling like an escaped convict in a safe house. Natasha came in from work and found the story hilarious.

The next morning, Oksana phoned and confirmed that she had organised an appointment for an emergency visa registration. I would need to meet her at one of the central police stations to get it. This meant travelling on the underground to *Klovska*, only two metro stations from *Druzhbi Narodiv*. I would meet Oksana at the metro at 11am. Although a short journey, I had to get there without being stopped by the *militsia* in the first place.

"Just look at your feet," Natasha said jokingly. I was reminded of the old man at the snowy tram stop who had given the same advice. She was finding this amusing, possibly not realizing the consequences. I couldn't leave Ukraine now, not for this. *Now I had met Yulia, did I want to?*

I headed out of the flat, fully focussed on getting to *Klovska* without catching anyone's eye. Fifteen minutes later, I was coming up the escalator at *Klovska* when I spotted two *militsia* coming down the opposite escalator. I stared at my shoes until I had reached the top. As soon as I passed through the barrier and saw Oksana, I let out an audible sigh of relief. But she didn't greet me with the usual beaming smile. Something was wrong. She immediately asked for my passport which I pulled out of my breast pocket and gave to her. We walked a couple of minutes from the metro station towards a large building, my local central police station.

"Richard, can you wait outside, please," she said with a reassuring degree of seriousness. I let Oksana take control of the situation. She entered the police station; I nervously waited outside the adjacent building, trying not to appear as though I were loitering. Ten minutes later, Oksana came back.

"All good. But you owe me a hundred hryvnia and you still need to go to the visa office to pay a minor fine." She continued, "but you are now registered for a further year."

"Great, no problem. Thank you." I passed her the money. I was just happy that I was a legal again. We had a coffee at *Klovska* before departing in opposite directions on the green line. The experience had shaken me. I knew how devastated I would be, if I were forced to leave Ukraine: a country and its people I was getting to know and love. One person, in particular.

After all of the visa fun, I was relieved that it was Friday night, *Rock Café* night. I arrived early as I was eager to have a few beers in celebration at my re-established non-illegal status. As I arrived, I was greeted by the *Crazy Frenchmen,* noticing that none of the British crowd had yet arrived. There was another birthday being celebrated and the atmosphere was already relaxed. Thibaut tactfully introduced me to Murielle, who apparently was the *French Attache* in Kyiv; she was exceptionally fluent in English with an enchanting accent. The conversation quickly moved from Ukrainian politics to French politics then to English politics. I understood in this brief exchange that she was a social Gaullist.

"What do you think of Tony Blair?" Murielle asked. She asked in such a way that she knew that this was a man who was destined to become Prime Minister.

"He seems like a decent enough chap. I think he'll make a good Prime Minister if he wins the election next month," I said, focussing on the man rather than the policies. To be honest, I had lost touch with some of the more recent British politics, being starved of the BBC news in Ukraine. The current Prime Minister, John Major, was looking rather forlorn and grey in some of the newspaper photos I had seen, in comparison to the young, smiley Tony Blair.

"Will he be good for Europe?" she asked as she drank a glass of *Obolon.* This was always going to be the comparison between Major and Blair. Major had spent the last five years struggling with his own party splits on Europe, creating a lot of tension with the European Union leaders and institutions. All of Europe seemed to think that Tony Blair was the 'golden boy' of British politics and expected he would bring Britain and Europe forward together.

"Yes, I think he will," I said optimistically. "But if you're asking me if he can be trusted, I wouldn't be able to tell you." I knew that the Conservative governments under Margaret Thatcher and John Major held power for eighteen years, too long for any government. Governments get stale and run out of steam. Tony Blair and the New Labour government seemed to be buzzing with new ideas, but anyone who smiles so much must be hiding something.

"Maybe you can't trust the politician but the people who voted for the politician?" she asked rhetorically.

"I don't disagree with you there", I responded, "and so, conversely, it becomes the people's fault when a politician does something wrong?"

"Definitely not. You can never blame the people, only the politicians can be blamed for their actions," she said even more assertively. "The people give the politicians their chance to do good things."

I liked Murielle; she had clarity of thought. We chatted long and hard about current affairs that evening. She would be pleased when Tony Blair became Prime Minister in two weeks' time. Afterwards, I went out with all the *Frenchies*, including Luda, an honorary French girl since she had started dating Thibault, to our regular go-to nightclub, *New York*.

25th April 1997

Sadly, Oksana called before breakfast to tell me that her marriage had broken down. Never mentioning him before, I hadn't really thought about her having a husband. *Another mystery husband.* She was distraught. Not about the split but because her ex-husband had taken their shared laptop and scrubbed off all her important files. She was devastated about losing much of her important work with Misha, as she had been preparing another *big project* with him. I hoped he would record a *Queen* song next time so maybe it would be *Project Freddie*.

"He is so spiteful," she cried down the phone. I withheld judgement because there are two sides to any relationship break down and I didn't want to speculate. She also reminded me that the fine for the expired registration had to be paid and so I went into town and paid it.

I met Chris in town and we decided to buy tickets for 'La Traviata' at the Opera House. As soon as a couple of us had bought tickets, there was the usual momentum and the rest of our European gang joined us. We had become regular theatre goers. *What was the alternative for entertainment in Kyiv?* There were several other theatres in Kyiv, and cinemas, but language often acted as a barrier. Moreover, the Opera House was a central meeting point with a good bar.

The following day, Natasha's sister, Teofila, invited me to accompany her and Snezana to a memorial service for the 11th anniversary of the *Chernobyl* nuclear disaster. The commemoration and remembrance service taught the importance of acknowledging and commemorating the tragic events of the *26th April 1986*. I was honoured to be invited and, without hesitation, agreed to go with them. We travelled together via *Percherska* to the Chernobyl monument on the Dnipro riverbank. Many families affected by the disaster were already gathering. Naturally, Teofila and Snezana were included in this. Of course, the immediate impact of the explosion was devastating; two plant workers died on the day of the accident and twenty-nine more people succumbed to acute radiation sickness in the following weeks. However, the long-term effect of the disaster was felt for years. Thousands of people suffered from radiation-related illnesses and the area surrounding the Chernobyl plant remained heavily contaminated.

The service was beautifully choreographed with lots of children, many orphans from the disaster, flowers and songs. I couldn't help but feel deeply touched by the thoughts expressed by these children. It was an unimaginable episode in the history of Ukraine. The sentiment expressed by many Ukrainians firmly placed blame for the disaster on the Soviet system which didn't acknowledge that the disaster had happened until it was too late. *Never again.*

After the gathering, we all travelled into a church near the Golden Gate for a formal memorial service. The memorial service was a more solemn and meaningful experience, highlighting the human impact of the Chernobyl disaster. It served as a reminder of the lives that were affected, the suffering endured by the survivors, and the sacrifices made by those involved in the rescue and recovery efforts. The service lasted an hour at which point we all moved into a hall for food and drinks. The service shed light on the long-term effects of the disaster on the environment, emphasizing the importance of protecting and preserving our natural surroundings. Large areas had become contaminated and ecosystems were disrupted. The children drew pictures of the environmental consequences of the Chernobyl disaster.

I remembered the Chernobyl disaster as a boy at Burford School in England, safely watching the news from one thousand six hundred miles away. Never then could I have imagined that I would be attending a memorial service to the victims and their children. I remembered how the leader of the Soviet Union, Mikhail Gorbachev, had visited the UK three years after that, in July 1989, flying into nearby Brize Norton air base. He visited the Queen and Prime Minister Margaret Thatcher. I was in the sixth form doing my A-levels and his visit generated enormous excitement amongst all of us. *At that time, he was considered as someone who could change, or even end, the Soviet Union.*

Chapter 17. Victory Day and the Actress

2nd May 1997

In the morning, I went into the central post office in *Independence Square*. I sat for several hours in the upstairs internet hall, reading all the results as they came through. Tony Blair was the new UK Prime Minister; the youngest for 185 years. New Labour won a landslide victory with a stonking one hundred and seventy-seven seat majority. The Ukrainian news channels were unanimously reporting that his election was good for Europe. The election was highly anticipated and had generated a lot of interest among voters, as Blair had campaigned on a platform of modernization and change. *Murielle would be pleased.* His campaign resonated with the electorate, particularly with younger voters who were looking for a fresh approach to governance. The Labour Party's message of 'New Labour' appealed to many as a departure from the traditional left-wing policies of the past. Both Ron and I had called it correctly back in the hotel room in Odessa a whole year ago. Everyone was talking about the dawn of a new era now that the Conservative Party's rule under Margaret Thatcher and John Major had come to an end. I enjoyed my politics and was beginning to understand the equivalent struggle between the parties in the Ukrainian parliament, including their views on the expanding European Union. Under President Kuchma, Ukraine had begun exploring closer ties with the European Union with ambitions to step towards deeper cooperation and integration.

In the warm spring afternoon, I grabbed my trainers I had bought from *Kontraktova* market and went for a run around the *Respublikanski Stadium* running track. It felt amazing to run in the beautiful weather. I was starting to get used to Ukraine not being just frozen or snowing all the time. It was good to be on a running track again, having been a half decent runner in the Reading University Athletics Club, two years earlier. Eight laps of the track were enough for me before I felt how unfit I had become. This was my local track, only three stations from my flat; I could get here, have a run, get back and have a shower, all within the space of an hour. That evening it was great to catch up with everyone for a drink outside the *Rock Café*, including Murielle who was delighted about the 'Tony Blair Victory Day' as she referred to it.

On Saturday morning, Natasha had begun preparing for a picnic. She asked me the day before not to stay out too late at the *Rock Café* as she wanted to go on a picnic with an old school friend. At 10am we met Anya and her friend Artyom at *Hydropark* metro station and walked over the bridge connecting the two islands. We found a nice spot on the banks of the river on *Trukhaniv Island* and Artyom began building a small campfire. I thought *we* had brought a lot of food for the picnic until I saw how much they had brought. *We could have camped there for the whole weekend!* Artyom and I cooked the mountain of meat on the campfire while Natasha and Anya talked and prepared the table.

"Anya is going to Canada," Natasha said.

"It's supposed to be nice this time of year. How long will she stay there?" I asked.

"Forever," Natasha said, suddenly watery-eyed. "She's emigrating and I'll probably never see her again."

"Oh, I see." I responded as sympathetically as I could. This picnic was a big deal for Natasha; Anya was her best friend at school. Many Ukrainians were leaving to find a new life in Europe, US or Canada. Anya, like many others, wanted to make a new life in Canada.

We ate, drank and laughed all day and only left *Hydropark* just before dark. Natasha and Anya had a big final hug on the platform before we departed in opposite directions. The reality was that Ukrainians could leave the country whenever they wanted to; a luxury they did not have only six short years before, under the Soviet Union. I sensed that Natasha loved Ukraine, loved her family, too much to leave.

On the way back, I jumped out at *Kreshchatik* to have another hour in the post office internet café, checking the BBC election newsfeed. While there, I bumped into Luda, who was there writing emails. We spent an hour in the internet café before sitting out by the fountains in Independence Square supping *Obolon* together. The warm evenings were here to stay, and it felt fantastic. Kyiv was a completely different place; it felt like a Mediterranean resort.

Suddenly, the air was filled with a peculiar melody from the great digital clock above Independence Square. The clock was across the square from the central post office and on the hour would send out haunting music from the clock's loudspeakers. The sound could stop any conversation in its tracks. It reminded me of an old film called the *The Time Machine* from the novel written by H.G. Wells. Wells' character travels eight hundred thousand years into the future to a civilisation split in two; there are the monstrous *Morlocks* and the hunted *Eloi*. One controls the other using hypnotic eerie sounds generated from hidden speakers. The *Eloi* are herded, trance-like, into a big cave under the ground never to be seen again. Luda and I agreed that this was the purpose of the Independence Square clock: the Russians were the *Morlocks* and the Ukrainians the *Eloi*. Luda and I laughed about this until we had run out of *Obolon* then we bid each other goodnight.

Sunday began with a lie-in and a plan to complete the draft of my second research paper. I had to review it with Korolyuk in the coming week. Oksana phoned to talk about UK elections; it seemed that everyone was thrilled that Tony Blair was now the UK Prime Minister. Then she changed the subject.

"Would you like to come and see a film tonight?" she asked. I couldn't quite grasp the context. *Was this a film at the cinema or on her television at home? Did it have to be tonight? What was the urgency? Was she asking me because her husband had just left her? Why did I feel like I was being disloyal to Yulia?* 'Stop panicking,' I told myself, 'I'm sure it's innocent'.

"Yes, I'd love to," I replied, not really knowing what I was agreeing to. I had noticed that whenever Oksana invited me to anything it was always same day. "What are we watching?" I enquired.

"The film is in Russian, but it translates as *Friend of the Deceased*," Oksana explained, not really selling it.

"OK... not a film I've heard of but let's go for it!" I joked.

"You might have heard of it," she insisted. "It is the CIS entry to this year's *Cannes Film Festival*."

"*CIS* as in Commonwealth of Independent States and *Cannes* as in France?" I was trying my best to understand.

"Yes, that's right. This evening is the Ukrainian premier."

"I'm assuming I should wear a tie," I blustered, making me sound very English and much like my dad. Dad wore a tie everywhere, including the beach.

"No, you can just dress smartly and quite cool. This is Cannes, not the Labour Party," she joked to herself.

I had never been asked to dress 'quite cool' in my life so just interpreted that as 'no tie'. I couldn't quite grasp how *Cannes* and the *Labour Party* had appeared in the same sentence.

"Where and when do you want me?" I was beginning to sound like a gigolo.

"7pm at *Palats Sportu*. We can walk from there. See you then!" She signed off the phone call with an excited yelp.

I was at *Palats Sportu* for 7pm. It was a warm spring evening and the sunset was still an hour away. It felt like Cannes. Oksana arrived dressed for the occasion. I just hoped they let me in. We walked five minutes and arrived at the *Artists House* as it was known. This was the equivalent to the *Empire* cinema in *Leicester Square*, London, where all film premiers were watched by the local glitterati. On the outside, the building could've been empty. There were two doormen at the entrance who looked at me when asking to see our tickets. I indicated that Oksana probably had them, taking half a step back. Oksana showed them our tickets. As soon as we entered the grand foyer, everything was decorated for a premier film. She gave in her coat to the cloakroom and we were shown to an entrance into the auditorium, already full of beautiful people. Oksana said that everyone in the audience was most likely an actor, a director or a celebrity.

We settled into our seats just as a compère walked out onto the stage to introduce the film. Oksana pointed out it was the director of the film we were about to see. He spoke about the film and indicated several people in the audience, including the cast. Not knowing who anyone was in the Ukrainian glitterati, I didn't know who I was supposed to be looking at. The lights went down and a wide curtain opened to reveal the cinema screen. The whirring sound of a projector could be heard somewhere behind us and then the sound and then the film titles appeared. I knew I had to concentrate as I would probably only understand one out of every ten words spoken anyway.

The film lasted about an hour and a half, I was relieved when it was over. I vaguely understood the story but most of the dialogue went completely over my head.

"Did you enjoy it?" Oksana turned to me as the lights came back on.

"Loved it!" I replied. I would try and find a video of it with English subtitles.

The buzz in the front row was audible; there were a lot of congratulatory hugs and kisses going on between some of the cast members. Oksana indicated that we move towards the exit.

"There is a drinks reception in the bar; we are allowed to go there." This was becoming interesting, a drinks reception at a Cannes film entry premier. We were rubbing shoulders with the film celebrities of Kyiv as we squeezed into the drinks' reception. Drinks were waiting for us on the bar and tables around the edge of the room. After a few minutes, a tall glamourous-looking woman walked into the reception. She had extraordinary charisma and was followed by several other people trying to stay close to her.

"That's Olga Sumskaya," Oksana said, indicating with a nod from her champagne glass. I had no idea who she was but she looked stunning.

"Was she in the film?" I asked, still not recognizing her.

"No, but she is the star of *Roxalana,*" she replied. I was still none the wiser so sought clarification.

"Roxalana?" I enquired subtly.

"Yes, it is a very popular drama series on television here in Ukraine. Everyone watches it and Olga is very famous because of it," she insisted. It seems I needed to find another video for my collection. "If I can, I would like to speak with her," she continued.

"Does she speak English?" I asked hoping to talk with her too.

"Come on!" Oksana grabbed my hand, pulling me in the direction of Olga.

"Good evening, Olga!" I was impressed with Oksana's assertiveness.

"Good evening, Oksana! It's so good to see you," Olga responded. So, they already knew each other. Olga turned to me.

"Hello Olga, I'm Richard. Very pleased to meet you," I said. The entourage that followed Olga into the reception were still around her, glaring at both Oksana and me, as if we had stolen Olga's attention from them.

"Very pleased to meet you, Richard. And where are you from?" She was my height in her heels, so our eyes were on the same level.

"I'm from England," I replied. This was my trump card. Olga and I continued chatting, all the time being watched by half a dozen minor celebrities. Oksana seemed glad that Olga and I were chatting and acted as standby translator.

"Did you enjoy the film? Please let me introduce you to the cast," Olga said as she tapped a few people on the shoulder. I wasn't quite sure what I could say to the cast of the film, especially if they didn't speak any English at all. Olga introduced me as 'Oksana's English friend' which I settled for. They seemed to never have met an English person, so I was starting to feel a bit of celebrity myself, getting my own gathering around me. After fifteen minutes, Olga's attention was required elsewhere. I felt that I had done well to chat with her for as long as I had.

"Nice to meet you, Richard. Oksana we must catch up sometime soon." Olga glided off to another corner of the reception, followed by her entourage. That was it. It was just Oksana and me again. *Celebrity is so fickle.*

"She was great," I said, turning to Oksana. "How do you know her?"

"She is a friend of Misha's and we met a few times already. When you have finished your champagne, we can go." Apparently, job done.

The next few days were spent getting my second research paper ready for Korolyuk's review. I split the time by popping into the British Council to read the papers about UK elections and visiting Inna in the British Consular. Inna was fascinated by British politics. I assume this is why she had the job that she had; she was even more fascinated that I had met *Olga Sumskaya*, she was a big *Roxalana* fan. We chatted for an hour until she left to have a meeting with the British Ambassador. In the sunny Spring evening, I met with Greg and Eugene in Independence Square for *Obolon* and eerie music. We then went to Respublikanski Stadium to watch Ukraine draw with Armenia.

By Thursday morning, Professor Korolyuk had approved my second paper; this would need to be presented to my peers, again. In the afternoon, I went to the National Athletics meeting at Respublikanski

Stadium and sat in a place directly in the sun, blissfully unaware that the next day I would suffer from bad sunburn.

9th May 1997

Today was 'Victory in Europe Day' in Ukraine, *oddly VE day in Europe is the day before*. This is a public holiday and a big deal in Ukraine. The event is for the people of Kyiv to pay tribute to the bravery and sacrifice of those who fought for freedom during the war. *I was nursing a nice shade of lobster.*

In the morning, all the English teachers and our Ukrainian friends met on *Kreshchatik* ahead of the VE Day military parade. The parade typically involved various military units, as well as veterans of war, including Natasha's father, the Colonel. The march began at *Kreshchatik* and proceeded towards the *Park of Eternal Glory,* where the Memorial Complex honouring the fallen soldiers is located.

We were there early enough to take a position at an outdoor café near the entrance to the *Passazh,* which provided an excellent view down *Kreshchatik* and across Independence Square. From here, we witnessed soldiers marching in uniform, military vehicles on display, and aircraft flyovers.

The parade took a couple of hours to march past and we had lunch. We noticed several scuffles breaking out in the crowd, but nothing more than that. After the tail of the parade had passed through *Kreshchatik*, another scuffle broke out and this one appeared to be worse than before. Suddenly, there were screams.

"He's got a knife!" someone shouted. In the panic, people started running down the pavement. We all stood and watched the melee. There was another scream and a dozen *Berkut*, the special *militsia,* arrived from nowhere. The crowd dispersed and ran away. We noticed a man lying on the ground covered in blood. The *Berkut* were around him now, but the man wasn't moving; he had been stabbed. Sadly, we learned later that the man had died.

This shook everyone up and it reminded us of the dangers that lingered in Kyiv, like any city in the world. We spent the rest of the day drinking *Obolon* and talking about what we had just witnessed. So, we finished VE Day celebrations commiserating by the big Independence Square fountain with *Obolon* and the eerie music. By evening, we all headed home feeling solemn after the events of the day.

The next day, I went to the central post office to check my emails. I had received an email from my brother. The email said, he *hoped everything was going well in Kyiv and he wanted to visit in June for my 25th birthday.* I replied to say he would be very welcome, and I thought it better to not tell him about the stabbing the day before.

It was Saturday. Greg, Chris and I all met up to buy tickets for *Romeo and Juliet* at the Opera House. We made a pact not to tell anyone at home of this, *especially not to put it in a future book.*

"Three lads going to *Romeo and Juliet* together is *not* a good look," Greg agreed. However, the purpose was to facilitate a triple date with three Ukrainian ladies. One of them was Yulia. As much as I enjoyed the banter with the lads, I was secretly excited to show Yulia my cultured side, hoping to impress her. We had managed to obtain tickets for the *Tsar's Balcony.* Yulia wore a beautiful dress and she fitted in perfectly on the balcony; never had I seen "true beauty till this night". We held hands when the curtain went down and I thanked my lucky stars. Greg and Chris had varying degrees of success with their respective ladies, but I was oblivious to anything but Yulia.

The following day, Natasha and I went to the Botanical Gardens for a Sunday walk. I noticed how different it looked to the day when Funtik disappeared in February. The scent and colour of the flowers was overwhelming. Natasha gave me a Russian lesson as I had brought my book with me, I took it everywhere: *Colloquial Russian* Chapter Eleven.

On Tuesday, I arranged a meeting at Korolyuk's apartment to finalize the second paper ahead of presentation. Arriving at his apartment, Nina answered the door as usual, but advised that Professor Korolyuk had another appointment and wasn't likely to get home until late. He had just phoned to apologise.

"Now that you're here, you may as well come in for tea," Nina said assertively, in such a way that I had no choice.

I entered the grand apartment and slipped on the Donald Duck slippers presented to me. Nina then directed me into the living room while she went into the kitchen to prepare some tea. I didn't sit down but, instead, took the opportunity to look more closely at some of the contents of the room. There were so many pieces of artwork and porcelain that this must represent two lifetimes of collection.

As I slowly swept around the room, I noticed some black and white photos at the back of a cabinet. One of them showed four young men. Visible now only because of the space left by the goat herder porcelain which had been given to Mum. Before I could read the names underneath, I recognized Korolyuk in the bottom right of the photo. Next to him was a man called Kustjuchenko; behind him was Michalevich and, to his left, Skorokhod. My mind immediately recalled Professor Harris' story about the four geniuses recognized at the highest level in Moscow during the 1950s. This could be them. So, this was what *Skorokhod* looked like. *Where was he now? What happened to the other two men?*

Nina entered with a tray of tea and Napoleon cake. She lay the tray on the table and sat down, preparing to cut the cake.

"Have you found anything interesting?" she said without looking away from the cake. *I wanted to know about the three other men in the picture but was this the right time to ask? Was Nina too close to everything?* I didn't wish to offend.

"Who are these men in the photo with Korolyuk?" I asked, my heart immediately missing a beat. Nina looked up to see to which photo I was referring to. She continued to pour the tea and started to explain.

"Oh, that's a very old photo of Korolyuk and his old university friends when he was your age. They all lived together in Moscow, except Kustjuchenko. He was separate from the other three."

I sat down on the sofa and poured milk into my tea, taking a large slice of Napoleon cake.

"The three of them lived as a commune; they were all on duty for two days a week, cooking breakfast in the morning and boiling tea in the evening." She took a sip of tea but she didn't eat any cake. "These 'three pilgrims' travelled to Moscow, which was the scientific and cultural centre of the USSR. Not only the best scientific institutions located there but also some of the world's best theatres and museums."

I took a giant bite of Napoleon, aware that half the cream had gone up my nose.

"In those days, the bright lights of Moscow attracted many young and energetic people, including these four young, talented and innocent men." She took another sip of tea. "They planned to take full advantage of these cultural and spiritual treasures." I took another giant bite of Napoleon. "But when Korolyuk returned home to Kyiv in 1954, Skorokhod stayed in Moscow for another three years. They were split up and really missed each other."

"Where are they now?" I spluttered through the cream feeling another missed heartbeat.

"Michalevich glittered with wit, Skorokhod sparkled with intellect and Korolyuk possessed inexhaustible enthusiasm and energy.", Nina recalled. "He hasn't changed," she said smiling, "that's why I married him." *Had she heard my question?*

"What about the fourth one?" I asked.

"He drank himself to death very young. Not long after this photo was taken."

"What a waste of a young talent," I said.

"There are only two of them left now. Korolyuk, of course, and Skorokhod." She glanced across to the photo.

"Where is Skorokhod?" I asked, feeling that I was showing too much interest and asking too many questions.

"Skorokhod is in Chicago. He works at the university there." She took another sip of tea. "He got out straight after the end of the USSR. He visits Moscow more now, but he occasionally visits us. He'll be coming in a few weeks."

I thought how I would love to meet him.

"Didn't you or Korolyuk want to leave too?" I was really asking too many questions now.

"No. He loves Ukraine, as I do, and we both wanted to stay with what was familiar...to help Ukraine at a difficult time. But our son left. He is a professor in Rome now."

My goodness, the whole family were professors. I looked at my watch. An hour had passed.

"Thank you so much for the tea. I should probably go now."

"Have you had enough cake?", Nina asked, waiting to cut another slice.

"I'm full and that's the tastiest Napoleon I've had in Kyiv." I gritted my teeth. It was still laced with condensed milk, lingering long after I tried to wash it down with tea. I left the apartment with a lot of information going through my head, Professor Harris' words ringing in my ears.

Afterwards I returned to *Druzhbi Narodiv,* shortly before Greg phoned to see if I could meet him in Independence Square for an *Obolon*. It was another hot sunny Spring evening; it was becoming an easy meeting point next to the *Obolon* seller and the fountains. I immediately saw Greg and Rory sitting on the edge of one of the fountains with *Obolons* in hand. Next to them was a red-haired girl.

"Rory got himself sacked," Greg said. "And he was nearly deported for being drunk on vodka in class."

"That's not good. Our visas are linked to the place of work," I sympathized. "You will have to go home unless you can find another place of work."

"That's what I told him," Greg said.

Rory didn't say anything.

"Hello, I'm Chloe, you must be Richard," said the red-headed girl.

"Pleased to meet you. Welcome to Ukraine. I used to be a teacher here," I said.

"Yes, I know," Chloe smiled.

I bought a round of *Obolon*. We sat and drank, pondering Rory's options. We concluded that they were limited.

14th May 1997

It was the hottest day of the year: a sweltering thirty degrees centigrade. I noticed, while passing through *Palats Sportu* last week, before we saw the film premier, that there was an Italian Business Exhibition on there. Under the heading of '*ITAL at Palats Sportu*', this was a big exhibition of Italian companies here in Ukraine or companies who were planning to set up in Ukraine. Ukraine was on course to invite more and more foreign, especially European, companies into the country. After breakfast, and the usual phone call with Oksana, I prepared to go to *ITAL*. Oksana had been interested to hear that I'd had tea alone with Nina the day before.

"Nina must really like you," Oksana said, "what are you planning to do today? She was prying. "I'm writing," which was true, deliberately not mentioning my intention to visit '*ITAL at Palats Sportu*'. *Oksana didn't need to know everything.*

I arrived at the *ITAL* exhibition by 11am and was immediately struck by how professional everything looked; in some ways, very un-Ukrainian: smart exhibition stands, fancy spotlights and smartly dressed Europeans. I was swamped with offers of goody bags, sweets and stationery from various Ukrainian students employed by the exhibition centre for the day. Halfway around the hall, near the centre, was an *Eni* stall, the Italian oil company. I began chatting to one of the representatives who was, unsurprisingly, Italian. I was really impressed with their ambitions for Ukraine. While we were talking, I noticed a couple of suited Ukrainians standing nearby, evidently listening in to our conversation.

"Hello, we are representatives of *Naftogaz*, the Ukrainian oil company," they said," maybe you know about us already?". I knew one thing.

"Your offices are on Shevchenko Boulevard," I replied, recalling the trip to *SwissAir* office to confirm mum's ticket.

"We're impressed that you know this," they said. They became very engaged in our conversation about Ukraine's future ambitions and what their thoughts were. They were very happy to see so much European interest and seemed very interested to hear that I, as a young western student, was living in Kyiv.

"Would you like to come and work for *Naftogaz*?" asked the female representative.

"Do you have a business card? I'll certainly think about it. Thank you," I replied.

"Yes of course, we are very happy to hear this," as she passed me her card which I added to the several other business cards I'd received, and the obligatory bag of goodies. I had often thought about a career in the oil industry, it seemed to be very interesting. Ukraine had a wealth of natural resources. As I promised to the lady from *Naftogaz*, I would genuinely consider it. After four hours at the exhibition, it was getting hot and the air conditioning in the building wasn't brilliant. It had been an entirely worthwhile experience and I left with a lot of goody bags full of new stationery equipment which I now wouldn't need to buy.

By early afternoon, the city was hot and I went back to the flat to cool down. Natasha gave me a letter from Poland. I was happy to see it was from Slacky, saying that he was now over the border, in Warsaw. He invited me to come and stay. I immediately replied with a letter by return post, saying that I would if I could, as I'd be travelling back across Poland next month.

By the evening, I didn't feel like a Friday evening at Rock Café. Instead, Natasha and I watched James Bond *'From Russia with Love'* prompting Natasha to ask me if I was a *British spy*.

It was an FA Cup Saturday in England: Chelsea v Middlesborough. Greg was a big fan of Middlesborough and this was the first time 'Boro had ever reached the final. We headed to O'Brien's pub to watch the game. He brought a new teacher with him; Ben, like many others, had just finished his A-levels and was taking a year out ahead of university. He was a Chelsea fan so there was some local in-pub rivalry immediately. Yulia had joined our little gang and she started to enjoy the gentle banter of the group. I liked how she fitted in with my friends and slowly grew to feel more for her as time went on. That afternoon, the Guinness flowed throughout the game and the most vocal fan in the pub, Greg, was enjoying the match for the first minute, at least. Chelsea's Di Matteo scored within forty-three seconds. Sadly for 'Boro, and Greg, Chelsea won *two-nil*. We consoled his grief by spending the evening in New York night club with a happy Ben, Chloe and Yulia. But Middlesborough losing the FA Cup was not to be the only grief we experienced that weekend.

On Sunday morning there was a knock on the door from our neighbour to say that the 'old woman' upstairs had died.

"Please can we use your dinner table for the body?" asked the neighbour freely, as if she were asking to borrow a bowl of sugar. The neighbour also happened to be the dead woman's niece.

"Yes of course," Natasha said, without hesitation. Natasha asked me to clear the dining room table, from which we had eaten many delicious Ukrainian meals, and help carry it upstairs to the dead woman's flat. I had been brought into the flat under false pretences as the niece then asked me to lift her dead aunt so that she could wrap a blanket around her. In all honesty, I had never lifted a dead person's body before and couldn't wait to put her down. The niece was spending so much time trying to organize the blanket in the correct way that I just stood there holding a corpse. She wasn't heavy but I could feel her bones sticking out. The smell in the flat was grim. I was beginning to wonder if she hadn't been dead for a couple of days already. We lay the dead woman in blanket onto the dining table. It would be several months before I would eat off that table again.

"Thank you for your help," she said, "do you know my aunt, as a younger woman, had been an actress on stage and screen." I was suddenly reminded of the beautiful Olga Sumskaya. It struck me that even she would be like that one day. I shook the thought out for my mind and returned downstairs.

After completing my undertaking duties that morning, I decided to skip breakfast, due to the lingering smell of death in my nostrils. Greg phoned to say that he was feeling dejected after the double blowouts of the match and nightclub yesterday.

"Blown out more times than a candle in 'urricane!" he complained down the phone.

"Greg, life isn't so bad," I said," I've been holding a dead actress' smelly corpse this morning." *The comment cheered him up no end.*

Chapter 18. The King, the Godfather and the Guard

26*th* May 1997

The start of summer in Kyiv brings a vibrant and energetic atmosphere to the city. With the warmer weather and the celebrations, Kyivites flocked to the numerous parks and took advantage of the river, relaxing on the beach at Hydropark. Kyivites eagerly embraced the arrival of the season, and the city hosted a variety of fledgling festivals. That weekend was a celebration for *Kyiv Day*, two full days of events, celebrating its *1515th* anniversary. A new statue of *King Yaroslav the Wise* was unveiled next to the Golden Gate in direct view of Korolyuk's balcony.

Korolyuk had taught me that "King Yaroslav was most famous for forming alliances with Scandinavia in the 11th century while simultaneously weakening links with the Byzantine influence in Kyiv," and that," he had constructed the St Sophia cathedral in 1037." More controversially he said that "he had even rejected Islam because his people loved their vodka too much; and was known to have supported the preparation for the *Viking* invasion of Britain in 1066 soon after his death." We had contested this over a vodka in his living room, I'd never heard this perspective of British history before, which didn't mean it wasn't true.

The vibrant café culture, much like Paris, had come alive. Yulia and I, with Greg and the others met at *Golden Gate*. We headed for some pizza where Greg danced with a waitress. When he'd put her down, we made our way down to Europa Square where we watched a fashion show filled with stunning Ukrainian models. We all enjoyed it for different reasons, Greg seemed to enjoy it most of all, before returning to Independence Square for the fireworks.

The following day, Yulia and I walked around the Botanical Gardens before going to a concert at the Arch of Unification and more fireworks. *It had been a wonderful time for us in Kyiv.* As I got to know Yulia, this added to the magic of the holiday atmosphere and the summer nights.

However, by Monday, I found myself in the Mathematics Institute. It was a scorching hot day and the last place in Kyiv I should be, but there was a special reason why I had to be there. Having presented my second research paper in the morning, there was a rumour that *Professor Skorokhod* was in the Institute to give a, so-called, *Kyiv Day Lecture* on his latest results. *I had to see him to believe it!*

At 2pm, the lecture hall on the top fourth floor, *a floor I had never dared venture on to before*, was filling up in huge anticipation of 'the great one' as he was known. Special permission had been given to anyone who wanted to attend, and seating was limited. Skorokhod always gave Korolyuk's students permission to attend his lectures, which was reciprocated by Korolyuk. I sat halfway up the lecture hall near an open window. The bright sunlight created window-shaped shadows across the audience. The hall was sweltering; there was no air-conditioning, only fans turning to push the warm air around. A tangible anticipation hung from the audience, then quiet.

When the mysterious figure of Professor Skorokhod entered the hall, he seemed to emerge from the shadows. No one dared make a sound. I wouldn't have recognized him from the photo I had seen in Korolyuk's apartment but that was taken forty-five years earlier. He entered the lecture hall with a godfather-like presence, his black jacket and sunglasses creating a menacing illusion. He exuded an air of power and authority, his presence commanding attention from everyone around him. As he stepped forward, the glint of his dark sunglasses caught the flickering sunlight, reflecting an enigmatic aura. The sunglasses, reminiscent of those worn by the infamous *Godfather* in 1972, completely concealed his eyes, adding to the air of mystique around him. They shielded his gaze, hiding his true intentions and emotions from prying eyes. Behind those impenetrable shades, he held secrets and knowledge that could shape destinies. His presence spoke volumes without uttering a word, conveying a sense of danger and intrigue. The mere sight of those sunglasses sent shivers down the spines of those that crossed him and earned respect from his allies.

Skorokhod put down his briefcase on the floor to one side of the stage. Silently, he walked to the blackboard and picked up a piece of chalk from the tray.

"You may take notes," he said, without expecting a reply. He began to write. There was a shuffle of notepads and clicking of pens from the audience. He exuded an air of confidence and control. With each calculated movement, like a chess master, he always stayed one step ahead of his adversaries. Those who crossed paths would think twice before challenging him, knowing that behind those shades lay a formidable force. *He had, after all, been a favourite of Stalin!*

What a contrast to his lifelong friend Korolyuk, always open and friendly but with the same sharp, ruthless determination. They were diamonds from the same rock face that Kolmogorov had unearthed so many decades before, under the most difficult of circumstances after the Second World War.

"Please can I ask a question, Professor Skorokhod?" one exceptionally brave member of the audience asked with their hand hanging in the air, as if suspended from the ceiling by an invisible string. Skorokhod stopped writing with his chalk still in contact with the board.

"Is there a problem?" he said, turning his head menacingly towards the floor. There was silence, the audience waiting to hear the question that had disrupted the flow of 'The Great One'.

"Is that the *Boruk-Ulam theorem*?" came the question. Everyone turned back towards Skorokhod as if watching a return winner at Wimbledon.

"Yes. Do you have another question?"

The audience watched the tennis ball slammed back over the net.

"No, thank you," came the response.

The audience murmured with the point won. After the minor inconvenience, Skorokhod turned his head back to his writing. Chalk dust dropped from the board and the equations continued coming. Skorokhod covered three blackboards with complex equations without reference to a single note. With each step he took, his legend grew; he moved like a shadow, leaving a trail of mystery and intrigue in his wake. With each element of each equation, his aura grew, and his name became synonymous with genius in the hall. He came to the end of the third board, banged a big full stop before placing the chalk back into its tray. He turned towards the audience.

"I think that's clear," he stated nonchalantly.

As he stood there, donning those dark sunglasses, the audience stared in awe. They knew they were in the presence of a force to be reckoned with. And as the shadows danced across his face, the mystery behind those sunglasses remained, forever shrouded in darkness.

Professor Skorokhod picked up his briefcase and walked out of the hall to rapturous applause from the audience. The whole experience was dazzling and surreal. The lecture was a masterclass from the greatest showman. The students loved Skorokhod and the legend that he had become.

As I left the lecture hall, Galina invited me to come with her in her office. This was unusual; it felt like I was going to be told off by her for being on the top floor, or in Skorokhod's lecture without her specific permission.

"I have very exciting news for you," Galina said. I had learned to treat Galina with suspicion. So, when she said she had 'exciting' news for me, I took it cautiously.

"I'm all ears," I replied.

"*Excuse, me?*" she replied, again a stern tone to her question.

"I'm listening," I said, not wanting to explain the English saying.

"Skorokhod wants you to proofread his book," she said. On the face of it, that wasn't the exciting news I was expecting. But coming from Galina, I did acknowledge that it was an honour to be considered by Skorokhod.

"*Korolyuk* recommended you," she said. I couldn't imagine anything worse than trying to present Skorokhod's work back to him, especially after the performance I just saw him give. *My instincts were screaming not to trust her!*

"Can I think about it? I'm travelling back to England at the end of June so I won't have that much time," I said with a hint that I might be trying to wriggle out of it.

"That's OK. You can take it with you and fax anything you've completed to me or the Institute." Galina had an answer for everything. There was no way out of this one. It was too hot. *I agreed.*

30th May 1997

The first *McDonald's* opened in Ukraine, at *Lukiyanivska* metro, and Natasha made me promise to take her there to experience the taste of a *Big Mac*. Natasha gave me a Russian lesson: *Colloquial Russian* Chapter Twelve in exchange for a *Big Mac*. By lunchtime, the massive queue of Kyivites, which had been there since early morning, had subsided and Natasha had her *Big Mac*. She loved the new taste, but we both agreed that it wasn't as good as Ukrainian *varenyky*. After lunch, I popped over to the British Consular where Inna had prepared a list of British companies with offices in Ukraine at my request after the *ITAL exhibition*.

"If you make your way to *Mariinsky Palace,* you'll see Boris Yeltsin," she said. Inna knew everything that was going on in Kyiv and she had become a good friend who was able to trust me with the more sensitive diplomatic information.

"He is here for talks with President Kuchma about Crimea," she continued. The Russian fleet still had a naval base in Sevastopol in Crimea and Russia paid Ukraine rent to use it. It was an amicable agreement but sometimes a cause of tension between the two countries.

"Thanks for the tip-off," I responded and hastily made my way from *Arsenalna* to *Mariinsky Park,* headed for the palace. As I arrived, I could see President Kuchma standing at the great iron gates awaiting his guest. It didn't take long for the motorcade of black Mercedes cars to arrive. The Russian flag flew from several cars; only one of them stopped outside the gate and the white hair of Boris Yeltsin appeared. He was larger in stature than Kuchma and they stood together for the national anthem of Russia, standard for visiting dignitaries. *I was interested to know what they agreed about Crimea.*

In the evening, I met with Yulia and others at Jaap's leaving party. Yulia was now firmly part of the *gang.* Jaap was thrilled to hear that I had seen Boris Yeltsin and wished he had been there. As loud and annoying as he could be, he would be missed; the Dutch element of our cosy European group would be no longer with us. *Any member of our group was sorely missed when they departed Kyiv.*

2nd June 1997

Murielle phoned to talk about the French election results. She was a passionate political enthusiast, it seemed, with all elections in any country. She was in the right place. We would continue the conversation at the Rock Café later in the week.

Oksana called immediately after I put the phone down on Murielle. "I have a favour to ask of you. Would you be able write an article about Misha?" This really confused me.

"What would I write about Misha that you don't already know better than I do?" I questioned, trying not to sound ungrateful for being asked.

"I want you to write about your impression of him as a *visiting Englishman.* You have a fresh view of Ukraine, and Misha, that I do not have. Would you, do it?" she pleaded. Again, I was having my arm twisted. Again, I was a little honoured that he would ask me to do this. I agreed. Again.

"When do you need it?"

"Tomorrow," came her reply. I set about writing something but didn't really know what. I put the phone down. The phone rang again. Natasha answered it, she always answered it, it was her phone.

"It's for you," she said, smiling.

"Hello! It's me," said Yulia. "Want to go and watch Germany play?" My heart, as usual these days when Yulia was involved, skipped a beat. Germany was set to play Ukraine on 7th June in the World Cup qualifiers.

"Yes. We can go and get tickets today." I couldn't wait. This was heaven. Apart from being invited to an international game of football by a beautiful girl, I was able to buy the tickets for a few pounds each. And the matches were all being played ten minutes from my flat. I had no doubt that Greg and the others would be coming too. The only problem was, as usual, that I had this article to write for tomorrow. No part of me could say no to Yulia (or the football!).

"OK. Meet me after university and we can go together."

"It's a deal," I said. The phone went down for a third time in an hour. Natasha, still watching this soap opera, smiled. The Germany training session would be Friday evening and if it had been anything like Northern Ireland's last month, I'd be sitting on the bench having a chat with Jurgen Klinsmann.

The following day, I met Oksana for a coffee and gave her the hastily written draft of my article about Misha to read. It was shaky at best. The headline was, 'Misha or not Misha, is there a question at all?' immediately paraphrasing a Shakespearian quote. It read like this; *"Giuseppe Verdi's gaze must surely be shining down upon Kyiv from composers' heaven in the knowledge that his 'Rigoletto' is in safe hands. For having found and settled upon a supremely worthy artist, the performance of tenor Misha, 33, as the duke in 'Rigoletto' has revealed a young man at the height of his career as one of Ukraine's most talented gems".* And furthermore, I recalled the words of the Tomato Man *"to promote Misha is to promote Ukraine",* finishing off with *"What an achievement it would be for Ukraine to have its own homegrown superstar with such a portfolio!"* The full article went on for over three hundred words.

"If it's not what you're looking for, I can re-write it," I said, hoping and expecting that she would say so.

"I love it as it is," Oksana said. She was reading it and re-reading it as if she had just found missing pages from The Bible. She claimed that the first draft was the most instinctive and from the heart; it shouldn't be re-written. Imagine my surprise to see the article printed in the Ukrainian equivalent of the *Weekly Mirror* newspaper the same week. Further surprise then to see it published in the Opera House programmes for all of Misha's performances.

5th June 1997

5th June 1997

I visited Korolyuk for the first time since seeing Professor Skorokhod give his lecture the previous week.

"What do you know of *Professor Skorokhod*," he asked. I assumed Nina had told him about my enquiries during our tea in his absence.

"He looked and behaved like the *Godfather*," I insisted," and that he neither wanted nor cared that anyone understood his theorem."

Korolyuk sought clarification, I felt I had overstepped the mark. He suddenly started laughing.

"One of my favourite films," Korolyuk smiled. "Yes, he has always been smarter than anyone else, at least this is what he tells us." Korolyuk continued to smile as if I had hit the sweet spot in Skorokhod's character.

"Please can you read my speech for a conference next week," he asked. I proofread, and ultimately re-wrote, a speech that Korolyuk was giving to a Swedish conference as a keynote speaker. We celebrated *successful speeches* with a couple of glasses of his secret vodka in his living room.

Suddenly, it seemed the week had ended. After chatting with *Jurgen Klinsmann* at the Germany training session the day before, we were all off to see Ukraine v Germany on a warm summer's evening in Respublikanski Stadium. We sat together as a large European contingent high up on the second tier, drinking *Obolon*. We had organized a sweepstake and chatted with Ukrainians all around us, we were their supporters too and part of their team. It was a great occasion. The score was 'nil-nil', which suited Ukraine, and Chloe who won ten hryvnia.

The following Monday I commenced work on my third research paper, consuming most of the day. Late in the afternoon, I popped over to talk with Inna at the British Consular to talk about the possibility of inviting Misha over to the British Embassy to sing one evening. This had been a suggestion of Oksana's the day before. She wanted to get some sponsorship for him singing a *Concert of European Music* early next year.

"I love the idea," Inna said, "let's make it happen." She suggested we meet in the *Cave Inn* tomorrow evening to discuss it further with the Embassy.

14th June 1997

My 25th birthday which I could've taken as a meaningful milestone in adulthood. For ten minutes, over a strong coffee, I reflected on my life so far and evaluated my experiences, relationships and goals. *I had certainly made it out of the village!*

I wasn't going to dwell, but I felt optimistic about the possibilities that lay ahead and the potential for new and meaningful connections. I woke up with all these feelings in this unique city on this day and was thankful to have taken the direction and the risks that I had.

Everyone's experiences and emotions can differ, and age milestones don't dictate the course of anyone's life. Although I was really enjoying Yulia's company, I didn't want to put a label on our relationship. Luckily, Yulia was laid back and seemed to feel the same. That's why it worked. It's important to embrace personal growth, communicate openly, and follow one's own unique path in matters of the heart. I snapped out of it and began living the next twenty-five years of my life.

My brother was due to arrive at *Borispil* airport later this morning; not the *ideal* birthday present but I needed to meet him otherwise he'd get lost. Before then I had a birthday Russian lesson from Natasha: *Colloquial Russian* Chapter Thirteen. I arrived at *Borispil* as he came through Arrivals ready to go. We had a 'welcome to Ukraine-happy birthday vodka', which he described as 'petrol'. He would be here for a *week* and I had organized several things for him to do while he was here. I'd also warned him he needed to look after himself for half the time. This meant providing him with a map, some geography lessons and basic language training.

"You need to learn the underground system like the back of your hand so you can get back to *Druzhbi Narodiv* by yourself," I implored. His language training included how to say the Russian name for Independence Square which was *Maidan Nezalezhnosti;* he felt comfortable that the only way he would remember it was breaking it down to *'My-mate-Dan-Neza-Leza-and-Steve'*. Whatever worked. He could test it out on Natasha. That evening, we celebrated my birthday in the usual *Rock Café New York* combo.

232

Over the course of the week, my brother was able to visit the Opera House, go for training runs around the Respublikanski Stadium track, swim in the river at Hydropark and attend a few concerts. Of course, he was also introduced to the European gang at the *Rock Café* and drank several litres of *Obolon,* which in his words was *gnat's piss.* He also visited *Koncha Zaspa* to see the Colonel's dacha. This was a particular treat; the Colonel dressed up in full military uniform with medals and took him to the same memorial in the forest, including the photo and a home-made vodka. He felt he'd had the full tourist experience but there was more to come.

Towards the end of the week, Oksana and her mother invited my brother to their flat in *Nyvky* for lunch. I was busy with Korolyuk who had returned from a successful conference in Sweden. Oksana had studied Physics at university as my brother. Indeed, Oksana's mother, I discovered, was also a *Doctor of Physics. So they had lots to talk about.* Having put my brother on the right train at *Teatralna,* I left him to find his own way while I went for an extended meeting with Korolyuk. This would be the last before I departed back home for the summer.

After several hours of working, Korolyuk put down his pen and directed me to his living room; there was a table full of meat, cheese and bread. He pulled out his secret vodka bottle and we drank to the work completed which amounted to two research papers and the start of the third.

"Forward, and only forward!" he toasted before necking our third vodka, one for each paper.

By the time I got back to *Druzhbi Narodiv,* my brother was already there, lying on the sofa as if he'd had a hard day.

"How was lunch at Oksana's flat," I asked. He sat up and began recounting the day.

"I met Oksana at *Nyvky* station and arrived at her flat. When I entered her living room, I saw a table overflowing with food and bottles of drink. I asked Oksana if this was going to be a party and if she was expecting others. She replied 'no' it was just her and her mother joining me for lunch. I sat down and began eating and Oksana's mother just kept my glass continually topped up. I have never eaten so much in my life. All the food on the table was for me. I went through several phases of feeling full and must have had several glasses of brandy."

I smiled as this was so typical of Ukrainian hospitality. My brother continued, "By the time I left at 3pm, that's three hours of eating, I'll have you know, I was ready to burst and staggered back down to the underground station. Finding my way back to *Duzhbi Narodiv* was the easy bit."

He looked to see if Natsha was around. He could see me laughing already.

"When I knocked on the door of Natasha's flat, I came in and found that her table was full of food. She told me to sit down and eat. It was physically impossible." He burped as if proving he was under digestive trauma. "Natasha then told me that Oksana had phoned her after I had left her flat to say that I *hadn't eaten much and would be hungry by the time I returned here*. So, she prepared a table of food which I ate. I feel like the bloody *Vicar of Dibley*." I didn't mention the dead body on the table. I didn't want him to throw up.

I was already in tears laughing. "How have you survived Ukraine for six months and why aren't you twenty stone?", he joked. We both laughed until he released a huge burp and *farted* before rolling on to his bed in his clothes and didn't wake up until the following morning. Farting was a big no-no in Ukraine. *What must Natasha think of my family?* One gets locked in her bedroom and needs saving; another can't handle a traditional Ukrainian lunch, or two.

On the way to *Borispil* airport, my brother said that he was glad he was leaving Ukraine. "I wouldn't have survived another week of eating and drinking," he laughed. He went through Passport Control with some vodka and tins of caviar and back to England. It made me glad that, by the end of next week, I would be home too. *It had been a long time to be away.*

The next two days were a series of farewells. The day after my brother left, I met Greg, Chris and Chloe for a drink at the *Camel* café before they headed off for a trip to Crimea. Then it was farewell to Oksana and Misha until my return in September. The hardest part was saying goodbye to Yulia. We spent some time on *Andriivski's Uzviz* for a glorious summer evening of drink and live folk music. It was a dream. We didn't dwell on the goodbye as we both knew it was only temporary and our feelings for each other were solid.

25th June 1997

Departure day. My train would depart from *Voxalna* at 10:14pm and the trains were incredibly punctual in Ukraine, certainly in comparison to British trains. I was able to spend most of the day getting ready. Natasha had set up a full lunch with her, the Colonel and old-Natasha.

"You won't need to eat again until you get back to England," she said. Well, that was forty-eight hours away.

At 9pm, I arrived at *Voxalna,* with Natasha and Yulia to see me off, still in the hot summer evening sun. I hugged Natasha and she subtly departed when she could see my bags firmly on board the train. Yulia and I had five minutes to say goodbye before the guards shouted the train was about to leave. I took her hand and gave her a long kiss; we'd see each other soon and I'd already promised this to her.

"*All aboard!*" was the cry along the platform for the full length of the giant train. The train slowly heaved its own weight away from the platform. Yulia stood alone at the end of the platform, in tears. I watched as she became more and more distant until she was gone in a haze of heat fumes and glorious dusk.

Twelve hours later, after a good night's sleep, we slowed down to a crawl as we approached the Ukrainian Polish border at a small town stop of *Yagodin*. The Ukrainian border guards boarded the train with the usual machine guns and dogs, requesting everyone hand over passports for checking. I handed mine over.

Ten minutes later "Collect your bags and follow me please!" he ordered, and I came off the train with them. This was scary stuff as I was aware we were in the middle of nowhere; I wasn't sure why they had asked me to get off the train. For a further hour, I sat in a guard house adjacent to the line, becoming increasingly agitated that the train would leave without me, worried I would be left behind, missing my onward connection from *Berlin*.

"I need to get back on the train," I told the guard on duty in the guardhouse.

"You are not leaving this evening," the guard eyeballed me before telling me to sit back down. As I sat and watched the train from the small open side window, the guards shouted for the train to move. That was it: I was left, stuck on the Ukrainian border. After the train had gone out of sight, I watched the space that it had once occupied.

"You need to return to Kyiv," said a new guard that had appeared in the guardhouse. "Your visa is not correct," he continued. *I was in disbelief!*

"But I renewed the visa for a year only a month ago," I implored. I immediately felt that there must have been some mistake.

"Your local police visa to *stay* in Kyiv is in order but your Ukraine visa has expired. You need to return to Kyiv and get an extension," he ordered. I started to realise there hadn't been a mistake, the border guard was trying to help. My Ukraine country exit visa had not been renewed, meaning I couldn't leave the country. I needed to renew it from the visa office back in Kyiv. I had to return to Kyiv on the next train at 7pm that evening, *another twelve hours to get back where I had started.*

"I will miss my train in Berlin," I pathetically implored the border guard.

"We will return your Berlin ticket to you when you return to *Yagodin*," he said calmly. Return to *Yagodin*! That was at least twenty-four hours away. My mind was frantically working out the new timetable. If I was back in Kyiv by 7am the following morning, immediately got my visa then get back on the same train at 10:14pm to get back to *Yagodin*, that was midday on the 28th June.

In the meantime, I had to sit in the guard house until 7pm, apparently with no food. At this point, I was thankful to Natasha who had told me to *fill up* yesterday. More guards entered the room, placing their guns into the rack on the wall; the dogs, left elsewhere, were released when the next train passed through. It was a regimented operation as one would expect. I counted nine border guards in the room with me, all now talking about my nationality. They had a *British* prisoner, temporarily at least.

"What are you doing in Ukraine?" a different guard asked. He turned a chair around and straddled it leaning on the back. I suddenly felt like a prisoner of war about to be interrogated. "Studying at the National Academy of Science," I said, not wanting to create any ambiguity with these guys.

"Are you from London?" More guards entered the room bringing the total to twelve. They all started to listen to our conversation.

"No, Oxford," I replied.

"Oxford University?" he said immediately. This was an area of ambiguity I didn't want to get into since I had talked to Professor Harris.

"No, Reading," I clarified. If any proof were required, I had it in my rucksack.

"Oh, I don't know this place," he said disappointedly.

"Who is your Prime Minister, Major?" he asked, moving into the realms of general knowledge. This had stopped being about me but about their source of entertainment for the rest of the afternoon.

"Actually, it's not John Major. We have a new Prime Minister called Tony Blair," I clarified, conscious I didn't want to be contradicting them too often.

"*Ah, yes of course, Mr Blair,*" he said, looking around at the others for acknowledgement. The conversation was in Russian only; I was glad of the *Colloquial Russian* lessons I'd been having with Natasha over the last six months. I was getting thirsty.

"*You speak Russian?*" he asked.

"I try," was the answer. This amused him. "Please can I have some more water?" I asked. The guard nodded to one of his colleagues to get me some more water. The guards in the room totalled nearly twenty by now. All were standing around listening into our conversation.

"*Queen Elizabeth!*" He said rather randomly. The second guard passed me the glass of water. I downed it straight away, indicating for him to refill it for me.

"Yes, Queen Elizabeth," I acknowledged, swallowing a last gulp of water.

"*Prince Charles!*" His random naming of senior members of the British royal family continued.

"Yes, Prince Charles," I acknowledged. Another glass of water came back to me and I took a sip.

"*Prince Charles and Princess Diana!*" called out another guard in English. This was surreal. Here I was, sitting in a guard house on the Ukrainian border, with twenty guards having a conversation about Prince Charles in Russian. I felt the urge to clarify.

"Princess Diana is divorced from Prince Charles," I said. As soon as they heard the words *Princess Diana*, they all sprang to attention. They were delighted to hear from me that she was now divorced; news obviously doesn't travel well here.

"Princess Diana, beautiful," another guard said in his best English. I had to agree that she was, if only to strengthen the growing relationship between me and my twenty new friends. I was getting the impression that they didn't know any more royals so I thought I would quiz them to keep the conversation going.

"Do you know Prince Philip?" I asked in Russian. They conferred amongst themselves.

"The Queen's husband," another guard said correctly.

"Correct!" I exclaimed. The guard smiled proudly that he had got it right.

"Prince Edward?" I said next. They all looked at each other quizzically.

"We don't know him. Who is he?" The guard sitting on the chair spoke for everyone.

"The Queen's youngest son," I confirmed giving the answer.

"Would you like some lunch?" the guard on the chair asked.

"Yes please." I wasn't feeling hungry but was aware of the extra journey I had to make over the next few days. I needed to keep my strength up until I got out of Ukraine. He indicated for me to leave my rucksack on the bench and to follow him. I was reluctant to be separated from my rucksack but I had no choice. I followed him and most of the other guards out of the building. We walked across a dirt track into the vicinity of a large single storey building, entering a large food hall. There were at least fifty other guards in there.

"Please take a tray and you can have some borscht and bread," the guard indicated. I picked up a tray and bizarrely joined a queue of

guards, queueing towards a hatch to pick up plates of food. I felt conscious that I was becoming a visible spectacle to everyone in the food hall, every one of them uniformed.

Sitting down at one of the long trestle tables, with the same guards I had been talking with, we continued our conversation about the British royals. Thankfully, I was able to keep this going indefinitely.

By 7pm, my train to Kyiv had arrived from Poland. I collected my rucksack and ticket back to Kyiv but without my ticket to Berlin which the guards were holding back. I bade farewell to the most royalist group of border guards in Ukraine and boarded the train. As the train pulled out of *Yagodin* headed East, I thought, if all went well, I would be back here in thirty-six hours.

Natasha got the shock of her life when I appeared at the door of her flat at 8am the following morning, white as a ghost.

"What are you doing here?" she couldn't express her confusion. *"You should be in Germany now!"*

I explained the situation and told her about my twenty new friends on the border. I phoned Oksana straightaway who immediately assisted with my visa renewal. She was equally surprised to see me back so soon and apologised profusely. She felt it was her fault for not checking that all my paperwork was in good order.

"No problem," I insisted. "If it wasn't for this mistake, you wouldn't have a contingent of border guards who know who *Prince Edward* is!"

"This is a story for another day," she laughed.

By lunchtime, I collected the new updated visa from the Ukrainian visa office with the assistance of Inna from the Consular. I was back at *Voxalna* at 10:14pm for the same train that I had taken two days before – *déjà vu* sprang to mind. Although, thankfully, I didn't have to say goodbye to Yulia again; it would have been too much for both of us. I entered a carriage and put my rucksack onto the top bunk.

"Hello Richard! It is good to see you again," said Anna.

"Hi Anna, what a coincidence!" I was glad to see a friendly face on the train. She was travelling back to Germany with her new husband, Tobias. I had met Tobias only a few weeks before in the Rock Café not realizing he had now married Anna. "Congratulations to you both," I said. Anna and I immediately joked about our trip to Odessa, it seemed a lifetime ago.

"You're lucky to still be alive," she insisted," have you been ice skating recently?" Her sense of humour as dry as ever.

The train pulled out of *Voxalna* and I told them both of my experience over the last two days. Twelve hours later, I was back in *Yagodin*. The border guards came onto the train with the same machine guns and dogs. I knew where these guns were stored when not in use and where the dogs were kennelled when not on a lead. The border guard asked for my passport.

"Ah, Richard! Welcome back. Please can I have your passport?"

Tobias and Anna were perplexed as if I were some sort of frequent traveller but understood that I had been there only thirty-six hours before. The next ten minutes were agonizing; I dreaded being pulled off the train again and returned to Kyiv for a second time. Natasha wouldn't recover from the shock another time. Thankfully, the border guard returned with my passport and my Berlin ticket tucked inside. He shook my hand and smiled; several other border guards who I recognized from the royal debate stuck their heads around the corner to say goodbye. *I didn't tell them that I would be back in September.*

This time, I passed through to the train depot on the border and sat as the carriage was lifted to replace the gauge on the undercarriage. The old Soviet train gauge was six percent wider than the European gauge; this process occurred every time a train crossed the border to and from Ukraine. In a strange way, I felt that as soon as the gauge had been replaced, I was home. But it only meant that we were now able to cross the two kilometre stretch of No-Man's Land between the two countries. This was a slow journey of one hour. At last, we arrived in the Polish border town of *Dorohusk*. By 7pm that same evening, we arrived in *Warsaw*. I took the opportunity to have a welcome wash in the shower facilities under the platform. *It wasn't worth calling Slack, this was now about survival.*

Tobias, Anna and I shared a Polish beer and we pulled out of *Warsaw* headed to *Berlin*. I slept until 6am the following morning as we crossed the *Oder River* into Frankfurt. Tobias cracked open another beer.

"Willkommen in Deutschland!" he said and an hour later we were pulling into *Berlin East* station.

"Can I offer you a lift to *Berlin West* station," he offered. I needed to catch my train to Amsterdam from there. I had one hour to get onto the connecting train.

"Let's go!" I replied. We climbed into his Mini parked at the Long Stay and he drove like the *Italian Job* to get me to Berlin West in time. *I could not miss this connecting train.*

"Thank you for all your help," I thanked both Tobias and Anna, as I rushed through the barriers of the station and onto the train with only minutes to spare. It was seven hours to Amsterdam; I could relax at last.

I arrived in Amsterdam at around 3pm. I immediately found a train to Vlissingen from where I could catch a ferry to Sheerness. I had cycled from London to Amsterdam via Sheerness and Vlissingen, in 1992 for a VSO charity fundraiser so knew the route already. However, five years later, I found that upon arrival in Vlissingen, there were *no more ferry services.* So, I headed straight back to Amsterdam. Arriving back in Amsterdam in late evening, I phoned Jaap who lived nearby. I told him of my week so far and he came out to meet me at Amsterdam station, offering me a place to stay for the night.

"It's either that or I sleep on the platform," I said. It was great to see him again and he was generous with his hospitality.

"Welkom in Nederland!" Jaap said warmly. *A friend in need is a friend indeed!* He took me out and we had several pints of *Amstel Bitter* with his friends who were amazed that I was still standing. After a good night's sleep, I departed Amsterdam again at 2pm to *Hoek van Holland* ferry port. At 7pm that evening, I had landed at Harwich ferry port only to jump on a train to Liverpool Street Station. I travelled on to Greenwich station to meet my brother.

"You look like shit," was his gracious welcome home. After a night recovering at his flat, I got on a train back to Oxford. It was late evening on 1st July, Yulia's birthday, by the time I returned home to *Altarnun*, Fifield, in the Cotswolds.

As I enjoyed the simple pleasure of being back, I phoned Yulia to wish her a 'Happy birthday!' and that I had just arrived home. Since waving goodbye to her on the Kyiv platform, I'd travelled for a *hundred and thirty-nine hours.*

"I'm celebrating with my family," she said," I wish you were here too." It was good to hear Yulia's voice and I already missed her. It was a mistake not to leave until after her birthday. As I spoke to her on the phone, I had turned on *BBC Radio 4* to a show about *'recent long journeys'*. I phoned in and recounted the whole story on the radio, there and then. It made me feel better. *It was a great to be home!*

Chapter 19. The Princess and the Attaché

12th August 1997

After returning home for two months, spending ample time relaxing on Burford golf course, or drinking with friends in Oxford, I was glad of the rest and relaxation. The six months in Ukraine had taken a lot out of me. Of course, I'd had regular phone calls and *love letters* from Yulia, but I also stayed in contact with some of my other friends in Kyiv. I'd even had a corresponding postcard from Greg. It read:

"Rich! Now then, mate, how in the name of all that rocks are you? I'm still ripping the quaff of Kyiv, although all my mates are dropping off one by one. Crimea was magnificent, we had such a sorted time, night swimming, guzzling wine, seeing the sights. Sound. As far as gossip goes (we both know you like a bit of squalid scandal Rich, don't deny it). Chris got off with Veronica on his last night, I've got off with the delectable Chloe, even Ben found himself a Ukrainian morsel. Me, Liliya, Chloe, and Michael went to Lviv the other week, went to a hotel for a weekend, and I'll tell you this for nowt – the place is pompously palatial, there's an authentic atmosphere clinging to the tops of the buildings. I just had to 'love it'. There's troops of new teachers now and I'm feeling I'm coming to the end of my time – me, Greg the muss, even I must leave Kyiv, and (unimaginable now) leave Independence Square and Obolon beer. But I've got three weeks left, and I plan to make like a barbarian – carnage an' tha'. Oh yes. When you come back, you'll find the new generation in Rock Café. Where else? Take care of yourself, mate, give us a ring when you get back – from Gregage. I missed them all and when I returned, they would be gone.

I had regularly visited the *Pitt Rivers* library in Oxford to access papers for my own research and made some time to proofread Skorokhod's new book. Professor Harris and I met in the *Lamb & Flag* to discuss Korolyuk and Skorokhod over a pint of Morrells bitter. He was able to provide an outside view which I greatly appreciated.

"When you're in the eye of the storm, it is difficult to determine what is true and what is not," Harris said. "Your insights are fascinating and help us to assess what they are thinking about. I mean really thinking about."

"They are both cut from the same gib but are also different." I wanted to express my own feelings but knew that feelings were unhelpful. "Skorokhod seems more absorbed by his own thoughts than Korolyuk. Korolyuk is open, relaxed and friendly. I sense there is a darker side to Skorokhod; he reminded me of the *Godfather.* The way he dismissed the students in the Institute was impressive."

"You say that Korolyuk's wife said that Skorokhod spends more time in Moscow than in Kyiv?" he asked rhetorically. I confirmed without saying anything.

"Personally, I would be wary of Skorokhod. Don't trust him as you do Korolyuk. You say you haven't spoken with him, yet he wants you to proofread one of his new books." Professor Harris was very clear in his thinking. "Why would he entrust this to you?" He swigged down his Morrells and then indicated to the barman for another two. The barman putdown his tea towel and started pouring.

"Maybe he thinks my English is better than anyone else's in the Institute?" I suggested.

"Or maybe he wants to know how much you understand about Korolyuk's research? Both Korolyuk and Skorokhod were privy to Kolmogorov's work on the *Moscow Defence Theorem*, as we discussed in my office last Easter. I believe a similar work would have been carried out for other major Soviet cities including Kyiv. The other two, Kustjuchenko and Michalevich, both died you say. So, they are out of it," he added.

"What would Skorokhod be interested in, about me understanding Korolyuk's work?" I asked as this was getting deeper and deeper.

"Maybe Korolyuk is concerned that he may need to update the *Kyiv Defence Theorem*. There is a lot of discussion and discontentment about Russia's relationship with Crimea now. Russia is unhappy about the large sums of money that they are paying to lease the base at Sevastopol. They are even unhappier about the prospect of NATO taking hold of some aspects of Ukrainian thought. It is unlikely that the *Moscow Defence Theorem* would ever be required again, but Kyiv could be attacked, theoretically by NATO."

"But surely Moscow wouldn't allow NATO to attack Kyiv?" I stated the obvious.

"No, you're right. But just supposing that it wasn't NATO attacking Kyiv but defending them." I felt that Professor Harris was enjoying this conversation too much. Or maybe it was the beer beginning to talk.

"Well, who would NATO be defending Kyiv from?" I enquired, at least humouring his train of thought.

"Well Moscow, of course," he said, as if this was likely.

"Moscow would never attack Kyiv, surely." I stated trying to bring some grounding to the conversation.

"What if Moscow considered that Kyiv was slipping towards NATO, or the EU?" he proposed. "If the right, or the wrong, leader was in power, then who knows what Moscow might do."

"But... what has this got to do with Skorokhod and Korolyuk?" I asked.

"Maybe Skorokhod thinks that Korolyuk is updating the *Kyiv Defence Theorem* to account for a Moscow attack scenario. Maybe Skorokhod thinks Korolyuk is updating this through you...and he wants to understand the people in contact with Korolyuk." Harris looked at me, trying to wager where I was in this scenario.

"This all sounds like Cold War supposition," I said.

"The Cold War and the Soviet Union both ended, we know this. But the prospect of losing influence over Kyiv troubles Moscow. Indeed, Moscow may be able to tolerate losing influence over Kyiv if they became a truly independent state but it could not tolerate another entity like NATO or the EU replacing them as Kyiv's key sphere of influence," he stated. So, in terms of Skorokhod and Korolyuk, you ask, then Skorokhod is Moscow and Korolyuk is Kyiv," he concluded.

"Can you let me have Skorokhod's proofed document so I can check any traps that he may have set? We both know he is supremely intelligent and will know what you could be capable of understanding with very few facts," said Professor Harris calmly. I had it in my rucksack and passed it to him.

"But what would I do with Korolyuk's defence theorem?" I asked.

"You might bring it to NATO," he said.

"I don't think I would," I stated categorically. "I don't know anyone in NATO."

"You may not know that you have," he warned. "I'll post this back to you before the end of August. In any case, you must return the fully proofread document to Kyiv, to Professor Skorokhod to make him believe you have done it."

31st August 1997

I received the posted document from Professor Harris; I immediately opened it. Inside, paper clipped to the document, was a small handwritten note saying, "Over to you. H." I reviewed his comments and set about replicating Professor Harris' comments in my handwriting. This took me all day and all evening. It was getting late, around 2am, when the news broke on the television that *Princess Diana* had been involved in a car crash in Paris. I put down the document, distracted by the extraordinary events unfolding by the hour. I went to bed thinking that she would be taken to a hospital in Paris and remain there until airlifted back to England. At 7am, I awoke and turned the news on to hear that she had died. I was as shocked as anyone else and watched the news all day, forgetting about the document.

A week later, I found myself standing outside the west door of Westminster Abbey, next to a wall of media, watching the funeral cortege with Princess Diana's coffin resting on a gun carriage roll past me. Walking behind the carriage, were two future kings of England, all within touching distance. The first week of September was a week in most people's lives that were consumed by the news events and little else was noticed.

5th September 1997

With the world's attention on the events in Paris and London that week no attention was given to the significant events in Kyiv. The First Summit in Kyiv between Ukraine and the European Union had taken place. With the European Union already expanding to other Eastern European countries, this would be fundamental to the direction Ukraine could take within the next twenty-five years. The European Commission stated, for the first time, that future EU membership for Ukraine would not be ruled out.

12th September 1997

I flew into *Borispil* from Gatwick Airport to see that the grief in London was replicated in Kyiv. Messages and flowers spoke to British people as they came through Arrivals: 'We love you, Diana!' and 'We miss you, Diana!' The Russian and Ukrainian media were already blaming the British security services for her death. As the only British person in the Institute, this would naturally increase interest in me for a few weeks; *attention I didn't need*.

It was fantastic to see both Yulia and Natasha after two and a half months away. I'd really missed Yulia which made us both realise it was more than a passing romance. Ivan had become a father, Natasha a grandmother and the Colonel a great-grandfather. Natasha and I went into *Kreshchatik* during the day, which had become part building site and part pedestrianized zone over the summer. There was a complete refurbishment of the city centre going on; *I hoped the eerie music would be refurbished.* It was Friday evening, so Yulia and I decided to check out the Rock Café to see who was still around. It became immediately obvious how many of the old gang had returned to England and there was a little hole in our social lives. Greg, Chris, Chloe, Ben, Rory and Lucy were all gone now. But it was great to see that Veronica, Eugene, Luda and all the Ukrainians were still coming. *Time was passing; Kyiv was changing; the world was changing.*

I brought a new Oasis CD called *Be Here Now* which I played repeatedly. The music seemed to represent everything that was going on in those first few weeks of September. A lot of things had changed, but some things hadn't. One of those was Oksana feeling upbeat about promoting Misha as part of a campaign promoting Ukrainian national identity, stemming from my article. My mind briefly flashed back to Professor Harris' last comments about Kyiv and Moscow.

In the first few days back in Kyiv, I completed *Colloquial Russian* Chapters Fourteen and Fifteen to get my spoken language working again. I had also picked up a book from Gatwick Airport which I started reading on the plane. *J. Archer's 'The Fourth Estate'* revolved around journalism. The story explored the power, influence and ethical dilemmas faced by the media industry. In the light of Princess Diana's death, widely attributed to the pressures of the media for a good photo story, I thought it a book well worth reading. Eventually, I recommended work on my third paper.

I had missed Inna at the Consular too. I went to see her at the earliest opportunity to discuss the impact of Princess Diana's death in Ukraine. She was quite emotional.

"It is a huge event in Ukraine because she was the first real international superstar here after the end of the Soviet Union. Everyone is so sad about it, even though she never visited Ukraine,"

249

said Inna. We talked for two hours about these events; I was able to give her a first-hand account of Diana's funeral cortege. In exchange, she gave me real insight into Kyiv's mindset on this matter, and the growing storm around Russia leasing Crimean ports.

19th September 1997

I hadn't seen Oksana since my return but when I did, she was firing on all cylinders. I met her on Kreshchatik at 10am outside the new European Commission building as she wanted to make an appointment with the cultural attaché. She developed the idea of linking Misha as the face, and the voice, of an independent Ukrainian.

"I'm nervous. Do you think they will listen to us?" Oksana asked, clearly frightened of their rejection.

"If you don't ask, you don't get. And besides, Misha is a National Artist of Ukraine. What's not to like? Of course, they will listen to us," I insisted. Oksana appeared to be reassured.

We entered the building and waited patiently in the Reception area for an attaché to materialize. After an hour, a smart young lady appeared and introduced herself.

"Hello, I'm Elizabeth," she announced. She was very executive-looking and assertive, as you would expect someone working as a cultural attaché. "I'm working as the Press Officer for the European Commission in Kyiv. How may I help you?" she continued. Oksana began to describe her plan for a concert involving Misha, as the tenor singer, with the National Philharmonic Orchestra in Kyiv – venue to be determined. He would be singing only songs and arias from European culture to promote it in Ukraine.

"Do you think the European Commission would sponsor the concert?" Oksana enquired. This was possibly bolder than I would have done, but she said it, nevertheless.

"This certainly sounds like a very interesting idea," Elizabeth sounded genuinely interested. "Would I be able to hear some of his arias in order to get an impression of how it could work?" she enquired.

"Of course," Oksana said, suddenly realizing her doubts had been unfounded.

"Maybe we could invite Elizabeth to tonight's performance of *Rigoletto*?" I interjected with the same boldness. "Would you be available at around 7pm?"

"Oh, that's very short notice. Let me check and I'll confirm with you, if that's OK? I can call Oksana and let her know later today."

"Perfect," I said, driving the request forward without conferring with Oksana. She seemed happy with the outcome. We left the building and stood outside the Commission building, initially in stunned silence.

"Wonderful, I can't believe it," bubbled Oksana. "Did that really happen?"

"We should always strike while the iron is hot!" I said. "We need to plan meticulously for this evening just in case she agrees to come. Let's talk over a coffee." We agreed that we must have *Tsar's Balcony* tickets as well as an audience with Misha after the show.

"We need to blow her away," I insisted. "We are likely only to have one shot at this."

After we agreed the plan, and Oksana had phoned Misha to confirm his involvement; we were just waiting for one thing and that was for Elizabeth to phone and confirm.

"We may as well get home," I suggested, "so that if Elizabeth phones you, we can get ready and come out straightaway." Oksana agreed and we parted at *Kreshchatik* station.

After lunch, I received a phone call from Oksana.

"She is coming," Oksana said excitedly. "She has agreed to come and will meet us outside the Opera House at 6:40pm. We can't be late."

"That's fantastic, well done," I said, "make sure Misha knows to sing his best performance as we want Elizabeth to report this very positively within the Commission."

"I've reserved three tickets in my name, which can be collected from the ticket office. I will let Misha know now," Oksana confirmed before hanging up.

Since January, I had seen three performances of *Rigoletto*; four of *La Traviata*; three of *The Queen of Spades*; two of *Nabucco* and two of *Swan Lake*. But none would be more important than tonight's performance of *Rigoletto,* including the opening night with the Professors Korolyuk in attendance.

I arrived at the Opera House foyer by 6:30pm, just in case Elizabeth was early. We didn't want anything to deflect from a smooth-running evening. With the goal of Elizabeth's positive impression of Misha, the prize could be European Commission sponsorship.

"Good evening, Richard," Elizabeth said, as she entered through the main door. "I'm so excited to see this opera."

"Good evening, Elizabeth. I'm so glad you could make it this evening", I responded aware that Oksana had not yet arrived.

"What is the opera about?" she asked. "I've never seen it before." I was glad that I had seen the opera three times and was able give her a brief summary of the story. I found this always helped, especially with opera as often I didn't have the faintest idea what was going on when they were singing in another language.

"It's basically a 16th-century soap opera, but with more singing and less drama. It revolves around the misadventures of *Rigoletto*, a witty and sarcastic jester with a hunchback. He's the king of one-liners and zingers, always ready to mock," I said, pausing to give Elizabeth opportunity to speak.

"Go on," she said.

"But things take a turn for the worse when he gets tangled up in a curse that brings tragedy and heartbreak into his life. I don't want to ruin the ending for you," I interjected, smiling.

"Carry on, otherwise I won't know what's happening," she said.

"Amidst all the chaos, Rigoletto tries to protect his daughter, Gilda, from the smooth-talking *Duke of Mantua,* who's a real ladies' man. That's Misha," I concluded. "I'm not going to tell you the ending."

"Great, I think I've got it," she said smiling. "It sounds like the European Commission."

Surprised by her comment, I laughed. I noticed that Oksana hadn't appeared and must be running late. So I asked the ticket office for two of the tickets under Oksana's name; she would not want Elizabeth to miss the opening scene. Elizabeth and I entered the *Tsar's Balcony;* it never failed to impress. *So far, so good.* We sat down with five minutes to go, then the orchestra started playing and the curtain went up.

By the time Act One had finished, Oksana still hadn't appeared. Act Two came and went and still no Oksana. I certainly couldn't abandon Elizabeth and go looking for her. I had no idea where to look. It would be a diplomatic disaster. Act Three came and went; the show finished.

"That was fantastic," Elizabeth said as everyone stood to applause. The usual cries of '*Bravo, Bravo'* rang out across the auditorium. I thought, 'What happens now? Do I hang around waiting for Oksana?' But that would appear awful in front of the European Commission's attaché. Before Elizabeth could ask, I indicated for us to head out of the *Tsar's Balcony* to the second-floor reception. I opened the door and was surprised and relieved, to suddenly see both Oksana and Misha standing there waiting for us to come out. Misha still in full costume and make-up.

"Welcome to *Rigoletto!*" Oksana said. "We hope you enjoyed the performance." She continued, "Please may I introduce you to Misha, who played the Duke of Mantua."

"Thank you, I thought that was marvellous." Elizabeth beamed, "and I'm very happy to meet you, my Duke." Elizabeth clearly had a sense of humour and occasion.

If that hadn't been enough, two waiters appeared: one with a tray of champagne filled glasses and the other with a tray of nibbles. Oksana had laid on the silver service for Elizabeth; that's why she hadn't appeared for the show. She was busy getting things organized for afterwards. We drank champagne until there was none left.

"I must go." Elizabeth said, "otherwise you will be carrying me home."

"Oksana, I will give you a call by the end of next week to confirm plans," she said optimistically.

As soon as Elizabeth had left the Opera House, we congratulated each other for the parts we had played. Misha thanked us and departed to his dressing room where he still had to de-make up.

"I knew you would look after her," Oksana said. "I thought she would enjoy your company more without me."

"Very shrewd," I replied, "I was getting quite worried there for a second but knew that you would want me to keep the show moving."

"That's why we are such a great team," she said, the champagne talking. I signalled my intention to leave and go home too.

"I look forward to your telephone call tomorrow morning," I said sarcastically and left; Oksana turned towards the direction of Misha's dressing room.

The following week, Professor Korolyuk was away in Romania so I spent most of my time in the Institute, working privately. I wanted to hand in the proofreading for Skorokhod before Korolyuk returned. The first day back, Galina told me that I was able to enter the Institute unaccompanied by permission of Professor Samoilenko, the Institute Director. However, I was still not allowed to be unaccompanied beyond the second floor. I entered the Administrators' Office to reacquaint myself with the staff. Galina appeared to be friendlier since my return, which I welcomed, but I still had my suspicions about trusting her.

"Welcome back, Richard," Galina said. I thanked her and spoke with the two ladies in the office, hoping to elicit a response, but all I got was a smile and a nod. Clearly Galina was still firmly in control.

"Please can you work in Professor Skorokhod's department for any work associated with Professor Skorokhod's book," she said. "I understand you have provided the English proofreading for it." This surprised me as I had only ever received instructions from Oksana or Korolyuk up until now. I realized that I hadn't mentioned Galina's request to Oksana. Given everything that had been going on in June with the ITAL conference, Misha's article, my brother's visit, then the long journey back home, I'd completely forgotten to mention it to her.

"This is Alan, from Professor Skorokhod's department," Galina said. "He will show you where to go." *Who's Alan? No one in Ukraine was called 'Alan'.* I turned around to see a young man, slightly younger than me, standing behind me. *When did he enter the room?* I was beginning to feel slightly unnerved but let Alan show me where to go. If Professor Samoilenko had given the green light, then all must be fine.

Alan was a first-year research student, like me. And he was very friendly and talkative. He took me left down the corridor and then right down the parallel corridor to the end. There was a small study, only just large enough for two seated people. Alan sat down at the far end, and I sat at the desk nearest the door. Like all the rooms, this one smelt slightly stuffy. None of them had good ventilation and there was no air conditioning.

"Are there many *'Alans'* in Ukraine?" I asked. It was a serious question that had been bothering me on the walk to the room.

"No, not many. My Mum just liked the name. It's Scottish," he said, taking no offence. Yes, I thought so. It was most bizarre and he made me smile whenever I called him by his name. He was a very likeable chap.

For the rest of the week, I typed up the English proofreading that Professor Harris had sent me. I just had to trust what he had written. I slotted in the floppy disc and worked off that directly. I was wary of copying the disc to an unfamiliar computer. Alan worked quietly on the other computer, on a research paper of his own. By the end of the week, the work for Skorokhod had been completed.

26th September 1997

Oksana phoned on Friday evening. Natasha answered, smiled and gave me the receiver. We had just finished *Colloquial Russian* Chapters Sixteen and Seventeen.

"You caught me just before I was heading out for a beer," I said before she had a chance to speak.

"I have some news for you," Oksana said. "The European Commission have agreed to sponsor our concert." I could sense she could hardly contain her emotions.

"That's great news," I said. "What did Elizabeth say?"

"She gave Misha a glowing report and recommended that the European Commission approve Misha as a cultural partner...the Commission agreed."

"Amazing," I said. "So what is the timeline for the concert?" I felt strongly that Oksana was making it up as she was going along.

"9th February in the Hall of Columns at the National Philharmonic Concert Hall on Europa Square," she reeled off. So maybe she wasn't making it up.

"Wow. But that's only four months away," I said.

"We have a lot of work to do in the meantime. We need to confirm the orchestra, the conductor and the presenters," she replied, with purpose. "Elizabeth has requested that *Amazing Grace* be included somewhere on the concert song list; please can you order this music sheet from London. Misha will need to learn it as he learned *Strangers in the Night*."

"Not a problem," I said obligingly. I was delighted for Oksana as she had worked extremely hard to secure this partnership. *I just wondered how the Russian Embassy would view this alliance.*

The weekend was a combination of watching the *Ryder Cup* golf and going out to *Derek's Bar* which was a new bar nightclub at *Ploscha Lva Tolstogo*. Derek was an American entrepreneur who had brought big money, and big personality, over to Kyiv as he could see commercial opportunities opening everywhere. Yulia and I, and several other Ukrainian friends enjoyed the new club scene emerging in Kyiv, and *Derek's Bar* made a change from *New York*. After a late night which led to a long lie-in on Sunday morning, I was thrilled to see Monty winning the *Ryder Cup* for Europe in Spain. *Maybe one day Ukraine will have a home-grown player in the European team.*

On Tuesday, I went into the British Consular to chat with Inna about the weekend's events, including the concert developments with the European Commission.

"We will give you any support that you need, Richard. It looks like a very exciting project for Ukraine." Inna was invaluable to be able to offload any thoughts, and she would always give something in return.

"In the meantime, can I offer you the Newcastle United training schedule we received from St. James' Park this morning?" She smiled, "it's the European Cup group match fixture." *I loved Inna for this.*

"That would be brilliant, thank you," I said. I supposed that if there was no issue handing out the Premier League training schedule in advance, then the players also didn't need any security around them during training sessions. Training was at Dynamo Stadium the following morning at 10am; the game was 9pm in Respublikanski Stadium. I turned up at the training session at 10am sharp to see an astonishing array of Premier League footballers at close range, even standing on the training pitch with them. Unfortunately, Alan Shearer was injured so was missing from the squad. *Newcastle TV* were there commentating at the training session. I even overheard them talking about the oppression of Dynamo Kyiv under Soviet times. I managed to speak with the great John Barnes, Keith Gallespie, Faustino Asprillo, Stuart Pearce and the legendary *Kenny Dalglish.*

"What the hell are you doing out in Ukraine?" asked Kenny, *this sounded familiar*, but he was thankful, nevertheless, that I'd come to support them. It was a cracking 'Two-All' draw at the Stadium later that evening. This was followed by a few drinks at the *Rock Café* with Luda, Veronica, the *Frenchies* and a couple of the new English teachers, *fresh out of the box.*

The following morning, I received my regular post from Dad. Every fortnight, without fail, he would send me some newspaper clippings of the stories that he thought I would find interesting with a personal cover note. I treasured these notes and missed both Mum and Dad; I felt far away from them. *However, talking to the Premier League players did make me feel at home.*

7th October 1997

There was a lot of coming and going. At the British Embassy, Fraser was leaving Ukraine and heading to a new posting in Singapore. He invited Inna and me to his drinks do at *The Cave Inn*. We talked about how cooperation with the Ukrainian army had been restricted; Fraser suspected it was a condition from Russia after Yeltsin's visit to discuss Crimea. The Colonel and Old-Natasha had gone to the Carpathian Mountains for some rest and relaxation. Professor Korolyuk returned from a week in Romania. Oksana came back from Moscow, where Misha was performing at the *Bolshoi Theatre* and had been a huge success, all good for the European Commission concert sponsorship. The first phone call I received from Oksana, rather than basking in Misha's glory, was very agitated.

"I understand that you have been working in Skorokhod's department. Is this true?" she asked. There was no point in denying it. I was working there with Alan as a witness.

"Yes. I spent a week there typing up the English proofing for Skorokhod's new book," I openly declared, eager to understand the cause of her agitation. "As I recall it was Galina who passed me the Skorokhod request in the first place."

"*Skorokhod is not to be trusted,*" she warned, "and you answer only to Korolyuk. You should have passed any request, seemingly from Skorokhod, or any notes on Skorokhod's book back to me." I had to ask, "What is the issue here?" I knew the question was likely to fuel the fire.

"The issue is that there are still members of the Institute who would have you out because of where you come from. Your movements always need to be controlled and, by working in Skorokhod's department, we don't know who may have viewed your notes. Who was with you?" she asked.

"Alan," I replied. I had to bite my tongue otherwise I would laugh and now was not the time.

"Did you stay with your computer and notes all the time?" she enquired.

"Generally, yes," I said, "possibly leaving them unattended for five minutes on the odd occasion to get a drink of water or fresh air from the smell of the study."

"Who said you could work with Alan?" She started to interrogate me.

"Galina, of course," I said. The phone went quiet.

"OK Richard, I understand," she said, "They are getting closer than I had thought. Alan and Galina both work for Skorokhod."

"Closer to what? I thought she was the Head Administrator working for the Institute," I asked naively.

"They are trying to trip you up, to force you out," Oksana said. "Remember the vote was only three to two in your favour. Only Professor Samoilenko or Professor Goosack need to abstain and you will be out."

"I still don't understand what they could've found in my notes that could've been incriminating," I pleaded.

"Did you save anything on the hard drive while you were sitting with Alan," she asked.

"I could've done," I said. "Certainly the proof reading for Skorokhod." And that was the end of the conversation. Nothing conclusive apart from understanding that there was a clear paranoia between the Korolyuk and Skorokhod camps. After that exchange, I paid particular attention to what Galina may be asking me to do and with whom. *I wouldn't fall into that trap twice, especially with anyone called Alan.*

21st October 1997

Professor Korolyuk invited me into the Institute to meet with him and a representative from Bern University he met in Sweden. Coincidently, his son was visiting from Rome. Bern University had offered to give the Institute a dozen computers. We all ate lunch together. I saw how Korolyuk often used his foreign conferences to request technical assistance for the Institute in Kyiv. The Institute was becoming linked to many European universities. Korolyuk and Korolyuk Junior were both real ambassadors for Ukraine travelling around Europe like European footballers.

I had come to value the football, especially the European Champions League games at Respublikanski Stadium, to escape from some of the swirling politics going on around me. This evening, I was watching Barcelona FC in a training session and the following day I was to go and watch them play. It had become normal to do this now and tickets were about twenty hryvnia, or five pounds. In England, tickets would be over a hundred pounds, that's assuming I could get hold of a ticket. I even found that I could watch the first half of the game at the flat and get into Respublikanski Stadium during the half time interval. The return leg in Barcelona, two weeks later, would be a defining moment; *Dynamo Kyiv thrashed Barcelona 'Four-Nil' with a hattrick by Andriy Shevchenko.*

The name *Shevchenko* was becoming known around the world because of what he could do to teams like Barcelona. At the same time, the Ukrainian poet and writer with the same name was growing as a symbol of Ukraine's own heritage. I mentioned Shevchenko to Yulia several times and she had the sense of humour to give me a present: *a book of verses by Taras Shevchenko.*

"This Shevchenko is more important than that Shevchenko," Yulia joked. Yulia was smart and was studying hard at her university; she was a top student, she wanted to be a lawyer. Her studies had now been interspersed with her modelling training and she even had modelling exams. This seemed a popular alternative route for a lot of Ukrainian students of her age. It sounded like an enviable lifestyle, but it was not; it was stressful and a nasty business. There was an underlying anxiety in Ukrainian student life that their futures were insecure or unstable, but they held out great hope. *It was a time of great hope and optimism.* The students were typically smart, savvy, multilingual and aware of the world they were entering, using every single resource to get the experience they needed to get ahead. There was a drive from this generation of young Ukrainians. The new independent Ukraine found itself in a similar position: uncertain and anxious, with great hope and ambition for the future. While Russia, under Yeltsin, stewed in its own societal chaos, they seemed to be indifferent to Ukraine, *except when it came to matters around Crimea.*

31st October 1997

It was Hallowe'en; this required a bit of explaining to Ukrainians for whom it wasn't a traditional celebration. Younger Ukrainians embraced the holiday for the sake of the Hallowe'en costume extravaganza. I managed to get hold of several pumpkins from the local market which I then carved in the kitchen, producing some vaguely scary faces. These were of huge interest to Natasha and the neighbours.

Yulia and I, and other Ukrainian friends and English teachers, decided to go back to *Derek's Bar* where we had been a month earlier for the opening. Derek had themed the night, of course, and most people had come in something that at least acknowledged it was Hallowe'en. We all had a great night.

It was after midnight and on the way back to Yulia's house we rode the metro back to *Kharkivska*. The carriage was empty apart from us and two other girls, who had also come from a nightclub, sat right at the other end. At *Palats Sportu,* four young men got onto the same carriage near the two girls, clearly showing signs that they'd been drinking. They immediately began intimidating the girls verbally, then physically assaulting them. One girl hit the Communications Button above her seat and screamed that they were being attacked. I felt Yulia's hand grip mine downwards, as if to say, 'don't get involved'. But this was getting uncomfortable, and the girls were now screaming and crying. *What could I do?*

The train slowed to the next station *Klovska*. The doors burst open and two men in black head-to-toe uniforms entered the carriage and pulled the men off the girls by their hair. The attackers had no chance. The men in black were members of the *Berkut*, licensed to freely roam the metro system, maintaining law and order under any circumstances.

"*Berkut* can kill you without repercussion," Yulia said. "Best not to get involved. They are very tough."

I recalled that the man at the snowy tram stop had told me that *Berkut* had been introduced into Kyiv by President Kuchma to clean up the city. *They were cleaning up the city by making a mess of their victims.*

The men lay in a pool of blood on the station platform, one of them with his nose shattered and hanging off his face. His face now looked like a Hallowe'en mask, slightly distorted like one of my pumpkin carvings. Three of them were unconscious on the platform floor. The two *Berkut* had taken the men down with efficient kick-boxing punches in the brief time that the metro train had paused at the station. The train doors closed and continued through *Druzhbi Narodiv* as if nothing had happened. I was becoming more accustomed to incidents like this and was becoming more aware all the time. I dropped off Yulia at *Kharkivska* and returned to *Druzhbi Narodiv* and straight to the flat. This episode was horrific and demonstrated the beauty and the horror that Ukraine could dish up; *it was a Hallowe'en to remember.*

12th November 1997

It was Sunday. Natasha and I spent the day reading *Colloquial Russian* Chapters Eighteen and Nineteen. In the evening I was accompanying Professor Goosack and his wife to the Opera House to watch *Rigoletto*. We had officially never met and so Korolyuk asked me to accompany him, as one of my sponsors, it may be important. Korolyuk was also aware that I had seen *Rigoletto* half a dozen times and I was a bit of an expert. Strangely, I didn't even know what Professor Goosack looked like. I was beginning to think that he wasn't real, although I only knew him as *the other professor who had voted me into the Institute.*

Upon arrival at the Opera House, I instantly recognized him from somewhere but couldn't recall from when or where. Both he and his wife were good English speakers, so we were able to chat quite freely about the opera and life in Kyiv. He was great company with a similar outlook to Korolyuk, and we enjoyed the evening. I could understand why they were good friends. Professor Goosack enquired whether I would be staying in Ukraine for New Year.

"Not this year. I've done it once and that almost killed me," I joked. This reminded me to book my flight home. I certainly would not be returning on the train.

Only after we had departed the Opera House, as I was walking toward the *Golden Gate* metro, did I suddenly remember where I had seen him. He was the man who had passed me on the stairs the day I first visited Korolyuk's apartment; I'd guessed he'd come out of Korolyuk's apartment. That was Professor Goosack. I wonder what they had been meeting about, given that academics would usually meet at the Institute to discuss their ideas. The following day, I booked my return flight for the 14th December which gave me about a month to try and complete my third paper with the plan that I could then present it in the new year.

4th December 1997

I met Korolyuk at the Institute and we discussed the finalization of my third paper. He considered that it would not be finished until the new year as the research had taken us into a different *strange* direction; he needed to think and apply some new considerations including a new layer of equations until then. He advised me that next week he would be busy chairing the Presidential elections for the *National Academy of Science*. As such, this was likely to be the last time we would meet before my return in January. We had the customary glass of vodka in his study and wished each other a 'Happy New Year'. He asked me to drink with him to a friend of his from the Red Army who had died that day. I would miss Korolyuk and his warmth and humanity; I had got used to his mentorship and friendship since returning after the summer. Our understanding of each other and the growing realization of our joint research was bringing us closer every day, turning him into a grandfather figure, certainly someone in Ukraine who I totally trusted and relied upon.

Afterwards, I met Yulia at *Druzhbi Narodiv;* she was supporting some of her friends who were taking part in the *Miss Student Kyiv* competition in the *Hotel Rus.* This was part of the larger *Miss Ukraine* competition that was taking place over a couple of days. Her older sister was a young reporter working for one of the Kyiv newspapers and had managed to get us both press passes for the front row seats. Yulia and I had fun naming them based on their outstanding attributes and appearance. Politically incorrect would have been an understatement but in Ukraine, then, it seemed to be the wholly acceptable norm. There was *Twiggy, The Pyjama Twins*, *Skin 'n' Bones*, *Top Heavy* and *Miss Angry* to mention but a few. The competition was intense. Miss Angry became less angry when she won. Afterwards, Yulia invited me to come backstage with her to visit some of her colleagues who worked at the same agency. As we entered backstage, it was a case of not knowing where to look. Some models were still in a state of partial undress. I ended up looking at my shoes a lot. Yulia thought it cute that I was embarrassed to be in such an environment.

Yulia and I were getting closer all the time; we were both aware that we would miss each other over the Christmas and New Year period. Ukraine had started to become everything to me, and I would be eager to return as soon as I could.

The following morning, Oksana phoned to say that she and Misha had returned from another successful trip in Moscow.

"Misha will become a member of the Bolshoi Theatre," she told me excitedly.

"Congratulations," I responded. "Is that good news for his new association with the European Commission and the concert in February?" I continued.

"That is a good point, Richard," Oksana's tone changed. "I would like you not to mention this to Elizabeth or the European Commission as it may complicate the relationship. When any artist is offered membership of the *Bolshoi Theatre,* it would be career-ending to turn it down." She paused, then further justified what she had said, "Indeed, the European Commission want to develop Ukraine's identity as an independent European nation, with Misha. That may be compromised if he is seen as a singer who is not wholly affiliated with Ukrainian institutions."

"I understand, of course. I won't say anything," I said, imagining that it was unlikely that I would ever be able to divulge such sensitive information. Things were getting complicated and I wondered how much deeper I could go into the politics of the Kyiv musical conservatoire. *As it would turn out, a lot deeper.*

"One more thing, Richard, another favour if you can?" she asked. "Would you be able to visit the Opera House tonight and accompany the team from the Finnish Embassy who are going to see *La Traviata.* Misha wants you there as you were able to provide him with the DVDs, which really helped him. You can collect tickets from the entrance as usual. Please also put any drinks you have in the bar on Misha's account," she insisted.

"Agreed, I'll be there," I said. Oksana was relying on me now as her Opera House attaché, a role that I found a lot of fun. Clearly, she was raising awareness amongst the Kyiv foreign political community ahead of Misha's European Music concert in February. This became a regular occurrence with teams from different embassies. I had become quite the attaché. I was happy to act on her behalf, *especially if it meant free drinks at the Opera House bar.*

After the conversation with Oksana, I sought sanctuary in the draw for France's World Cup 1998. England would play Romania, Columbia and Tunisia. Sadly, Ukraine did not qualify, *so the world would not see Shevchenko or Ukraine just yet.*

10th December 1997

I had less than a week left before returning home for Christmas. Oksana had travelled with Misha to sing a concert in Crimea, so they were both away. I would not see them again before New Year. Crimea was risky for Misha and he had nothing to gain by going there, I felt that it was political. *Oksana was playing politics, she had to be careful.*

"It is important that Misha visits all parts of Ukraine," Oksana insisted before they left. I wondered whether it was Misha or Oksana driving this current concert schedule. Either way, they both were aligned with each other's goals.

In the morning, I visited Inna at the British Consular and she processed my latest exit visa. *There would be no one hundred and thirty-nine hour journey via Yagodin this time!* We had coffee while discussing the latest news events about President Yeltsin who had reportedly fallen ill with a respiratory virus.

"I'm worried about the consequences if he doesn't recover," she said. "There are some worrying possibilities who could take over."

"Let's hope he recovers then," I replied knowing what she was referring to. There was a fear in Ukraine that there were Russian politicians who were angry about the end of the Soviet Union and would reverse it if they could get into the Kremlin. Natasha and I completed *Colloquial Russian* Chapter Twenty. *Done.*

14th December 1997

Today, I was flying back home. The first snow fall of the winter had been particularly heavy. Now all Kyiv was covered in a thick layer of snow. It looked magical again.

The last few days had been all about catching up with friends to wish them a 'Happy Christmas' and a 'Happy New Year'. I was a sad not to have stayed. I visited Sveta at the British Council, Inna at the Consular and Fraser for the last time at the Embassy. Natasha and I went to see

Carmen at the *Ivano Franka Theatre,* near the Rock Café, which was beautifully decorated in snow and Christmas lights. She loved it. *I still hadn't found out about Ivan's father, it wasn't important for me.* Yulia and I went out together the following evening, my last. We had dinner and a few drinks. This goodbye was even more painful than the *train platform farewell* a year before but I knew I'd be back.

Yulia and I arrived at Borispil airport at midday for the usual afternoon flight. The temperature had dropped to a cool minus twenty-three degrees Celsius. After having purchased a couple of bottles of vodka for Christmas gifts, we said our *goodbyes* and I departed Ukraine for the third time with a sense of sadness. However, I was confident I would return in January after a rest and with a growing sense of purpose, not only to conclude my work with Korolyuk, but to help drive forward Oksana's and Misha's European mission for Ukraine. *I understood it had become my mission too.*

Chapter 20. The Concert

30th January 1998

I left my brother's flat in Greenwich for Deptford station at 8am, headed for Gatwick airport. It was a bleak icy morning but I knew this was not as cold as Kyiv would be. Six hours later, Yulia and I were hugging at Borispil Airport. I was right; it was minus ten degrees and heavy snow there. We had a drink at the airport then travelled straight to *Druzhbi Narodiv* in a taxi where Natasha greeted me with the same warmth. Ten minutes later, Oksana appeared. They had set up a welcome party for me and it felt amazing to be back. I pulled the *Best of the Lightening Seeds* CD, a Christmas present, out of my rucksack and played it on the player in the flat. After the party, Oksana pulled out another CD from her bag and began talking about the *Concert of European Music* which was now only nine days away.

"The European Commission would like Misha to sing to Beethoven's 9th Symphony at the end of the concert," Oksana began. "Elizabeth said it was a requirement of the Commission as it is the anthem of the European Union." She removed the *Lightening Seeds* CD and replaced with her CD and pressed 'Play'. Beethoven bellowed out from the speakers.

"They are getting serious," I joked. "If the anthem is requested, it usually means it is a formal event sanctioned by Head Office in Brussels. They will be asking to fly the European Union flag next!"

"The European Union flag has already been agreed and formalized. It will be placed above the orchestra at centre stage and below the choir balcony," Oksana confirmed. *This was real.*

269

"OK, so we are dealing with a major European Commission event now," I commented. "Do we have any important guests coming?" Clearly a lot of preparatory work had been done by Oksana and Elizabeth between the time Oksana and Misha had returned from Crimea and now.

"Yes, all the invitations went out to all the embassies in Kyiv before New Year," Oksana said as a matter of fact.

"Any responses?" I asked, clearly not expecting the answer that I received.

"Yes. They responded and all will send a representative," Oksana said gleefully. This was marvellous. Oksana had performed a diplomatic miracle.

"So, the concert is ready to go," I said, joining Oksana with a gleeful smile.

"Not quite. We are seeking an English language speaker to co-host the concert," Oksana said in a conciliatory tone. "The European Commission had suggested a name but this was rejected by the Musical Conservatoire."

"On what basis?" I asked quizzically.

"On the basis that the person had no real understanding or experience in Kyiv or of Ukraine," Oksana responded. "So the Conservatoire asked them to find someone else."

"You mentioned that this was the 'co-host' so who is the other 'co-host'?" I asked. Before Oksana could say the name, I had worked it out.

"*Olga Sumskaya* will be the Ukrainian language host," Oksana confirmed. Oksana looked like she was about to burst with the excitement. I knew it; she had engineered the meeting with *Olga Sumskaya* at the film premier in May for this purpose. And now the most famous actress in Ukraine would be co-hosting our European concert. This was getting better and better.

"That's fantastic! How did you manage that?" I asked.

"Misha managed to convince her that it would spread her name to a wider European audience; that it would be good for her career, so she said 'yes'," Oksana said.

"Very clever," I responded. "So, just the small matter of the other co-host to find."

"Yes. The problem is that the European Commission and Musical Conservatoire both have to agree as the main interested parties," she clarified. "But Elizabeth and I are working on it."

"How is Professor Korolyuk?" I asked. I had not spoken with him for nearly two months.

"Korolyuk is ill now," she said with a sad tone. "It could be pneumonia which would be very dangerous for him."

"That's terrible. Where is he now?" I asked. I would visit him if I could. I was immediately concerned for his wellbeing and ultimately our work together. What would happen if he died? *There would be no formal reason for me to remain in Ukraine.*

"He is in his apartment being looked after by Nina and a nurse. I saw him two weeks ago and he looked very ill."

I'd only been in Ukraine for six hours and already I had been bombarded with a whole raft of news which I wasn't expecting. Great news about the concert but terrible news about Professor Korolyuk. The party finished at 10pm and I took Yulia back to *Kharkivska* metro before returning to my flat and straight to bed. It had been a long day.

1st February 1998

Sunday morning and the phone rang after breakfast. It was Oksana. These days it would usually be Yulia, but that day it was Oksana.

"Please can I ask you to help write some speeches for the concert next week," she asked immediately.

"Who do you want me to write speeches for?" I asked, rather confused by her request. *I wasn't a speech writer.*

"The Ukrainian representative for the European Commission in Kyiv might make a speech," she said, "and it would be good if he had a speech to pull out if required."

"You do realise I'm a Maths student not a political speech writer, Oksana?" I stated, slightly annoyed at some of the requests coming my way. *What would she be asking of me next?*

"Yes, but you wrote such a good article about Misha, in which, you first mentioned the phrase *'to promote Misha is to promote Ukraine',"* Oksana said. "And Professor Korolyuk told me you wrote his speech for the Sweden conference. That is speech writing."

"OK you've convinced me. I'll help you write some speeches, but I need to know exactly the message he wants to convey," I said, fully aware that the water was generally now lapping at my neck. Soon it could be above my head.

2nd February 1998

I spent the morning in the Institute, re-registering and generally making my presence known to the Administrators' Office. I wished the two administrators a 'Happy New Year' and they replied without too much fear in their voices.

"Professor Korolyuk is still very ill and has not been in the Institute since new year," Galina barked from her desk. "And everyone is worried about his health."

"Thank you for letting me know," I replied. "Oksana already told me."

"Where is she these days?" Galina stopped typing to hear my response.

"We haven't seen much of her since before New Year." Not wanting to drop Oksana into any trouble, I suggested she might be travelling. Galina didn't flinch.

"If you need a computer to work on, please use Skorokhod's department," Galina advised robotically. I was not going anywhere near Alan's office again, even if Korolyuk seemed to be on his death bed.

"Thanks, but I'll work from my flat until he recovers," I responded politely, knowing that Galina was still working for the powers that didn't want me there. The snow was falling heavily outside. People were making their way home from the office at lunch time, just in case traffic got stuck.

When I entered the flat, Natasha was also coming in; we knocked boots together to get the snow off. It was heavy, deep snow so we hurried in to have a hot chocolate to warm up. The phone rang. It was Oksana.

"Richard, you have been selected to co-host with Olga," was Oksana's opening line. The words didn't really make sense, so I sought clarification as I knocked the lumps of ice from my gloves.

"Sorry, did I hear that correctly," I queried.

"Yes, Richard. Nina suggested your name and was approved on behalf of the Musical Conservatoire. Elizabeth confirmed your name after an approval from another attaché called 'Sylvia'," she said.

"Who is Sylvia?" I replied with a question.

"She used to be a Cultural Attaché for the UN. She recalls you speaking to her school last year," Oksana said. "She moved across to the Commission just after New Year. Elizabeth and Sylvia both approved you on behalf of the Commission. A French attaché, called Murielle, vouched for you too. Which means the Conservatoire and Commission are in full agreement on one person. That's you!" Oksana was about to burst again. I did recall Sylvia as the lady who met me in the UN school when I saw the 'snow babushka'.

"Elizabeth had a small concern that a representative from the UK could pose more of an issue than other member states by appearing on a public stage in Ukraine. But this was considered a minor concern. So you were approved."

"That's very kind of them," I agreed, understatedly.

"The next question is, do you feel that you can do it?" Oksana asked. "You will have a script and you just follow Olga's lead."

"I suppose I could," I agreed. "After all, I have a whole week to rehearse," I said sarcastically.

"That's the spirit," Oksana replied. "Oh, but one thing. The British Embassy need to formally agree to your participation as it would be broadcast across the whole of Ukraine."

"Sorry, I thought you just said it would be broadcast across Ukraine? On radio?" I queried.

"On television," Oksana confirmed.

"So, let's get this right. You are saying that I will be co-hosting a Concert of European Music sponsored by the European Commission, with Olga Sumskaya, the hottest property in Ukraine, to promote Misha with the aim of promoting Ukraine. All on television. Did I get that right?"

"Not quite. It would be *live* television broadcast," Oksana confirmed. I dropped the phone. Then hurriedly picked it back up again.

"Live television! That's impossible and I don't even have a proper suit. I also need a haircut," I proclaimed.

"That's not a problem. We can borrow a suit from Taras Stonda, one of the other tenor singers from the Opera House. We can easily arrange a haircut for you on the day of the concert." *Oksana had an answer for everything.*

9th February 1998

The previous day had been my parents' 29th wedding anniversary. Times had changed. In 1969, Leonid Brezhnev was the leader of the Soviet Union. President Nixon sent a squadron of eighteen B-52s, loaded with nuclear weapons, to race to the border of Soviet airspace to convince the Soviet Union that he was capable of anything to end the Vietnam War. Today, my parents' son would be standing on a stage in the former Soviet Union to promote a former Soviet state with an identity that was not aligned with the former Soviet state of Russia. "There would be some backlash," Elizabeth had warned me of that, "The European Commission were ready and would be there to support me". It had been *a riddle wrapped in a mystery inside an enigma,* in the words of Mr Churchill's, how I had arrived in this position; but in this position I was. This had been signed off by Inna from the British Consular and Fraser in the British Embassy, the final approval for a British person to speak in public on behalf of Ukraine and the European Commission.

I woke up at 7am, ate some of Natasha's delicious chicken casserole for breakfast while watching a bit of the *Winter Olympics* in Japan. Hastily, I made my way on to the underground. I had to get to *Nyvky* metro station to meet Oksana and I was late for my hair appointment. We arrived at a hairdresser friend of hers in her apartment block, surrounded in deep snow drifts. The hairdresser friend was Antonina and her flat appeared to be quite normal, until you entered the living room. She had set up a full hair salon in there. Oksana thanked her for the appointment at short notice on her birthday.

"No problem at all. I'm happy to help," Antonina said cheerily.

"Which birthday are you celebrating?" Oksana asked. I thought that a question I couldn't possibly have asked.

"Twenty-five years young," she replied.

"Same as Richard," Oksana teased.

"Yes, but I'm starting to feel older than twenty-five because of what Oksana is doing to me," I joked.

"Twenty-five is an age better for men than for women," Antonina said. *That was Ukrainian society talking.* She changed the subject as hairdressers are so skilled at doing.

"I hear you have a big day today?" Antonina asked.

"Yes, I just hope to get through the day without starting a war," I quipped. Antonina smiled.

"Ukraine is a peace-loving country, I'm sure that won't happen."

By the time Antonina had finished with my hair, I looked somewhat different. *It was more boufant than I had anticipated.* It tried not to choke on the cheap *Elnett* hairspray she liberally covered me in. I thanked her all the same and wished her a 'Happy Birthday'. The snow was heavy again and moving around in a taxi was becoming challenging.

The hair appointment had taken nearly three hours. Oksana and I were ready for some lunch ahead of a quick visit to the Opera House to pick up my suit. By 3pm, I was back at the *Druzhbi Narodiv* metro feeling rather awkward with my new hairdo. Natasha opened the door and almost didn't recognize me, not helping with the awkwardness.

At 6:30pm, everything started to become surreal. Oksana phoned.

"There is a black car waiting for you outside," she said. "It will take you to Europa Square. I will meet you at the entrance."

Natasha wished me luck and I left the flat. The snow was particularly heavy now and I crunched my way through to the black Mercedes waiting for me. I wondered how the black Mercedes would get through the deep snow; but it did. I chuckled to myself; if it had been a *Zaporozhets*, I wouldn't be getting there, unless the Colonel had been at the wheel. I was beginning to feel that this was Ukraine at its finest. I had to pinch myself for what I was about to do.

We drove across Europa Square and into the front porch of the National Philharmonic Concert Hall. Oksana was waiting. I exited the Mercedes into heavy snow. Kyiv looked beautiful. *This was Kyiv's night and I really wanted to make it happen for her.*

We entered the Hall of Columns as the first invited guests began to arrive. We walked to the back of the stage. Olga arrived and looked stunning. I, on the other hand, was wearing smoking jacket and trousers slightly too big for me. Oksana provided me with my script; Olga and I practised our Ukrainian and English introductions. The hall filled up quickly. The Philharmonic Orchestra began filing on to the stage and taking their seats. I was briefly called off to the side of the stage where I had a couple of words of encouragement from the British Ambassador.

"Don't fuck it up," he said, casting me a menacing smile, his hands clasping both of my shoulders. To be honest, that didn't improve my nerves. I never imagined myself in this position: introducing a set of European music arias in front of a packed audience of foreign dignitaries and a live national television audience in the heart of Kyiv. The stakes were high and I knew that the success of this event could have far-reaching consequences for Ukraine and its relationship with the European Union.

Misha was ready; the conductor was ready; the orchestra was ready. The television cameras either side of the stage gave a thumbs up. Olga led the way on to the front of the stage with me in her wake. I felt like 'Billy' again going on stage for the start of Act One of *'Stags & Hens'*.

"Ladies and gentlemen, distinguished guests. Welcome to the Hall of Columns in the National Philharmonic Concert Hall of Ukraine," she opened in melodic Ukrainian language, "where tonight we have the honour of hosting the first-ever live nationally televised concert under a European Union flag." I repeated the same welcome in English, my voice echoing through the hall. *I was tempted to say "CAMRA The*

Campaign for Real Ale, I support that, I've got a badge" but I really didn't think the Ambassador would appreciate the diplomatic fallout.

"Tonight, we have a very special concert for you, featuring some of the most beautiful and beloved arias from across Europe. We are honoured to have so many distinguished guests here with us tonight and we hope that you enjoy the music as much as we do. We are here to celebrate the rich cultural heritage of Europe and Ukraine and to showcase the talent of a young Ukrainian singer who embodies the spirit of our shared values and aspirations." I paused for a moment, as Olga said her piece, taking in the sight of the packed hall and the flags of the various embassies displayed on either side of the stage. This was a momentous occasion; not just for me but for the entire country of Ukraine.

There had been a slight change to the proceedings since rehearsals. The Head of the European Commission Delegation in Ukraine wanted to come on stage and say a few words. I had noticed the insert in my folder.

"We would like to now welcome to the stage the Ambassador and Head of the Delegation of the European Commission in Ukraine, Mr. Luis Moreno," I had almost managed this in one breath. Olga repeated in Ukrainian. She was so professional. I was so amateur. Led by his translator, Mr Moreno mounted the stage and settled in front centre under the European Union flag. Olga and I shuffled to one side. He began the historic speech in his heavy Spanish accent.

"Before we begin, I would like to thank the European Commission for their support in making this concert possible. The Action Plan for Ukraine is a major step towards strengthening the ties between Ukraine and the European Union, and we are proud to be a part of this historic moment." The translator repeated in Ukrainian.

"I didn't realize when I came to Kyiv the number of tasks the European Commission were going to undertake in Ukraine. As some of you probably know, the European Commission is involved in all the economic sectors of Ukraine." The translator repeated.

"We are involved in every sector, even agriculture, we are involved in the environment and transport, we are involved in efforts of educational cooperation. The Commission are involved in the Action Plan to support the balance of payments of Ukraine." The translator repeated.

"This has only been possible with the friendship and cooperation of Presidents Kravchuk and now Kuchma, for which we get our combined strength. I think in 1998 we are living in the European Union one of the most important years of our history in a few months Europe will move towards economic and monetary union and nothing will be the same after the 4th May this year." The translator repeated.

"And also you may know, in March of this year, that we shall establish the enlargement into Eastern Europe. It means in a few years' time the borders of Western Ukraine will be the border of the European Union. This has been done at such a speed that it may be difficult for some people to understand how things can go so fast, I can tell you that in the EU the process of monetary union and economic enlargement will be our historical achievement." The translator repeated.

"In any case I think I have been very lucky, personally and professionally, to be present as a witness to this historical transformation work in Ukraine. We are very pleased with the support given to us by the President and the Parliament and by all the authorities of the structure of Kyiv." The translator repeated.

"And taking into account that Ukraine is a European country in the future our perspectives will much converge. Thank you very much." The translator repeated for the final time. As the audience showed their appreciation and approval for the European Commission's words, we shook hands with each other. It was clear from the translator's cold and clammy hands that she was suffering more than I was. Ambassador and his translator left the stage.

Sunflower Underground: A Kyiv Memoir

We were already twenty minutes in and we hadn't heard any music or singing, this was going to be a long evening. The concert programme was listed as follows;

1. W.A. Mozart
    Overture to the opera "The Magic Flute"
2. G. Donitzetti
    "Una furtiva Lacrima" from the opera "L'Elisir D'Amore"
3. G. Puccini
    "Che gelida manina" from the opera "La Boheme"
4. P.I. Tchaikovsky
    Waltz from the ballet "Sleeping Beauty"
5. P.I. Tchaikovsky
    Herman's Arioso from the opera "The Queen of Spades"
6. G. Puccini
    "Nessun Dorma" from the opera "Turandot"
7. G. Bizet
    Musical Interludes from the suite "L'Arlesienne"
8. G. Verdi
    "La donna e mobile" from the opera "Rigoletto"
9. G. Meyerbeer
    "O, Paradis!" from the opera "The African"
10. P. Mascagni
    Intermezzo from the opera "Cavalleria Rusticana"
11. V. Chiara
    "La Spagnola"
12. E.D. Curtis
    "Tu, ca nun chiagne!"
13. Ukrainian Folk Song
    "Black brows, brown eyes!"
14. S. Gulak-Artemovski
    Andrei's prayer from the opera "Zaporozhets za Dunayem"
15. L. van Beethoven
    "Ode to Joy" from Symphony No.9

I noticed the omission straightaway. There was no *Amazing Grace* on the programme. *Panic set in.* Elizabeth had made it explicitly clear that she wanted *Amazing Grace* included somewhere in the concert.

Did Oksana know? Did the orchestra have the music? Was Misha ready?

I looked over at Olga, who smiled encouragingly, and continued. "Music has the power to transcend borders and bring people together. Tonight, we are honoured to have with us a truly Ukrainian cast of musicians, representing the best of European classical music." I repeated with my introduction; my words were carefully chosen to convey the importance of this event and the significance it held for Ukraine and the European Union. I glanced over at Olga, who stood beside me, looking every inch the movie star in her stunning evening gown.

There was a round of applause from the audience and my nerves began to settle. Olga smiled at me. We turned to the side of the stage to allow the conductor to take his place. The lights dimmed. The orchestra burst into life as it began to play the haunting melody, the opening bars of the piece by Mozart. As the music from Mozart filled the hall, panic turned to excitement. *This was a far cry from my humble beginnings in a small village in the Cotswolds. But somehow, I managed to find my way here, to this moment, on this stage, in this country.*

Back in the wings, Oksana confirmed to Olga and me that *Amazing Grace* would be inserted somewhere into the concert programme but she would take instruction from Misha and let us know beforehand. *This introduced an unwelcome uncertainty for us into the proceedings. I tried to forget this was live television across Ukraine.*

After what seemed only a few short minutes to catch our breath, the orchestra finished, the conductor turned to acknowledge the applauding audience. This was Olga's and my cue to return to the stage. Our narrow path to the centre inhibited by an errant cello. Opening our black folders again, we introduced the next aria. Olga first, then me. As I finished my introduction, Misha took to the stage. The audience applauded politely. Olga and I returned to the wings, stage left. The conductor acknowledged Misha, and he turned to the orchestra, arms raised. Misha faced the hall and readied himself. The music began, the audience hushed, Misha's voice soared through the hall. The audience were mesmerized; I could feel the tension in the air slowly dissipating as the music took hold. Five minutes later the audience erupted into applause and I knew that this was going to be a night to remember.

By the time we had reached Tchaikovsky on the programme, I was becoming increasingly aware of a rather large lady in the centre of the front row, with a beaming smile. She must have been around seventy years old but looked every bit as glamorous as Olga Sumskaya.

"Who is the lady in the front row?" I asked Oksana in the wings, as Misha sang *Herman's Arioso*.

"That's Evgeniya Miroshnichenko," Oksana confirmed," Lady Miroshnichenko to you." *I was none the wiser.* "She is Misha's mentor. Misha is her protégé."

"Is she famous?"

"She was the most famous soprano in the Soviet Union," Oksana replied, "She was the People's Artist in 1965. She is also an ex-girlfriend of Fidel Castro." *I wish I hadn't asked. This was not helping my nerves.*

The audience applauded. Misha came off for a glass of water. Olga and I returned to the stage for the sixth time, cello still stubbornly rooted to the stage, to introduce *Nessun Dorma*. I couldn't take my eyes off Lady Miroshnichenko who was gazing back. She seemed to be looking straight through me. Olga and I headed back into our box, stage left. Misha bounded back on stage. The orchestra began. *The BBC theme tune for World Cup Italia 90 sprang to mind for a moment.* Misha sang and kicked this one out of the park. The audience were almost standing to applaud before he'd finished, then the pressure was released, and the applause was deafening. *This must look great at home on television.*

And so the same process repeated another ten times for the next couple of hours. Olga and I would manoeuvre ourselves through the narrow alley way through the orchestra, side stepping the cello. Misha would bounce onto the stage, sing, take the applause, we would come back on. For the audience of dignitaries, and the viewers at home, it may have appeared as one giant Swiss clock, with all the pieces on stage moving in conjunction with each other, eventually working *like clockwork.*

As Olga and I moved to introduce *Zaporozhets za Dunayem,* I thought it could have been a song about the Colonel's car. *I could imagine him driving, with his driving gloves, onto the stage and through the orchestra, cellos flying everywhere.* The song actually translated as *A Cossack beyond the Danube* and so Misha sung about the freedom-loving Zaporizhian Cossacks of Ukraine. Freedom. Freedom. *This is what Ukrainians wanted most of all.* Olga and I stood in the wings, Oksana passed us another insert for our black folders. *Amazing Grace* was confirmed as next. Misha came off stage left for a glass of water, amidst another standing ovation. *Ukrainians were in tears with this aria.*

Olga indicated that I should walk on to introduce *Amazing Grace* in English first, and so I led the way. As I reached the centre stage, I turned expecting to see Olga standing beside me. She had remained in the wings. She smiled cheekily as if to say *you're on your own.* I understood. "In an addition to the Concert programme this evening Misha will now sing *Amazing Grace* by English composer John Newton." The audience response was immediate. Olga hadn't even bothered translating. *Everyone knew this song.* It was about the abolition of slavery. The Ukrainians had adopted this as their own since their independence. *Never again would they be slaves to another master.* Misha returned. The orchestra began. Lady Miroshnichenko beamed even more than usual knowing that Misha, her protégé, would need to be singing in English, something he had never done before apart from *Strangers in the Night.* The concert was reaching an extraordinary crescendo. Oksana and I knew that this was a risk. Misha was very brave to attempt it. Five minutes later we could see Lady Miroshnichenko wiping tears from her eyes. Her makeup mildly smudged. Hugely proud of her protégé. She above all, knew the sheer intensity of the music and Misha's exceptional talent. It was a marvellous sight to see. As the final notes faded away, the hall erupted into thunderous applause, and I knew that we had were succeeding in our mission.

Olga joined me to introduce the last piece of music, Beethoven's *Ode to Joy,* the European Anthem. *A choir emerged from the balcony above the European Union flag.* The orchestra began playing. Misha was ready for one last effort in this marathon three-hour concert. We had no doubt that he could save his best performance for last. He lifted the roof off in a way I could have barely believed, he was singing for Ukraine. Singing in a way only a National Artist of Ukraine can. By then, Misha was flying and so were we all. The music came to an end and the audience stood and clapped their appreciation. The orchestra stood as one and Misha came to the stage for an encore. Bouquets of flowers began to pour onto the front of the stage. For the seventeenth time, sixteen for Olga, we moved through the narrow passage around the cello applauding Misha together. Olga had mentioned to look into the television cameras for the final goodbye, I was first up.

"We would like to thank Misha for his wonderful performance this evening. Thank you also to the National Philharmonic Orchestra and Choir of Ukraine. Thank you to the European Commission in Kyiv for your support. We truly hope you have enjoyed this *Evening of European Music* as much as we have. Goodnight!" Olga repeated. As the concert ended, Olga and I took our final bows and the audience erupted into applause. The cameramen gave a double thumbs up and signalled a cut. Filming was done. *We could relax.*

It was a moment I would never forget. We had presented sixteen pieces of music live on television.   Finding myself backstage, surrounded by the chaos of people rushing to pack up their instruments and equipment, the British Ambassador suddenly appeared beside me, a rare smile on his face.

"Well done," he said, his voice filled with pride. "You did us proud," he said simply, before turning and walking away. *I watched him go, a sense of relief washing over me.* I had done it. We had pulled off the biggest diplomatic event of the year, note by note, and it had gone off without a hitch. This was just the beginning, I thought. The beginning of a new era for Ukraine; one that would see it forging closer ties with the European Union and carving out its own independent identity on the world stage. As the final moments of the concert faded away, I couldn't help but wonder what the future held for Ukraine. The country was still transitioning out of its relationship with Russia. There were many challenges ahead. But as I looked out at the sea of faces in the audience, I saw hope and determination. These were people who believed in the power of music to bring European nations together, to bridge divides and create a better Ukraine.

The applause had died down, a loud excited murmuring echoed through the hall. The audience started to move out to the side of the hall where the European Commission had prepared drinks in the marbled reception area. Misha led the way out of the Hall of Columns; followed by Olga and me.

Lady Miroshnichenko greeted me with an enormous bear hug, clearly delighted with how everything had gone. I found myself almost being broken in two by her great arms. Oksana looked on in shock.

"You've been embraced by Evgeniya Miroshnichenko," she exclaimed. "That is a great sign and a huge honour." I understood that I had been hugged by Fidel Castro's ex-girlfriend; I just hoped he would not come looking for me.

I had several glasses of champagne as we circulated around the reception, bathing in the buzz and success of the concert and ultimately *the project*. This was Oksana's project; she had put it all together. But I knew that the original idea was sparked by the *Tomato Man* on a wintery Kyiv-street, over two years earlier. The rest of the evening passed in a blur of introductions and polite conversation. I tried to take it all in but it was overwhelming at times.

I finished the evening chatting with a Ukrainian businessman. He told me that he was currently sponsoring two young Ukrainian boxers at his gym in Kyiv, Vitali and Vladimir Klitschko. *"To promote Vitali and Vladimir is to promote Ukraine,"* he smiled. I wished him and his boxers all the luck in the world before stepping out into the deep snow.

As I walked out of the Hall of Columns that night, the snow crunching beneath my feet, I knew that I had just witnessed something truly remarkable. And I knew that, no matter what the future held, I would always be proud to have been a part of it. I felt a sense of excitement for the future; Ukraine was a land of opportunity, a land of promise, and I knew that I would do everything in my power to help it realize its full potential.

In the days and weeks that followed, the concert was the talk of the town, a symbol of the new era of Ukrainian-European relations that was dawning. Misha became an overnight sensation. And me? Well, I was hailed as an unlikely hero in diplomatic circles and received a personal 'thank-you' from the British Ambassador himself. *Of course I wasn't a hero, but they like their heroes in Ukraine.*

Looking back on that night, I realize it was a turning point, not just for Ukraine, but for me as well. It was a reminder that sometimes, the biggest risks can lead to the greatest rewards. With a little bit of courage and a lot of hard work, anything is possible.

The Mercedes was waiting outside. He skidded out to meet me under the canopy entrance, then continued to slip and slide through the Kyiv streets back to *Druzhbi Narodiv*. With huge relief, I entered the flat and had a coffee with Natasha, telling her all about it. *Back to reality.*

Chapter 21. The Trial

28th February 1998

I received a phone call from Ilda who I had met in the Arizona Bar last February. This was a surprise as I had not given her any of my contact details. But I was happy to hear her voice, nevertheless. She sounded agitated.

"I wanted to congratulate you on your success with the concert a few weeks ago," she said. "I saw you on television and couldn't believe it was you."

"Thank you," I said, trying to be as humble as possible. "It was really the hard work of others. I was just performing the English translation of it."

"Don't underestimate what you have done. It was hugely symbolic. Have you had any other feedback from the concert?" she asked.

"What do you mean?" I was slightly puzzled by the tone of the question.

"I have picked up some negative feedback in the Russian press to say that this sort of cultural stunt was not appreciated by them," she said. "I wanted to make sure there had been no threats to you and that you were safe. It was a very brave thing to do." *Brave or foolish?*

"I must admit I have not heard of any feedback like that since the concert. However, our sponsors in the European Commission did mention beforehand that not everyone would appreciate the sentiment behind the concert," I replied. Ilda then seemed to change the subject completely.

"Have you heard that another war in the Balkans has flared up?" she asked.

I had been aware of increasing tension between Serbia and Kosovo in recent weeks; it had been reported on the BBC and Ukrainian channels. The conflict had intensified significantly, with widespread human rights abuses committed on both sides. The Serbian military and police were conducting a brutal crackdown against the Albanian population, resulting in numerous civilian casualties and the displacement of thousands of people. Ron told me about the history and ongoing tensions between Serbians and Albanians after he had escaped from Tirana on a helicopter last year. He had warned of further trouble then.

"I'm aware of the situation. Do you have any family in Kosovo?" I asked sympathetically, based on my knowledge that both Bosnia and Kosovo Albanians are minority Christian populations. I knew that Ilda had come from a family in the Bosnian Christian community.

"No, but thank you very much for asking," she said. "The reason for my call is that I wanted to warn you about being in Kyiv at this time. I know that Russia is likely to put pressure on Ukraine to support Serbia. I hope that you will stay safe."

"Thank you for the heads up," I replied. "What is President Kuchma's position on this?"

"Kuchma will want Ukraine to stay neutral on this matter, especially if the situation escalates," she advised. "But I think Russia may force him to accept logistical support for aid to Serbia."

"And especially if NATO come to the defence of the Kosovo Albanians," I said, trying to join up the diplomatic dots.

"Exactly! Just imagine if NATO gets involved, then Russia would have a big influence on how Ukraine behaves," she said. "You will be on the wrong side of the battlefield." Ilda was smart and had already assessed the situation.

I understood now what she was saying. I would need to be extra vigilant in every aspect of my life in Kyiv. I thanked her and we promised to stay in touch if we needed anything from each other.

5th March 1998

A week later, I received a message via Galina requesting me to attend the Institute for an administrative matter. I assumed it was just a minor clarification on a document or a visa oversight on my behalf. At 11am, I entered Galina's office and wished everyone good morning. I realized something was wrong when I hadn't received the usual warm greeting from the junior administrators. Something was different. Galina looked up from her computer.

"Ah, Richard, good morning," she said. "Please take a seat in here while I let Professor Samoilenko know you are here."

This was unexpected and now I regretted not asking Oksana about it before. *Why would Samoilenko want to see me?* As the Head of the Institute, he was usually too busy to see anyone. I sat down and waited in silence with the two administrators. I sensed something I had not sensed before. I always used the junior administrators to gauge Galina's mood. This was the first time they had blanked me. I wondered what the reason was. Fifteen minutes passed.

"You may come through now," said Galina firmly as she had appeared from the connecting door to Samoilenko's office. I stood up, smiled at the unresponsive junior administrators and entered the passage to Samoilenko's office. I didn't expect to see Professor Korolyuk who greeted me as I walked into the office.

"Hello Richard, please take a seat," Korolyuk indicated to take a seat that had been placed in the middle of the room. In front of me sat Professor Samoilenko. To his left sat Professors Korolyuk and Goosack; to his right sat two other men in military uniforms. Galina closed the door behind me and took a seat at the back of the room, opening up a note pad and pen as if to take minutes of an official meeting. I felt unnerved. Where was Oksana? *I could do with her support now.*

"Thank you for attending this meeting," said Samoilenko. "I would like to introduce to you Colonels Smirnov and Petrov of the Institute's Projects Division," he indicated to his right.

I acknowledged them. I had never seen these men before and assumed they were part of the secret military projects on the prohibited floors. He then placed his right hand back on the desk and used his left hand.

"Here we have Professors Goosack and Korolyuk who you already know,", he concluded the introductions. I acknowledged them with a smile.

"It has come to our attention that you have been engaged with activities that may conflict with the Institute's policies, here in Kyiv," he advised. The atmosphere felt formal and intimidating, like a courtroom. I was being judged for something which I couldn't quite yet understand. I felt nervous that I couldn't see Galina from where I was sitting and would only respond once a question had been asked. I was certainly aware that I should only answer any questions truthfully and with brevity.

"What connection do you have with the European Commission?" he asked openly. I glanced at all five pairs of eyes staring back at me.

"I have no connection with the European Commission," I responded. "Apart from assisting them with a cultural project last month," I added truthfully. I made sure that I didn't respond to a question with a question; this was the surest way of creating suspicion. This felt serious. I had to keep it simple. *I was reminded of the Yagodin border guards.*

"What was the purpose of this concert?" asked Samoilenko.

"To promote a Ukrainian opera singer," I replied. This was true.

"Why were you involved?" he asked.

"I was invited to take the position of co-presenter to satisfy the English language requirement stipulated by the Commission," I answered. "Which I accepted."

"This was a publicly aired event, correct?" asked Samoilenko. The other eight eyes remained fixed on me.

"Correct," I maintained brevity.

"Under whose authority did you accept this invitation?" he probed. I glanced at Korolyuk, knowing that if I mentioned Nina's role, it may place him in a very difficult situation. He stared at me without reaction waiting for my answer.

"The European Commission and my Embassy," I replied, knowing that the answer was incomplete.

"At any time, did you seek the permission of the Institute to engage with this event?" he asked. This was clearly an interrogation. One wrong step and I would be out. My bet was that a wrong answer would be to lie.

"No," I said truthfully.

"Why didn't you seek permission?" he asked. I was now fully aware that Oksana was coming into focus. *Should I mention her?* She could be sacked by the Institute. I desperately thought of a truthful answer and needed to prepare the ground for some humility and maybe an apology.

"I was not aware that I needed permission from the Institute," I replied. I wanted to say that I strongly felt it may benefit Ukraine but knew this would get me into trouble with Smirnov and Petrov.

"We feel that, although it wasn't a requirement, it would have been appropriate to advise us beforehand," Samoilenko advised.

"I acknowledge this and apologise," I said, feeling that 'humble pie' was the way to go. I gave into the urge.

"I also felt that it would benefit Ukraine," I said, immediately regretting it.

At this stage, Colonel Smirnov interjected in Russian. Samoilenko translated the question into English.

"Who are you to know what may or may not benefit Ukraine?"

I was in trouble now and needed to think fast. I looked around the room; all eyes were on me waiting for my answer.

"I only know that Lady Miroshnichenko embraced me like a bear afterwards. It felt like I was being embraced by Ukraine herself. Nothing I have done has felt so right," I said, aware that the ice was quickly melting under my feet, knowing that I would probably be expelled on the spot. Mentally, I was already packing my bags and returning to England. Colonel Petrov raised his voice and spoke in Russian. Samoilenko asked Petrov to repeat the question. Samoilenko translated.

"Are you a spy, he asks?" said Samoilenko. My heart missed a beat. A rush of adrenaline exploded through my body. *Didn't they shoot spies here?*

"Absolutely not," I answered quickly and firmly.

"We have been made aware that you have been observed, on several occasions, on the upper floors of the Institute without permission," continued Samoilenko. "What is your explanation for this?"

I felt a strong urge to turn towards Galina, as only she could have mentioned this to him. Galina was the only person to have observed me on the day that I previewed the lecture hall ahead of my paper presentation and the day I visited Skorokhod's lecture. Of course, she did not speak up in my defence.

"I checked an empty lecture theatre in preparation for my presentation," I replied. "Also, I had permission to attend Skorokhod's lecture."

292

"Is this true Galina?" he asked.

"No formal specific permission was given," Galina replied.

The injustice of the comment sank to the bottom of my stomach. This was a lie. She had personally told me that Korolyuk's students could attend Skorokhod lectures, giving me implicit permission to visit the upper floors to attend his lecture. I couldn't possibly contest this without a lawyer and that was not an option here.

"Thank you," said Samoilenko. He paused to take notes and then continued. "Richard, we thank you for your time today," he began. "You may leave us now and I will advise you of the outcome of our decision by tomorrow."

I stood up and walked out of the office, feeling the gaze of six pairs of eyes searing into my back. The whole grilling had taken under an hour but it felt like an eternity.

My head was spinning. I immediately returned to *Druzhbi Narodiv* for sanctuary. Based on the last comments, I felt that I was out of the Institute. Out of Ukraine. *It was Galina's word against mine; of course, they would believe her.* Back at the flat, I phoned Oksana and repeated the whole episode to her.

"I apologise," said Oksana. "I didn't inform them about the concert. I hope you can forgive me. They would have been surprised to see you appear on the television in that role. Colonels Smirnov and Petrov were the two votes against you entering the Institute. I'm afraid they will hold another vote for you to remain."

"So tomorrow, I could be going home?" I said.

"Yes, without the mandate from the Institute you will have to leave Ukraine. I'm so sorry, it is my fault."

I didn't blame Oksana. I knew that the Institute was split down the middle regarding my presence there: UK presence there; *western presence there.* With the new tensions in the Balkans, Colonels

293

Smirnov and Petrov probably felt that I was NATO too. They clearly didn't want me there. *Ilda had been right.* Any excuse to get me out, all facilitated by Galina, the Head Administrator. I didn't know it yet but I was distraught. I phoned Yulia and we went out for a drink that evening. I stayed quiet about it as I knew this could be my last day in Ukraine. I didn't want to face another goodbye with Yulia just yet. I was sick with worry that the Institute would cancel my visa with immediate effect.

The next morning, I was summoned into the Institute by one of the junior administrators. *Clearly, Galina was not speaking to me.* "Please can you report to the Administrators' Office by 11am," the junior said. Natasha sensed the tension in me.

I arrived at the Institute under heavy snow. *Snow. Go away, now is not the right time.* I entered the Reception and began walking up the stairs. *Would they accuse me of spying again? I felt like an innocent man walking up the steps of the gallows.*

I entered the Administrators' Office and was shown straight through to Samoilenko's office. Surprisingly, Galina was not there, anywhere. No one else was in there except Samoilenko, who sat at his desk.

"Richard, please sit down," he said sternly.

"Thank you," I said. *I was waiting for the noose to go around my neck.*

"We have decided to let you stay and continue your work with Professor Korolyuk," he said. I thought I had heard the trap door open but the mechanism had clearly jammed. *Did I hear that correctly?*

"We accept your account," he said. "Thank you." I couldn't believe it. *I thought it was a certainty that I would be out. But what about the explanation about Skorokhod's lecture? How was that reconciled?* I dared not asked just in case Samoilenko changed his mind.

"You may go now," he said with a smile. I thanked him as I stood up and walked back out into the Administrators' Office. I thanked the two junior administrators who both responded with words and a smile. They had never done that before. Galina's absence nagged at me. *Where was she today?*

Instead of returning to *Druzhbi Narodiv*, I walked over to the internet café at the main post office in Independence Square. I was eager to read more about the Kosovo crisis; I needed to know when the Russians may bear down on Ukraine. I now knew that the greater the tension with Russia, the more problems I may have in the Institute.

'Thank God it's Friday' had never had greater significance for me. I phoned Oksana.

"Professor Samoilenko said that I could stay," I said.

"Yes, I heard. That's excellent news! In the re-vote, all votes remained the same. Samoilenko had the deciding vote again." Oksana had already spoken with Korolyuk about it.

"I was sure that Samoilenko would take Galina's side on the Skorokhod lecture," I said.

"Apparently, Skorokhod himself confirmed you had his personal permission to be at his lecture when Samoilenko asked him. Samoilenko phoned him in Chicago and spoke with him. That is, in itself, amazing as my assumption was that Skorokhod was against your presence here. Clearly, I was wrong, and it seems something had swayed him your way."

"So, what of Galina?" I asked.

"She was asked to take a month at home," Oksana confirmed. "She will be back and I would suggest you to steer clear of her for a while. Everyone knows the games that are being played."

Afterwards, I phoned Yulia who was ready for drinks after a long week of exams at university. We met at the Rock Café before heading off to check out a couple of the new bars appearing in Kyiv. I loved the energy in Kyiv. I felt that I had become a part of Kyiv and it was becoming a part of me. I was also relieved that I could stay longer with Yulia, not having to say goodbye to her just yet.

3rd April 1998

The story of the great ship *Titanic* fascinated me since I was a child. I was delighted to hear that James Cameron's new *Titanic* film had reached Kyiv cinemas. In particular, it was showing in a new cinema that had opened in Institute Street up the hill from Independence Square. It had been a full year since I first met Yulia; we both thought it would be nice to go to the new cinema for the premier of *Titanic* in Ukraine. There were only ever four Ukrainians who were confirmed to have died on the *Titanic* but everyone knew the story.

Yulia and I met at *Druzhbi Narodiv* and headed straight to the cinema. I was excited about the occasion: the film itself and about us. Our relationship had developed into a strong partnership over the year. We entered the new cinema which was one of the few places in Kyiv that felt like a modern western environment. The cinema seats were luxurious and the popcorn was fresh. Even the sound systems were Dolby surround sound. The cinema was full, with every seat taken; we enjoyed the stunning effects recreating the *Titanic* in realistic detail for the first time.

All going well I felt, until that is, the ship hit an iceberg and started to sink. Until this point, the Ukrainians in the audience had just expressed appreciation at various points in the film. As the *Titanic* began to break in half, and passengers began falling into the freezing cold sea, an audible sound of sobbing could be heard. There were even gasps of horror as funnels came tumbling down onto drowning passengers.

I gradually found myself in a cinema full of sobbing film-goers, including Yulia. I tried to explain that this was only a film, and these were actors but collectively they seemed to be right there, in the moment, on the *Titanic* with the passengers. The empathy felt by the film-goers for the *Titanic* passengers was astonishing. I took advantage of the situation, as always, and put all my efforts into consoling Yulia. I have never had a cinema experience like it and unlikely to ever again. *This was 5D Max. In hindsight, maybe it hadn't been the right place for a first anniversary.*

A week later, I began to feel ill.

The stress of the last two months began to take a toll on my health. The concert, the Institute, the work and the continued freezing weather had not helped. I was beginning to feel out of breath with a loss of appetite.

"You are looking pale and must rest up for a while," Natasha insisted. I took her advice and stayed in bed with several *Jeffery Archer* books I had found in the British Council offices. These were a huge comfort and I did begin to feel rested after several days.

Old-Natasha, who was still a senior Matron at the Kyiv hospital, suspected that it could be a form of pneumonia. One morning, after about five days in bed, I woke up feeling particularly weak. Even a walk to the kitchen to get a glass of water and back to my bed was traumatic. Natasha could see that I was suffering and was regularly on the phone to Old-Natasha for advice. By midday, I registered a temperature above forty degrees centigrade.

I lay in bed, pouring out sweat onto the sheets faster than Natasha could replace them. I began hallucinating, seeing myself in Jeffery Archer characters, repeating lines in Jeffery Archer books and generally feeling like I was at Death's door. I felt like I was in the film *Titanic,* gently slipping into the icy cold waters of the sea, losing my grip, never to return to the surface. This was it; I was leaving this world. One of my fears had always been to die away from England and this is what was happening to me now. I was gasping for air, burning up, sinking. As I sunk away, I began to feel a cooling around my chest, something was enveloping my lungs.

Slowly, I began to float up to the surface of reality. I opened my eyes and saw Natasha standing at the end of my bed. *Was she an angel?* I looked left and saw two paramedics in green, they had put a large needle into my arm and were injecting me with something. Whatever it was, it was working. I was starting to return to the surface. I could breathe again. *I would survive.*

A week after I had nearly succumbed to pneumonia, I was strong enough to attend the hospital for some tests and a check-up. I recall seeing Old-Natasha and hugging her. It was she who had instructed immediate attention by paramedics. She had saved my life. I understood now why she was considered one of Kyiv's finest nurses. Without the massive injection of antibiotics I had received, I would only have had hours to live. No more England. No more Yulia. *No more nothing.*

The experience allowed me to evaluate things through a new lens. I could freely consider whether it was the right time to leave Kyiv or stay. I had a deep feeling that I must stay for the people around me, including Yulia and Professor Korolyuk. *So, I chose to stay; to continue my personal battle for whatever it was I was fighting for in Kyiv, and for Ukraine.*

Chapter 22. Crimea

23rd June 1998

The weather was beautiful and warm. I had been able to enjoy a 26th birthday full of sun and sand on the beaches of Hydropark. In May, Mum visited Kyiv for a second time, primarily to see how my recovery from pneumonia was going; *I didn't tell her about the spying accusations.* We joined Natasha and her work colleagues on a boat party headed north up the Dnipro River, fortunately not as far up as Chernobyl. It was a day filled with vodka and anecdotes of how women were better off on their own.

I had recovered slowly over the last two months by taking regular outdoor exercise to get my lungs and body breathing again. "There will be scarring on your lungs which will take years to heal," advised my doctor, Dr. Scott at the Milton-under-Wychwood surgery on my next return home. Memories of childhood asthma had resurfaced but I was feeling fit again. The occasional run around the track at Respublikanski Stadium improved my stamina too. Yulia was a constant source of strength, despite being busy with university and modelling exams.

That day, Natasha and I travelled south to *Koncha Zaspa* under invitation of the Colonel. The forest was a comfortable retreat in the heat of summer. We arrived at the dacha with bags of sweet foods and drinks. The Colonel and Old-Natasha had set up their new wooden pergola covered in grapes above a large brick wood table, with a rustic brick oven at one end, all built by Ivan. *The Colonel was keeping him busy.* He appeared from the back gate and walked up the garden path, having been fishing in the lake behind. I remembered how different it had all looked when I had fallen in. Ivan also looked different since he'd separated from his wife. He had a baby daughter now and looked stressed. He would be joining the army after the summer with the pride of his grandfather.

The next day, Natasha would be travelling south to Crimea with her girlfriend Polina for two weeks of sun, sea and sand. The following week I would be travelling down with Yulia. So, today was an opportunity to eat and drink together as if we were in Crimea, minus the Black Sea.

We sat down under the shade of Ivan's pergola, the table covered with Ukrainian dishes. There was meat cooking in the brick oven. As usual, I was invited to sit on the right-hand side of the Colonel, who sat at the top end facing the oven. He poured a round of vodkas, which wasn't my first-choice drink on a hot day like this. But somehow, it was the best drink in Ukraine and I loved it. Ivan attended the meat diligently.

"I remember Crimea from my army days," the Colonel began. "Of course, the war was still on." He lifted his glass, prompting everyone else. "To our health and Crimea!" he toasted. We all threw the vodka down our throats and reached for the lemon slices. Ivan began lifting the meat out of the fire, fat spitting in all directions.

"February 1945," the Colonel continued, "I remember it well."

Ivan placed the meat onto a chopping board on a separate table next to the oven and began carving.

"Yalta!" the Colonel suddenly exclaimed. "That was a very important day," he said as he began pouring another round of vodkas.

"Of course, we learned about Yalta in History at school, the Conference at the end of the war. But I never actually thought I'd meet any of the people attending," I smiled. Natasha smiled.

The Conference was attended by the leaders of the three major Allied powers: Winston Churchill of Great Britain, Franklin D. Roosevelt of the United States and Joseph Stalin of the Soviet Union. The main purpose was to discuss the post-war reorganization of Europe and to plan for the establishment of a new world order after the defeat of Nazi Germany.

"I was a young corporal in those days," the Colonel continued. "I had to do what as I was told, else Mr Stalin would've shot me," he looked at me and grinned. I had no doubt he was being serious.

"We all drove down to the *Swallow's Nest* on the cliffs of the Black Sea," he said. "I remember it was freezing cold, not like now." The Swallow's Nest was a small castle perched on the edge of a sheer cliff overlooking the Black Sea. Ivan began plating up the meat and dampened the oven.

"My Commanding Officer placed me at the entrance to the cliff top path and we waited for three hours like that until our guests arrived," he recalled. Great chunks of meat now sat on the table and the smell of cooked meat was irresistible.

"The first black car arrived and stopped right opposite the clifftop gateway, where I was standing," the Colonel pondered and then smelt the meat on his plate. "The door opened and Churchill climbed out of the car. He stood there, took a cigar out of his left coat pocket then lit it, while marvelling at the sight of the Swallow's Nest. I stood rigid trying to keep my eyes forward. Of course, I wasn't allowed to stare at him. Then, puffing away on his new cigar, he walked towards the pathway entrance and breezed right under my nose. I can smell the smoke from his Cuban cigar now as I sit here with you. I'll never forget it." We all begun piling food on our plates but were fascinated by the Colonel's unique account of history.

"What happened then?" I asked, twiddling the vodka glass in circles between my right index finger and thumb.

"Well, Churchill carried on down the path towards the castle, puffing like a railway train down a valley. As soon as he disappeared, the second black car arrived and stopped at the path entrance," he said. "This time an American officer jumped out of the front of the car and opened the door for Mr Roosevelt. A second soldier appeared with a wheelchair and Mr Roosevelt climbed into it. They put a blanket around him and wheeled him past me. I dared not look down at him, else I'd be shot," he said.

I looked at Natasha for an acknowledgement we could begin eating. She had heard the account before and she knew what was coming next but nodded an approval to eat.

"That left Mr Stalin," the Colonel said, lifting his glass. I stopped twiddling and lifted mine. "The third car arrived. Stalin opened his own door before the car had stopped. He got out, waited for a couple of his officers and then marched past me like the conquering host that he was. By then, the war was already won. Herr Hitler was defeated. Just the race to Berlin remained."

The story was mesmerizing and I had no doubt that it had been told before at many a dinner table. It's not many soldiers who can say they have been within a hair's breadth of three of the most influential men of the twentieth century. Natasha sat there, vodka glass in hand, looking proud of her father.

"*Budmo!*" she said.

"*Budmo!*" echoed around the table and heads flicked back and glasses slammed down.

"The next time I was that close to Stalin, was in Moscow eight years later," the Colonel said. "He was honouring half a dozen mathematicians. That's right, about a week before he died." I almost spat my mouthful of vodka out across the table. Professor Harris had mentioned this. *How was I hearing it from Natasha's father?* There were only two possibilities: the Colonel knew Professor Harris or he knew Joseph Stalin. The latter was clearly the most likely. I had to ask.

"What were you doing at the meeting?" I enquired, suffering from the combined effects of the revelation with the vodka. I quickly put a lemon slice in my mouth.

"By then, I was already a Colonel, of course," he replied openly. "I was part of his security team in those days. He only really trusted officers who had been with him in Yalta. That day happened to be my shift." What a massive coincidence.

"Can you remember the names of the mathematicians being honoured?" I asked. He would never remember. *Why would he?*

"Yes, one of them was very well known. He had been involved in a scandal before the war with a scientist. The Luzin affair," he said. "I remember, his name was *Kolmogorov*." I was just about to fall off my chair. The Colonel had been present at the meeting with Stalin and Kolmogorov. Should I ask if he recalled someone called *Korolyuk*?

"What was he being honoured for?" I asked, just because I needed to confirm.

"He led the plans for the defence of Moscow," he confirmed, "and he did a bloody good job. I'll drink to that." The vodka went down his throat in an instant.

"Do you recall the names of the other junior mathematicians?" I asked as he started pouring a third round of vodkas, for the men only this time. The ladies sensibly stayed out of the hot-weather vodkas.

"No, I don't. They were just his students, really," the Colonel said. "But they were all about my age." Korolyuk and Skorokhod were the same age as each other. They must have been the same age as Natasha's father, all born around 1925. This was incredible. I was able to answer Professor Harris' question. Korolyuk had been there, with Skorokhod, and the other two. *Had Natasha already known this story? Is this why Korolyuk had placed me with this host family?*

"Do you recall anything else from that meeting?" I asked trying to squeeze everything out of him. I drank my vodka in solidarity and to keep up the momentum.

"Yes. Curiously, Stalin then gave each of the mathematicians a city to reapply Kolmogorov's *Moscow Defence Theorem*," he said. "One got Leningrad, now St. Petersburg because it was the next closest city to Moscow in the North; one got Moscow as the capital; one got Vladivostok, in case the Japanese invaded over Sakhalin Island in the East; and the last was Kyiv, in case the West invaded."

"I don't suppose you know who was guardian of which city?" I asked, already knowing that he couldn't remember their names.

"No, but I do recall reading later that two of the mathematicians died quite young and they were the guardians of Leningrad and Vladivostok." So that left Skorokhod and Korolyuk for Moscow and Kyiv. Nina had mentioned in her apartment that Skorokhod had stayed three years longer at Moscow State University than Korolyuk, after the meeting with Stalin. Stalin himself had ordered Skorokhod to stay in Moscow. *Maybe that's why he spent so much more time there than the other three.* "They really missed each other," Nina had said, when they were split up. Which means that Kyiv-born Korolyuk had been given Kyiv, returning there earlier in 1954 to resume his work at the Institute. It was all starting to make sense. Korolyuk was the guardian of the *Kyiv Defence Theorem* that Professor Harris had suggested but had had no proof. *Well now he did.*

1ˢᵗ July 1998

It was Yulia's birthday and we were on a train headed south to Crimea. Our destination was a seaside town called *Alushta*, about a one-hour drive from Yalta. Natasha and Polina had already been in Crimea for a week but they had travelled to a city in the eastern peninsula called *Feodosia*.

The train arrived at Simferopol, and it was a short bus trip for us to the coast. After a couple of days enjoying the coast that the Russian writer *Anton Chekhov* had enjoyed a hundred years earlier, we decided to take a trip down the coast to Yalta to visit the *Swallow's Nest*. I hadn't told Yulia much about Professor Korolyuk, or anything about his past, but I was increasingly feeling that there may come a time that I may have to.

We arrived in Yalta on the midday bus and enjoyed some lunch before heading to the *Livadia Palace*, which was the summer residence of the last Russian Tsar, Nicholas II. Then onward to the *Swallow's Nest*, the most recognizable symbol of the Crimean Peninsula. We stepped off the shuttle bus near the entrance to the clifftop pathway where the Colonel must have stood all those years ago. The sight of this magnificent castle perched on the clifftop was surreal and I could easily imagine the three great leaders wending their way past him and along the path.

"Come on let's have a drink," Yulia said as she pointed to a small café perched above us and overlooking the *Swallow's Nest*.

"We can get some great photos from their too," I replied. We jumped up the steps where suddenly we were caught in the clifftop breeze.

Distracted. I couldn't stop thinking about Korolyuk and the Kyiv Defence Theorem. Would he remember what it was? Should I ask him about it? All these questions passed through my mind. What had Professor Harris said? *"Maybe Skorokhod thinks that Korolyuk is updating the Kyiv Defence Theorem to account for a Russian attack scenario."* He had gone on to say, *"Moscow may be able to tolerate losing influence over Kyiv if they became a truly independent state, but it could not tolerate another entity like NATO or the EU replacing them as Kyiv's key sphere of influence."* What could Korolyuk be doing? Was he working on it now? Ukraine was clearly aligning itself more with Europe, I had witnessed that first hand during the concert. What would happen if Ukraine was more aligned with Europe than Russia? What would Russia think? More importantly, what would they do? Could there be a scenario where Russia felt it in their interests to bring Kyiv back into their spere of influence by force? In which case, Kyiv would need to be defended from the East, not the West.

A gust of wind blew up from the sea which lifted Yulia's skirt. She pulled it back down, slightly embarrassed. *I was back in the room.*

"Two glasses of Crimean wine please," I asked the waitress. The open-air café was big enough for two tables only. The view from the café was breathtaking. The waitress returned with two glasses and a small carafe of wine.

"Do you know we can go into the castle and have a look?" Yulia said as we clinked glasses and took a sip of the delicious wine.

"That would be fascinating," I replied. "The path looks pretty precarious and there are a few steps to get down then up at the end."

"It's not so bad," she said, "and anyway Churchill did it as an old man," she joked. She was right and she knew her history. I could envisage Churchill negotiating the steps, puffing away on his cigar. But how did Roosevelt manage it in his wheelchair. He must have had plenty of soldiers around him carrying him up. It was interesting how our perception of history was much simpler than the realities they must have experienced at the time.

When we arrived at the castle, it was much smaller than it looked from far away. A deliberate and clever optical illusion created by the architect in the 1920s. There were only four rooms and observation decks on several levels. I wondered in which room the three great leaders had sat and discussed the future of Europe. We exited onto the castle parapet, surrounding the castle. From there was a panoramic view of the nearby mountains and the sea. I understood why Mr Stalin had chosen this location; no-one would get in here unnoticed. That evening, back in *Alushta*, my mind was very much on to the vacation with Yulia. I had been satisfied with our experience of the *Swallow's Nest*.

The Colonel's account seemed real to me now. His account of the Moscow meeting with Stalin and Kolmogorov must have been true as it corroborated with Professor Harris'. I needed to know what Korolyuk was doing with the *Kyiv Defence Theorem* and, given that I had now completed my three research papers, I was starting to run out of time with him. Why had Skorokhod supported me at a time when he could have ended my time at the Institute, if he'd wanted to?

As with my visit to Odessa, the visit to Crimea provided me with a different perspective of Kyiv; a chance to breathe and to look at our Kyiv microcosm through a different lens. After the summer break, compiling my final thesis and publication would be my main task. I would need to spend as much time as I could with Korolyuk between now and the end of my mandated contract with the Institute in 1999. This would be subject to my remaining on good terms with the committee of Five who allowed me to be there, already on a knife edge. There could be no further conflict with the Institute; I would need to watch myself if Oksana or the European Commission wanted any more favours. Clearly, Colonels Smirnov and Petrov were not amused that I was close to the European Commission.

I wondered who else they would be reporting to.

Chapter 23. Millenium

31st Dec 1999

"President Yeltsin has resigned," I said to Yulia as we crossed Westminster Bridge. We swerved the crowds of people as they gathered for the New Year fireworks on the Embankment. The turn of the millennium promised to be massive fireworks display and everyone in London had come out on to the streets to watch. I thought about what Inna had told me in the Consular two years ago. *Now it was happening and we hoped the world was prepared.*

"That means Putin becomes Acting President," Yulia said. "He is a horrible little man. I don't trust him. And you know what they say about little men," she smiled. Immediately after the statement about Yeltsin, Acting President Putin said he was expecting to send a New Year message to the citizens of Russia.

We walked past Big Ben on our left as the big bell struck 6pm. The envelope was clasped firmly in my hand. Yulia knew the importance of the delivery. The contents of which could be critical for the defence of the Kyiv in years to come. The contents of which included a signed letter from Professor Korolyuk to the Prime Minister wrapped around a DVD of the European Commission concert. There was a second letter signed by Professor Korolyuk to Professor Harris which needed to be issued securely to him via the Prime Minister, to enable the government to decipher the well concealed theorem inside our Wright Fisher model research formula.

Prior to my return from Kyiv for the last time as a research student, Professor Korolyuk had confirmed that he had refined the *Kyiv Defence Theorem* to consider an attack from the East. This would be entrusted to the *Sunflower Underground* movement in Lviv as the guardians of the West of Ukraine. But I'd realized everyone I had met over the past four years had been part of a *sunflower underground* in their own way: *Lady Miroshnichenko, Misha, Oksana, the Korolyuks, Professor Goosack, Natasha, the Colonel, old-Natasha, Ivan, Sveta, Inna, the family Korol, Marina and even the students in School No. 17 - all wanted a free and independent Ukraine.* But guardians within Ukraine would not be enough; Korolyuk recognized that they would need guardians from outside Ukraine. He understood from the Second World War that the British would most likely respond to their call for help in their hour of need. It had been his gamble to identify a British student to accompany his work.

"I feel I can trust you," Korolyuk told me after the grilling from Professor Samoilenko and the committee of Five. "It would have been very easy for you to give Nina's name to Samoilenko and the others, but you didn't." After my return from Yalta eighteen months ago, Korolyuk began to tell me about the 'special theorem' he had been developing; how he had found a way of embedding it in the Wright-Fisher Model without disrupting either. This is what we had been writing all along. Korolyuk had developed this under mathematical stealth, a type of encryption; a skill that only a few of the most brilliant mathematicians could do. This was the art of concealing one formula inside another. I readily admitted that this was well beyond my ability.

"It will require a brilliant mind to interpret it though," Korolyuk said. "Do you know who could take this task?"

"I know exactly the right person," I said. "His name is Professor Harris." I continued, "Professor Harris was able to covertly send a proof to Skorokhod's theorem through the work that Skorokhod had given me via Galina. Skorokhod must have thought the proof was from me; it was on the file I deliberately saved on Alan's server, in Skorokhod's department. Galina had been assisting Skorokhod who was fishing for information about my role, as Korolyuk's student, in the *Kyiv Defence Theorem,* which will have conflicted with his *Moscow Defence Theorem*. Oksana confirmed that Galina did this deliberately to get me thrown out of the Institute, to get me away from Korolyuk, under the orders of Colonels Smirnov and Petrov. They had clearly influenced Skorokhod."

"But Skorokhod accepted Harris' proof," insisted Korolyuk, "and that's why he convinced Samoilenko to re-vote for you to stay in the Institute. Smirnov and Petrov were furious. Skorokhod was very pleased with Harris' theorem which he'd been trying to prove for several years. So, I gladly accept Professor Harris as our equal."

"The Russians can never know that the *Kyiv Defence Theorem* could be used against them," he said. "After all, it was Stalin himself who came up with the original idea, applied so well by my mentor Professor Kolmogorov in Moscow." These conversations I'd had with Korolyuk now seared into my memory. "If there is ever a need for my defence theorem to be applied for real, it will be a case of *'they know not what they do'* to describe the Russian leadership in the Kremlin who triggers it," Korolyuk stated. I had hugged him tightly upon my departure from Kyiv a week ago, not knowing when, if, I would see him again. *My only solace was that Yulia was by my side on the plane back to London.*

A week on, Yulia and I entered Parliament Square. I glanced across to Churchill's statue and felt I knew the man. I certainly knew his ghost. He helped Ukraine in its hour of need. We hurried and turned right into Whitehall. My heart was pumping now. *Would he be there?* I was not sure he would be.

The cenotaph came into sight.

The mysterious note I had received a week earlier at Gatwick Airport upon landing from Kyiv, read *'Get to the Downing Street gates at 18311299 and ask the officer on duty for the Prime Minister's post box. Will meet you there. W.'*

We crossed over Whitehall and approached the gates at Downing Street. There were two armed officers on duty.

"I have a letter for the Prime Minister," I said. "Tony Blair."

"I know who the Prime Minister is, Sir," the bigger armed police officer replied. "The Prime Minister's official mailbox is across the way, down the little alley next to the *Red Lion* pub. You can see it from here." I turned to look and could see the *Red Lion* pub still festooned in Christmas lights.

"Thank you," I said. "Come on Yulia let's go!"

"Happy New Year, Sir," said the police officer.

We turned the corner past the *Red Lion* pub into Derby Street and approached the doorway at the end, where Downing Street received its mail.

"You've done your country and Ukraine a great service, Richard," Warren said as he stepped out of the shadow. "Pleased to meet you, Yulia."

"Thank you," I replied. "It's been a long time." I hadn't seen Warren since he had taken me down to the Lviv underground club four years earlier.

"You may not have noticed me, but I've been pretty close to you since then," he said. "We just missed each other in the Hall of Columns then at least once in the Embassy."

"What were you doing in Ukraine?" I asked.

"Better if you don't ask," Warren replied, "but Sveta let me know how you were every step of your journey. We are married." Sveta. The lady from the British Council; it was all making sense.

"I have the package here," I said. "It contains everything the Prime Minister needs to make sense of Korolyuk's message. A partial theorem will be published in a Ukrainian Journal in March to test if anyone can work it out, test its resilience under scrutiny; Korolyuk will monitor this for the rest of his life."

311

"Excellent! Sign it in here so it is formally registered," Warren indicated to a metal secure box. I signed the form and put it in the secure box with the package. The click of the box ended the process. I had done all I could.

"Goodbye Richard," he said. "Go and enjoy the celebrations, you deserve it. Happy New Year!"

"Happy New Year to you!" I replied. "Will I see you again?"

"If ever you come back to Ukraine, most definitely," he said. "I'll know when you do."

We shook hands. Yulia and I headed back up Derby Street on to Whitehall. By the time I stopped and turned around to wave to Warren, he had gone.

"How did he know my name?" Yulia asked. "I've never met him."

"I think he knows everything about me," I answered. *Maybe he'd popped into the pub for a pint; it was New Year's Eve after all.*

"Let's get to the Embankment," I said. "we're meeting my Australian cousins there at 7pm, they've got the alcohol." I was reminded of Australia Day in the British Embassy nearly three years before. We hurried back towards Parliament Square then turned left and left again at Westminster Bridge. We turned into a throng of people drinking and all jockeying for their positions to see the new millennium in. We headed towards the Embankment and camped in a position right opposite the new Millenium wheel, in front of the Shell building.

By midnight, I felt the great twentieth century coming to an end, standing within sight of the parliament that had possibly done most to keep it from falling into tyranny. *I prayed that the new Russian leader would do the same with the next century, but if not, we would be ready.*

Epilogue

In the years that followed I visited Ukraine on numerous occasions and witnessed how the country began to develop on a path of its choosing. The Orange Revolution on Independence Square successfully overturned a fixed Presidential result in December 2004, in which the pro-Russian candidate President Yanukovych initially won. Ukraine's Supreme Court ordered a revote which subsequently gave victory to President Yushchenko. The Orange Revolution was viewed negatively by pro-government circles in Russia.

2004 Orange Revolution.

2005 President Yushchenko (elected).

2010 President Yanukovych (elected).

2012 Ukraine hosted European Football Championships.

20 Feb 2014 Euromaidan Revolution (clash with Berkut riot police).

22 Feb 2014 President Yanukovych removed from office.

23 Feb 2014 President Turchynov (appointed temporary leader).

27 Feb 2014 Russian invasion and annexation of Crimean Peninsula.

7 June 2014 President Poroshenko (elected).

27 June 2014 Ukraine EU Association Economic Agreement signed.

16 September 2014 EU Association Agreement ratified.

2019 President Zelenskyy (elected).

March 2020 First COVID-19 case in Ukraine.

April 2020 Professor Korolyuk died.

February 2022 Russia invaded Ukraine in an escalation of the Russo-Ukrainian War that started in 2014. The invasion was the biggest attack on a European country since the Second World War. Kyiv successfully defended itself from an attempt by Russia to take it. The plans for its defence were well established.

"The fool fears and retreats from evil,

Because he does not know how to

Overcome it, and the wise man trusts

Himself, fights evil and defeats it.

- *Taras Shevchenko*

Acknowledgements

This book is largely attributed to Professor Korolyuk and his many accomplishments. But the book, like the events it describes, would never have been possible without the help of others, to all of whom I am deeply indebted both then and now. Many of the friends and characters of those times are not referenced as much as I perhaps would have liked. I hope this is to no one's lasting distress, not least since I have tried to represent faithfully the events of those years as they appeared to me at the time, and to include those who were there as much as possible.

To all who made a contribution to the Evening of European Music in 1998, and surrounding organizations in whatever form, especially the European Commission in Ukraine, Musical Conservatoire of Kyiv, British Embassy, Consular and Council at the height of great hope and optimism. Please accept collective thanks for the roles that you played in our real-life script, and please also accept my own apologies for not having been able to include you all personally. Without you there would be no events to describe, and no history to salvage. To Mum and Dad. You are true role models. Your love, wisdom, humour and tolerance have never faltered, and those are the foundations that made my journey possible. My beloved Daniela, you gave me the time and space to be able to achieve this undertaking – it simply would not have been possible without you.

As a first-time author I am also indebted to some of the wonderful people one meets on the journey. In writing the book I have found the support and counsel of Max Gorlov, my editor, invaluable – I have learned so much. Alex Sweetlove our chance meeting enabled me to complete this work on time – you are wise, kind and patient. I fully acknowledge my friend Mario Creatura for the simple genius of the cover design. To old pal, Greg McGee for staying in touch with Ukrainian affairs, Ukrainian friends and sharing old stories. Our experiences were shared yet different, and I hope that your perspectives and contributions are faithfully represented. I could not have stayed sane without you. We continue to share the hope and pain in Ukraine. I profoundly hope this book sits well with the brave Ukrainian people. The brave, brave people of Ukraine! Slava Ukraini!